MASSACRE
IN COURTROOM 425

MASSACRE IN COURTOOM 425

By

Flannigan O'Rorke

RIVERCROSS PUBLISHING
NEW YORK ● ORLANDO

ISBN: 0: 944957-75-7

Library of Congress Catalog Card Number: 94-40952

First Printing

Library of Congress Cataloging-in-Publication Data

O'Rorke, Flannigan.
    Massacre in courtroom 425 / by Flannigan O'Rorke.
        p.   cm.
    ISBN 0-944957-75-7 : $15.95
    1. Winner, Charlie Bud—Trials, litigation, etc. 2. Trials (Child sexual abuse)—Pennsylvania—Philadelphia. 3. Child sexual abuse--Pennsylvania—Philadelphia. I. Title.
    KF224.W554076 1995
    364.1'536—dc20   94-40952
                                                              CIP

CONTENTS

THIS BOOK IS DEDICATED TO:

first and foremost, All Praise to Lord and Savior Jesus Christ, without whose help this book may never have been completed.

Thanks also to Mother and Father who have always "been there" for me. Thanks to my wife. I love you so much, my dear. I pray that you will always be with me, for I'm always with you. Thanks to my son and daughter; Daddy will forever "be there" for you.

Special thanks to Jennifer, all the employees of Thriftway Market, Pennsylvania's Ironworkers, members of twelve step recovery programs, my brother and sister-in-law, also to Mr. Cameron whose creative insight helped in the final production of this work.

A final thanks to Rivercross Publishing who waited for this inexperienced hand to re-write the drama you are about to experience.

MASSACRE
IN COURTROOM 425

1

Guilty Till Proven Innocent

Old head stirred peacefully in his sleep, awakened, opened his eyes, gratefully inhaled a deep blast of oxygen, arose to a sitting position, and prayed triumphantly: Come Holy Spirit, Fill the hearts of the Faithful, in Jesus' Name. Thank you Jehovah God for life. Then he vaulted from his bunk.

Charlie Bud Winner is a born again, Holy Spirit-led, child of God. He was a prisoner convicted of crimes that were fabricated by employees within the Commonwealth of Pennsylvania who subjected the innocent man to highly damaging, outrageous, insulting, malicious slander. Conjecture became the guiding light fueled by suspicion; perpetuated by wolves in sheep's clothing.

False witnesses, incompetent doctors, professional mental health care workers, therapists, attorneys, experts, biased judges and police officers conspired to create a modern, high tech, computerized lynch mob to prove their case.

Winner served the Saints within the Universal Body of Christ.

Biased, lopsided justice was presented by a legal cult within the justice system to produce the necessary animosity to convict. Libel, convincingly posed as authentic fact, fooled the jury which returned a unanimous guilty verdict.

Mob justice was alive and doing well in Philadelphia, Pennsylvania. Ministers of Justice spread perfidious beliefs and opinions to each other, creating a hypnotic obsession that filled their consciousness with visions and illusions.

Roughly, Winner rubbed his fingernails through grayish hair. Hundreds of white specks of dandruff flakes floated into the light from a sunbeam. He pulled the state-issued white undershirt away from his hot sweaty body, raised his forty-eight-year-old neck while massaging the adam's apple and noticed a bed full of notes that held the story spread haphazardly over the sheets. He picked up a blue Maxwell House coffee cup and took a sip of the lukewarm beverage.

Situations, circumstances, different realities, contain within the experience different elements of good or evil. One complains discontentedly while the other, observing the same visions, but with a different point of view, notices what is good and rejoices. Bad becomes worse; good gets better!

More than twenty thousand dollars is paid each year to incarcerate one person. Inmates touch no money, pay no taxes, drive no cars, nor have meaningful employment. The rat race is over. The free world is no more.

Those who work earn up to thirty-five dollars a month which gives them needed funds to shop at the commissary store once per week to stock up on smokes, chips, cookies, ice cream, coffee, and health and comfort items. Color television with cable TV. is available for a slight fee.

The prison cell is tiny and normally occupied by two people. Single cell classification is available but difficult to obtain. In each cell sits a desk with a shelf overhead and a sink and toilet. Two steel bunk beds fill up half of the room which has bars on the window and a door that is usually locked. A person standing in the center of the cell can touch both walls with his arms held out. Four steps north show you the distance from wall to wall.

The church is represented at chapel by different ministers.

Outdoor recreation is available three times per day in pleasant weather. The public address system announces at 8:30, 14:00 hrs. and 18:30, ''yard out'' which means inmates can leave their cells to go into the yard. The entire population can assemble at these times for physical activity. Guards surround the compound watching the inmates walk, run or jog on a huge circular track, play basketball, softball, football, pump iron, life weights, play guitars, listen to radios, sing in groups, play horseshoes, or walk silently contemplating brilliant cloud formations, the mountains and deer that inhabit the nearby forest.

Negatives exist in an unenlightened mind. One saved from the evils that overcome the good is continuously making spiritual progress no matter what the circumstances in the world. A patriot defends his country's best interest while traitors are disloyal to a trust. It is fit and proper at this time to proclaim the good news.

Hebrews 12:3 *Think diligently upon Him that endured such opposition from sinners against Himself; That you be not wearied, fainting in your minds.*

The Lord blessed Winner with a single cell, silent solitude, a clean mind and a sorrowful heart. All his needs met without any effort on his part. Three years of prison had taught him lessons that he wanted to share along with a heart-breaking, pride destroying, drama that needed to be told.

Justice sometimes errs. The law is ready to lock up a large segment of society. Be warned! You may be in a cell some day. Innocence means little. What matters is who the jury believes. Some may say, you're angry; to them I reply, "Yes, very angry", wouldn't you be? You certainly can sings song of Praise to a Wonderful God but the evil must be stopped.

In life from my childhood I was taught to honor the system, but when people in this system act like devils, try to ruin you to prove what they think is true, then I say, "It's time to fight the ones who are trying to destroy the spirit of freedom."

2

Mother's Prayer Answered.

Remember the point of this book is to share lessons learned from severe trials and tribulations. At any time a lesson learned may be interjected.

Meet Grandfather, called Poppe, and Grandmother, called Nanny, parents of Charlie Winner who had lived on Fairy Tale Lane for over forty years. In row homes that stretched thirty homes in a row on both sides of the street, Polish, Irish, Greek. Italians blended in with Germans and Jews.

Mayfair is served by two bus lines that cruised past area shopping centers, the bowling alley, pizza shops, banks, fast food joints. Poppe and Nanny purchased their home right after the Second World War. A mixed marriage it was, protestant man to catholic woman.

The neighbors were peaceful, avoiding pain, not seeking fame. Church, family, work, were held in high esteem. Silent solitude is a great relief for an overworked mind. Poppe demonstrated his good character by action. He worked every day of his life except when ill, attended church, supported the Democrats, paid his bills, didn't get drunk or use dope.

Seventy years of living had turned his jet black hair white. The death of his second son converted him to the catholic faith. The first major upset had come to the younger couple without warning. In his sleep his three-year-old baby son died. Here today, gone tomorrow.

Grandfather Winner, born in Ashland Kentucky, worked in the machine shop on train brakes at the Budd Company. He had one telephone number throughout life. He was loyal to his vows of marriage.

Each and every Sunday the couple attended mass at St. DeMontfort's church. They survived the poverty of the depression, the stock market collapse in the 20's, Hitler's war, Korea, the cold war, Vietnam, the sexual revolution, the war on drugs and the current underclared opposition to the values they held important.

Poppe was an Eagle Boy Scout who paid weekly his contributions to the church. He wallpapered houses, painted, was good in math. A union man whose heart was won over by the United Auto Workers Union, he loved to fish, make bass lures, and watch the Phillies baseball team from the comforts of his rocking chair.

Nanny was an in-house preacher with the salvation message preached right in the kitchen. "Jesus Christ" was crucified, died, was buried and resurrected for you." The older she became the more faithful was her stand. It was common to see Nanny in bed with a set of rosary beads in her hand.

She did all the deeds good women do for good men. She cooked, cleaned, washed clothes, had friends in for visits and kept a close eye on her only living son, correcting, directing, pushing young Winner Jr. to complete school. She kept a spotless home, was annoyed and enraged by sloppiness but wouldn't accept defeated negative attitudes.

Early in the 50's children learned from the TV: "Mickey Mouse Club," "Howdy Dowdy," "Romper Room," "Milton Berle," "Rin Tin Tin," "Princess Summer, Fall, Winter, Spring." Television was entertainment, not a political soapbox. Few, if any, spoke of abuse, of condoms, or sexuality.

Winner took to the streets early in life. Mass was then said in the Latin tongue. No words could be understood by kids who watched the back of the priest for an hour on Sunday.

Mickey Mouse had more influence on a boy who rejected religion, especially a disobedient lad with a desire to be important and who, at a young age, was self-willed.

Pride was growing, Spirituality was dead. Even from those early days Jesus was the one who had something to do with a boy going to hell forever for eating meat on Friday.

At thirteen he was going into bars to buy and drink beer, getting high in the park, running from cops. Arrested at 14, he was in court for contributing to the delinquency of minors. He had purchased alcohol for the kids in the neighborhood so they would think he was a big shot.

At fifteen, girls, sex, failing in school, fighting at home, boredom, cheating, pretending, looking for fun, pleasure. He was growing up without discipline.

At sixteen—driver's license, drive-in movies, motels, trips to the shore, breaking free, fearful, uptight, fat, ugly, pimples. Winner was out for pleasure. Selfishness controlled the young man who had kicked God out of his life when the top of his brother's coffin was closed.

At 17–18–19—high school over, graduated at the bottom, work, Poppe got Winner a job at the Budd Co. He was out in the world, inexperienced but with a big head. He saved money, bought a car, had dates, joined the service, got a honorable discharge.

In those days hippies were handing out flowers at Haight Ashbury in San Francisco. Vietnam divided the country, bell bottom trousers, long hair, Janis Joplin, the Beatles, Sgt. Pepper's Lonely Hearts Club Band, rebellion, riots, Black Panthers, women's liberation movement, Patty Hearst, sex, war on TV. Kent State, drugs, rock and roll, sexual revolution, Chicago Seven. Pornography invaded America; girls without bras were a special event, not ordinary.

At 20 he joined the Marine Corps, served as a clerk and went to Japan as part of an Honor Guard. The outside was fooling the people while the inside wanted to stay high. Winner traveled back to the old neighborhood. It was the same but he was different.

His ego was in need of constant feeding. He stayed in shape, ran three miles per day, and lifted weights until pot smoking put an end to health-related activities.

Frenchy the Barber, from South Philadelphia, had his shop on Fairy Tale Lane. Philip Balony, Republican Committeeman, discussed politics with the crowd who congregated inside French's place. Sara owned and operated the Bird's Nest, a gift store next to French's Barber Shop. Fred's Bar was on the other side of the driveway. Both young and old caught a slight buzz at the Drink Fast Tavern around the corner.

The kids in the neighborhood knew each other for years. Blueman had a hoagie shop that was a popular corner hang out. Across from Blueman's one could see Fred's Bar, a flower shop and a hair salon.

Winner started to take drugs, diet pills, speed, pot or beer on an everyday basis. Years went by, the addiction grew into a giant monkey on Winner's back saying, "Feed me, feed me."

The drug speed fed the evil personality and gave him false feelings of superiority, a feeling that "I can do anything." Six years of nonstop everyday use of meth qualified Winner to be called a dope addict, but never could he admit that truth. "He could stop anytime he pleased. All his friends were users, it makes you feel good. What's wrong?"

Poppe's wife Nanny was a new type of Catholic, a charismatic who prayed that her son would be saved. In fact, her prayer partners had been praying for years every Wednesday night that Winner would come to his right mind and get off the speed.

At age 30, after losing hundreds of jobs, going in and out of ruined relationships, fighting with society, Winner returned from working in Alaska on the Trans-Alaska Pipeline, and moved into a three-story rented home.

He gave party after party and rented the basement to a band that rehearsed there. Each night, 20, 30, 40 strangers would be in the living room. All high, or drunk. All desperate.

One night, after three months of this style of life, Winner's heart started beating faster than it had ever beat. He was suddenly aware of death. "I'm gonna die," thought Winner as he stood among the addicts. He quickly left the room. Tears fell from his eyes. He sat at a desk and picked up a pen that didn't have much ink and wrote "Jesus, Jesus, Jesus, forgive me Lord for not thinking of you for six years. I don't want to die or go crazy, help me!"

Winner was sitting at his desk, hearing the noise from the crowd in the living room, hoping nobody would see him so out of control. He noticed his heart beat slowed. His tears stopped but he continued to write with the pen that had no ink.

Paul, Paul, Paul; who was Paul? He didn't know any Pauls! Then, I want you to be a writer and write the truth for me.

This was his first honest prayer. It was the Beginning of the New Life, yet Satan was by no means finished. In the years ahead there were to be rescue missions, flings with strangers for a night, the never-ending always strong appetite for alcohol and dope; the hunt for something at different churches. He was restless, always moving on from town to town, from job to job, from girl to girl, always moving, never resting. And all the time writing like a madman, looking, learning, seeing, feeling bad, fighting with Nanny and Poppe, being lazy, couldn't, wouldn't, didn't work. The party wasn't over, the world still held out its neon signs of success.

15

3

For Better Or For Worse

Winner was coming to understand the reality of sin. God forgives me. He flashed back into the scenes from his past. Addicts enjoy living in a fantasy trip, pretending to the outside world that they are proper examples of mature adults while the uncontrolled impulses from within jerk their heads around. Truth, real truth, causes pain.

In humility one had a tendency to view oneself as less, low, base, even wicked. Could Winner admit his errors for the good of others? Clearly, one cannot be double-minded, that is living in the world, at times, seeking pleasure, advancement, sex, power, applause from others, recognition, dope, booze, money and things, and then, when that is finished, walk in the Spirit. You can't be a part timer. One world must have your complete attention. Winner was split into two parts. Good–evil, right--wrong, yes–no, will–won't, can–can't, do–don't, love–hate, faith–doubt, happy–sad, stop–start. The outer man was under the control of inner compulsions. The battlefield was the mind.

Jesus was soon relegated to pride's lip service which fell upon the other unrepentant sin. Time was consumed seeking wine, women and song. Responsible adult behavior was overwhelmed by addiction. Home life at Poppe's was one big argument over life styles. Winner was asked to leave his parent's home once more due to his refusal to live by their rules.

Out the door, nowhere to go, broke, angry, hurt, unhappy; traveling with a bag filled with notes. Walk down to the highway, stick out the thumb, wait for a ride, go on strange trips to shady places;

nobody understands. Oh good, a car stopped. "Get in. Where you goin'?" "Don't know!" "Do you want to get a beer?" "No money, I'm broke." "Don't worry about money, I'll buy."

"Okay, let's go. At the bar Winner saw Sabrina Brownski with her sister Flamingo drinking beer while playing pool. Winner was attracted to Sabrina; both were in a battle with the devil who was winning every round.

Winner noticed Sabrina's beauty, a magnificent face; she in turn was attracted to Winner; both struck up a conversation, and a relationship was born.

Sabrina had jumped off the horse that never yields to weariness; ride it must, ride it will. She had kicked heroin before she met Winner, but its aftereffects lingered–collapsed veins and a bad head. She lived with Flamingo, her sister, at Woody's house on Archer Street.

Sabrina asked, "What's in the bag?" Winner replied. "Notes. I'm writing a book." "What's your book about?", "Good question. It's about drug addiction, breaking free, Jesus, sin, sex, guilt, pain, stress, hate, life in general!" "Can I read it?" asked Sabrina. "Yes." Winner shoved a handful of pages across the table. She picked a page at random and read it out loud. "Falling leaves on other trees' branches; trees are beat with age; green moss covers a blown down tree, nature has become reality. The sounds in the woods are loud, indeed, footsteps stepping on falling leaves. Is this the life I ask of you—living your life in the morning dew? Living far away from the fast spinning pace? There are plenty of places for people to be, but people need to be able to see the positive side of reality."

Sabrina said she enjoyed the writing and asked permission to show Flamingo, who had a crowd of men around her teaching her how to play pool.

To make a long story short, the next three months were spent in courtship. Winner went back to Poppe's house and was let back in the house. An engagement ring was purchased, and a wedding planned.

Nanny knew her son was addicted to mind-altering substances and disapproved of his intentions towards Sabrina, who created a bad first impression when she spoke to Nanny for the first time on the telephone. Sabrina spoke for twenty five minutes straight. Nanny didn't have the opportunity to say one word. After Sabrina finished talking, she handed the telephone to Winner. Nanny asked "Winner, is this a joke or a bad dream? Are you crazy?"

The big day came, vows were exchanged, a reception followed. One of the guests committed a crime by robbing an aunt of $160.00 while the coats sat unwatched in a bedroom. The honeymoon was over right after the ceremony. Money was needed. Back to reality. Now Winner had to support a lady and he couldn't take care of himself.

Evil manifested itself shortly after marriage. Sabrina did her best to please a man who demanded more and contributed little. The weight of responsibility was placed on her tiny shoulders. Winner was an immature baby in a grown man's body, totally dependent on others, especially Nanny, Poppe and his pretty young wife.

The stork presented a child to the couple. Ann was born. Sabrina was now going in and out of mental hospitals three or four times a year. Winner grew resentful, thinking, "Why didn't she tell me she was nuts?" Ten months later Tony was born. Winner was pleasant with the children, offering them his better side. The kids and Winner enjoyed each other's company while Sabrina stood outside the group afraid to approach. She hid in the shelter of her bedroom, disgusted with married life. She had all she could stand. A house was rented around the corner from Poppe's house. The Winner family moved to Dreamer's Lane. By this time Winner knew he needed help and had been attending A.A. meetings. The children grew up at their grandparents' since his relationship with Sabrina wasn't good and perhaps would bring life-long problems to the children.

The man and woman who lived in the house with the foot high grass were plainly eccentric. They communicated displeasure with wordless ice cold silence that thundered within the minds of the hatebirds who always noticed each other's short comings.

Winner looked at Sabrina and saw a picture of what he thought about himself. The perceptions he formed were motivated by sin, so he saw evil in the woman he had promised to love. Sabrina developed mental problems due to Winner's trying to improve her mental health. Big mistake!

The fault-finding maniac would fly off the handle in a crocodile frenzy, snapping at his prey for her mental hypochondria. Peace officers appeared in the living room, called by somebody to calm the storm. Arguments thrilled the neighborhood! Sabrina's voice, when raised, could travel one hundred yards. Doors were slammed, voices screamed, tears fell, hate grew.

Hundreds, perhaps thousands of their neighbors were recovering from one addiction or double trouble, multi-addictions. Rehabilitation organizations with twelve-step recovery programs were fashionably accepted solutions founded to rescue the alcoholic or addict in the Torresdale, Frankford and Mayfair sections of Northeast Philadelphia.

Winner and Sabrina fit in well with the substance abuse crowd. Recovery hurts. Pain brings miserable side effects to the user. Getting high is normal. The fix removes the guilt but then the poor addict has to fix the fix. Few stick around long enough to take the necessary steps for sobriety. The program works when you work the program. Abstinence was short-lived, interrupted by drunken episodes, fights, arguments, blackouts, visits to the cop man, slips, falls, the detox., in and out of recovery, dry out, withdrawal, confession to the priest, forgiveness, back to the program.

Addicts and drunks battle one another in a close race for the title of most selfish person in the world. Meeting makers make it, so they say, but what do meeting makers make?

Alcohol and drugs were doing their best to destroy the family. A.A. brought hope, but it also brought separation. Winner and Sabrina were going their separate ways.

Wouldn't it be kinder to pray for people instead of pointing the finger? Your prayer will help in the rescue!

Winner saw Sabrina as mentally ill because he himself was mentally ill from years of addiction. He didn't know that what he perceived in his wife was what was in him. The wife was his mirror. He looked at her and viewed himself.

Addicts take those who love them hostage.

Often a person had no idea how to correct a situation that is bringing grief. You live through the ordeal and wait to see what happens. The mind thinks and keeps thinking uninterrupted. Thought after thought comes and goes.

Correct yourself, check your own conduct, leave others alone. The speaker always talks about his views towards himself. Criticizing a stranger is back biting against yourself.

Poor views of responsibility, bad work habits, dislike of marriage, paranoid superiority results in depressive potential schizophrenic symptoms: pot addiction, alcohol abuse, resentment, anger, bad ideas.

Sorrowful repentance for offending God and hurting others were replaced by lip service speaking the word of spiritual pride.

Compulsive impulses struck the brain. *Thought without thought.* Urges, desires and wants demanded to be satisfied. Again, the words of Jesus came to the rescue. St. Luke 5:31–32. "Jesus answering, said to them: 'They that are whole, need not the physician; but they that are sick. I come not to call the just, but sinners to repentance.'"

Selfish men say "yes" to the get-high impulse, "yes" to the have-a-good-time impulse thinking that pleasure is all important in the quest for happiness.

Foolish people believing they are wise become arrogant causing others to suffer.

Satan, the evil one, the tempter remains in control making suggestions to his servants of pleasure who obey until right becomes wrong and wrong is right.

Few will admit that their actions and conduct have them in a race car heading for hell. People like to appear as good, they also want the freedom to do as they wish.

Evil spirits mock the religious man creating false impressions that cause others to hold these same false impressions. This keeps the arrogant bound, tied, hitched, uprepentent, continually breaking God's law with mortal sins against Jehovah.

You can't use anything without it using you. A.A. meetings become an extension of pride that demanded recognition. The Word of God says, "Be strengthened in the Lord, and in the might of his power. Put on the armor of God, that you may be able to stand against the deceits of the devil. In all things, taking the shield of faith, where with you may be able to extinguish all the fiery darts of the most wicked one, and take unto you the helmet of salvation, and the sword of the Spirit which is the word of God." Ephesians 6

"I" mindedness never cease to drawl attention to itself is in control. I, I, I, me, me, me, I have, I am, I want, I will.

Hey! Look at me, I'm a handsome dude, thank you for your applause. That guy is really doing good, he works the program, helps others, is a good example, attends meetings, but underneath he is a snake pretending to be helpful to win a favorable impression from you.

This is how you work the program. Just do what I do. Follow me. You can't fix yourself so stop trying. Clean up the inside of your mind, admit your defects of character to God, yourself and other human beings. Pay the bills you now neglect, pray and meditate. Help around the group, get involved. Winner knew the language of recovery.

A fool will not stray close to a humble man. Saying and speaking is quite different from silently doing without the need to be noticed. *Pride seeks attention; humility does not.* Spiritual men who have been broken can see when a person is ready to accept the spiritual disciplines necessary for recovery.

Japanese proverb: Applause is the beginning of shame.

Sabrina had had troubles throughout her life. She was a quiet girl going to beauty school when Winner leaped into her life. She was a real fox, a good looker, slim and youthful, but her mental health was shaky. Professionals would supply the therapy, the pills, the in-patient counsel and at times, she'd go away for a few months.

The experts never convinced her that she needed a certain type of pill to keep her in balance.

One doctor recommended brain shocks for six thousand dollars. Iron Workers Insurance paid, so she had the shocks. She came home, didn't know who she was. She walked into walls. She gained seventy pounds, which upset Winner greatly.

Sabrina said, "There's nothing wrong with me. If I keep listening to these people, I'll really go nuts. I'm through with these pills!"

She went to Weight Watchers, and in several weeks all the fat was off, but the instability was back. At Mass one afternoon, she gave the faithful a piece of her mind. The priest called the authorities who took her to the hospital.

For some reason, Winner thought he had the skills to guide her in her life. He should have left her alone, but he couldn't, so he didn't and Sabrina kept getting worse.

Sabrina and the children depended on Winner to take care of the needs of the family. He had the load. Unfortunately he wanted to do other things besides work. Of course, since he didn't have a sense of responsibility, he'd get a job and lose the job.

4

Death, A Breath Away

Man's wisdom pointed to the symptom of the disease while not able to discern the cause, resulting in solutions that eventually become problems. The political system of the United States was in the dark. Light does not shine from political lamps. Mortal sin against God manifests itself to the discerning eye as tremendous, audacious, atrocities against holiness, purity, chastity, virtue and righteousness.

The horsemen were in the saddle, faithful and true, glancing behind for a look at past time, ratta tat tat. Because you don't, doesn't mean you can't. Anger holds the pistol in a mad man's hand. Hurricane Andrew has spoken to man! Addicts score their hidden pleasure. Saints announce the hidden treasure. Mother's fight for the right to choose. Hurt a sister we all lose. Sir, zippers up. Good news breaks my spell of melancholy. The evil one would like to take you straight to hell.

Winner was a union ironworker out of Local 401. Philadelphia Ironworkers built the skyscrapers, bridges and all the other buildings that are supported by structural steel beams. These were the men you see high in the air, walking the tops of six inch wide beams. Danger is present at all times.

Smoking pot before work produces slowed-down workmen who jeopardize the proficiency of the gang.

Drinking alcohol is no better, but more accepted among the men who erect the iron, plum up or square the building, stick the bolts, rattle them up with a yo-yo, lay the metal deck floors, load and unload trucks, climb columns, guide steel into place by hand signals and much more.

Home life was a mess, but working the iron paid well. Three days work and there was enough money to get high and pay some bills.

In the Union Hall, ironworkers sat in groups of four to a round table waiting for the business agent to come to the window and call out the jobs. A free coffee machine kept the men supplied with coffein, creating a comfortable mellow space. Nails, the business agent, entered the room with several work slips in his hand.

Getting a job is like being a seal being fed in the zoo. You had to be quick since it was first come first served. Whoever was the quickest to get Nails' attention went to work. The men sitting in the back of the hall had less chance than those sitting in front.

The B.A. called out the first job. "I need two connectors for American Bridge down at the Gallery." Several men shouted at once, "Here Nails." "I'll take it." "Hey Nails. "Yo Nails." "Give me that job," Some workers lifted their hand, but said nothing. The business agent looked around the room, saw two men and said, "Boots, you and Skip go down there and see Bobby the Steward."

"I need one man to go to work for Precast Erectors who are building a parking garage in Frankford. There's about three months worth, Robbie Pelson is the General Foreman. A hospital is being built."

Winner sitting at the first table right under the nose of the B.A. yelled. "I'll take that job." Nails looked up and saw Winner and said, "Okay go ahead down there. You'll need to help out connecting and welding." "Great," said Winner.

The job was a mile from home, would last three months and it was a safe job. No walking the iron or climbing it. Getting a job at the union hall was work.

As mentioned, Robbie Pelson was the boss and according to his own testimony he was the best prefabricated concrete plank erector on the east coast.

Modern science can get us to the moon, build bridges, turn theories into realities, develop a philosophy, conclude matter will respond in a certain way, but it cannot and never will be able to create a solution that will not turn into a problem. Only faith has that ability. Man cannot be God! Sorry boys, you have to be people. Pretty much like the bum in the street. The only difference between men is in the head.

Therapists have taken complete control over the ills of our

23

society. Actually, of course they had made matters worse by their "knowledge." Solutions have turned the troubled person into a pointer at others saying, "You did this to me, it's your fault." This takes all blame away from the sick but down the road the input is hate. Haters are selfish. Forgivers get blessed! Trouble sells, so it has to grow to succeed.

Billy and his brother Vince were connecting on the job. The Frankford el ran adjacent to the job site. Elevated trains traveled by twenty feet overhead, entering and exiting the Bridge and Pratt Street Station which was the first stop. This was the beginning of the transportation system that carried commuters throughout the city. A car wasn't necessary to reach this destination. A bike could be used and it was all downhill.

More than a hundred thousand Philadelphians passed through this location traveling to their place of work.

Early in the morning in the Frankford area, the streets would be cleaned by workers for S.E.P.T.A. S.E.P.T.A. was the transportation company that had their buses everywhere in this neighborhood. Four buses at a time would be trying to leave the station and get on to the street. Traffic was usually heavy. People stood in lines seventy deep waiting to board the bus. Thousands of pigeons flew from roof-tops to feed on soft pretzels fed to them by passers-by.

Non-stop people in motion; panhandlers, men, women with kids, cup in hand, seeking money.

Drinkers outside the Golden Bar looked into empty bottles of Jim Beam for a few drops to check the shakes. Older senior citizens were dumbfounded as runners ran away with their purses. Hungry people filled up the restaurants for breakfast. Rose sold newspapers from the newsstand. A hustler walked up and down the street shouting, "Hey Philadelphia Daily News." Street people were sleeping on the concrete. A lady walked past the intersection talking to herself.

Traffic moved on green, stopped on red. Bus drivers watched the riders fill up the bus.

Chuck, the pizza man, was open for business. In the morning instead of pizza sauce, Chuck used a scrambled egg mixture to pour over the dough, then added sausage or bacon. Hookers tried hard to attract a "John." A tuba player belted out the Marine Corps Hymn in hopes of receiving a tip, while Pastor John, microphone in hand, preached the Gospel to the people. Luke 6:27, "But to you who hear I say, 'Love your enemies, do good to those who hate you, bless those who curse you, pray for those who mistreat you. To the person who strikes you on one cheek, offer the other one as well.''

Entering and departing trains overhead filled the area with noise.

The man on the bike passed through the scene, not in a great big hurry, but slowly cruising along heading for Frankford Hospital. He stopped by the newsstand, purchased a cup of coffee from Rose, heard the public telephone ring, ring, ring. He picked up the phone. "Hello." "Hi" came from the other end. It was a girl who said, "Can you talk?" "Yes, I can talk!" "Oh good, do you like to . . . ?" He hung up the phone. It was a dirty phone call. Better get to work!

Five minutes later Robbie was shaking hands with Winner. "Good to see you." They were friends who had worked together on other jobs. Winner was to do some welding.

Crowds of people would gather on Frankford Avenue watching the construction operation. Poppe would bring Sabrina and the children, Tony, the baby at age four and Ann the seven-year-old, to the work-place to watch the building go up.

Flat-bed trucks arrived with heavy loads of fifty foot long concrete planks, eight feet wide, that were one foot thick. Robbie directed the movements of the crane through his microphone that was tied to a stick that he held in his hand, close to his lips, speaking commands into the ears of the operating engineer who pushed and pulled levers inside the cab of the crane.

"Operator, can you hear me clearly? . . . Good, swing your boom over to the flat-bed, we're gonna pick up the load, nice and easy, swing left!" The boom turned, Robbie, head bent backwards, looked high towards the jib, 100 feet from the ground. The 100 foot boom circled until it stopped in line with the flat-bed truck.

Son, you are a knight in God's kingdom. Protect your honor. Good will be attracted to you by your good actions.

Two ironworkers stood on the piece to be placed waiting for the hook. "Stop," said Robbie. He took another look at the boom. "Operator boom down." The boom lowered. "Stop! Bring the load ball down." The cable drum released the metal wire. "Hold that." The operation stopped. Men froze. "Down with the hook." The hook fell into the hands of a worker on the truck who stood over the center of the piece to be lifted.

The ground men snapped two steel lifting cables into the hook.

A hand signal was given, "Up load, easy, good, keep coming up." The men jumped off the truck as the load lifted. The driver of the truck stepped on the gas, pulled away while a crowd watched on the street.

Robbie watched with his full attention on the job at hand. "Boom up operator." The boom came up. "Swing right operator." The boom swung right. The gang was installing the second piece for the day. Production was good. After morning coffee break the second piece was ready for installation.

Vince and Billy waited with pry bars, come-alongs and heavy beaters. Winner stood watching the operation 25 feet away from Robbie, standing on the plank that had been installed before the morning coffee break.

The piece glided into the hands of the connectors who tried to steady the load. "Operator, boom down, good, down, down, hold that. Bring the load down, down." This is the last stop until we land the load. "Stop." The load hung inches away from the support. "Okay, the load looks good, let's bring her down!"

Vince said to Billy, "Looks good." Billy said to Robbie, "Bring the load down, we're ready." "Operator, we're coming off the load, easy now, like a baby, easy, down, down. . . ."

Silence. Perfect darkness. The welding shield snapped over Winner's eyes, both his arms lifted up into the air.

"Call the ambulance," yelled Robbie. He and Winner began their fall to the ground twenty feet below! Accident! Accident! Both men's bodies were falling into the hole. As soon as the piece landed on its support, the piece Winner and Robbie were standing on collapsed, and 50,000 pounds of concrete was falling earthbound, while 50,000 pounds was swinging overhead with Vince and Billy riding the swinging piece. They jumped onto the load at the last second and were saved from a serious fall.

On the way to the ground, Winner's mind was clear. This is death! Who will take care of the children? Jesus.

Winner's body fell backward away from the falling load that hit and vibrated. He fell like a baseball player sliding into second base, right leg extended, sliding over gravel and dirt. In full motion he landed hard, the right foot slid under a rod that locked his leg in place. His upper body was in full motion and couldn't be stopped. "CRACK!" Pain blasted the brain. Shock! Fear of death.

His right foot was flopping around, held together by skin alone. The big thick bone right before the ankle snapped, like two kids pulling at a turkey's wishbone. Winner's body came to a halt. He prayed. "Thank you Jesus, Praise to you Lord, I can take this pain."

Old Ray, another ironworker looked down at the injured brother saying, "You're gonna make it, the ambulance is on the way." Vince ran over, looked at the foot hanging by the skin and lifted up the leg. The foot flopped around just attached by skin. Vince said, "You ain't going anywhere." Winner attempted to get on his feet but that was impossible.

A voice said, "Call Al Flame." Al Flame was the attorney who represented ironworkers injured in accidents.

Both feet doubled in size and blackened.

Sirens alerted the people of trouble. The hospital was notified. Firemen arrived, walked to the injured man lying on the ground and said, "Today is the luckiest day of your life. You're still alive." Then they put him onto a sheet of plywood and carried him to the vehicle that drove 50 yards to the emergency entrance.

Robbie broke his arm, but he could walk. The ironworkers watched their brother squirm, twist, grit his teeth and make facial signs of extreme pain. A doctor arrived with a needle in hand. He attacked the pain with morphine. Lying there staring at the ceiling the drug entered the blood stream, travelled throughout the body and bought comfort. The broken bones were wrapped in an ace bandage that brought the foot in line with the leg.

A hand holding a slip of paper was in front of his eyes. "Winner, can you hear me? My name is Al Flame. You have very serious injuries. I am an attorney and will represent you. some of your friends called my office. I came to the hospital to see if you would like me to represent you while you recover from your injuries." Winner said, "Yes, sure."

"Okay, sign this paper for me, and I'll do the rest." The paper said, "Al Flame forty percent." Mr. Flame left a basket of peanuts and filed a lawsuit against those responsible for 1.5 million dollars. Workers compensation sent checks for $347.00 dollars a week tax free. All hospital bills would be paid by insurance.

27

5

Into The Slimy Pit

The higher power was about to strike the final blow that was strong enough to double a person over with uncontrollable sorrow for years.

What are the benefits of telling the truth?

1) A clear conscience.

2) No fear of being exposed as a false witness.

3) Strength of character.

4) Courage to resist and attack error.

5) Honesty in all affairs.

Worldly experience changes you. What was true a year ago may not be true today. Within you is another you, the man of spirit, not like flesh. Spirit man wars with the man of flesh for victory. One is ruler, the other a slave. One is real and true; the other is false and an illusion.

Suddenly, without warning a snarling beast may startle you. Show no fear! Look him in the eye, retreat slowly, pull back, re-group, get out of there, but be confident.

You are learning how to relax. Count each breath like this: in one, out one, in two, out two, in three, out three, in four, out four, do this to the count of ten. Your eyes are closed, it will be dark. Bring your attention right to the center of your forehead; note the breath at the tip of your nose. Bring the breath up to the center of the forehead. Watch it at the tip of the nose, let the air come out the nose. Keep breathing in and out. When you are aware of thoughts, simply come back to the breath coming and going. As you continue to practice your body will go deeper into relaxation

29

while your conscious mind watches the subconscious thoughts rising and falling. Thoughts will flow. You won't get stuck on one.

Practice until you get it right. You'll make mistakes. Nevertheless, steady aim on the goal brings forth the product.

Frankford Hospital's nurses insisted Winner get out of bed and into a wheel chair once the operation was over. Self pity should not be a part of aftercare. Demerol was ordered three times per day.

Twenty-eight days after the fall it was time to go home. Two health care workers lifted up the stretcher and placed the patient on a hospital bed in the living room. Anthony was happy to have his Winner home and came running. He jumped on the bed and fell on Winner who said, "Tony no! Don't jump on me, I'm hurt. I love you pal. You're a great little boy. Give me a kiss." Sabrina had the job of bedpan girl. Going to the toilet in bed is no fun.

The surgeon had made two one-inch cuts at the right ankle and inserted a steel plate to hold the bone together. Two plaster casts were built around both legs six inches above the knee.

Physical therapists were ordered for home care. The living room looked like a hospital room: crutches, a walker, porta-toilet, wheel chair, hospital bed.

Ann and Tony loved to go to Poppe's and Nanny's house. Poppe played with Tony in the park, took him for rides in the car and for walks. They played mechanic in the basement. Tony had his own tool box. Ann played with Nanny. She had a room in her house.

Sabrina thought Charlie, Poppe and Nanny were trying to take her children away from her. She said, "Those children are my children, they came out of my belly. You and your parents aren't stealing those kids from me!" Winner answered, "Are you taking your pills? Nobody wants to take the kids from you. You're thinking stupid? How can we make the kids not like you? Be nice to the children, they will love you, but if you yell, scare them and don't talk to them kindly, they will be frightened. That's why they want to go to their grandparents." Again, stupid Winner made the wrong decisions but thought he was right and Sabrina wrong.

Proverbs 12:25 "Anxiety in a man's heart depresses it, but a kindly word makes it glad."

Dual natures coexist simultaneously. Spiritual or worldly mindedness. One sleeps while the other is awake.

Family relationships were strained. Sabrina was upset with

Winner, Nanny, Poppe and Ann. Poppe was upset with *Winner, Sabrina and Ann.* Nanny was upset with *Winner and Sabrina.* Winner was upset with *Poppe, Nanny and Sabrina.* Tony loved everybody. Ann was upset with *Poppe, Sabrina and Tony.* The accident occurred April 15, 1986. By Christmas time, with the help of a wall, Winner could slip his pants on.

Winner fancied himself a song writer and spent his time in bed writing songs. One song he sent to a recording company that agreed to put the words to music for three hundred and fifty dollars. Rainbow records, from California, put outs its Alleluia album. They had the singers, musicians and the experience to produce.

"Jesus gave joy in the spirit today come on give his joy away, give, give, give, give, it away," that was the song. Sabrina didn't like Winner preaching a gospel he didn't follow. One day she wrote a song that went like this, "You call me master but obey me not."

Be ye kind, Be ye friendly; Be ye good.

Be ye disposed to peace among men.

Be ye one who favors others; Be ye honest.

Be ye perfect in your thoughts concerning others.

Be ye a watcher of Man's good.

Sabrina was sneaking brews in the basement. Beer! Still family life had its good points. In the morning Sabrina and the kids would dance before school. The children loved their mother. Ann and Tony would watch Sabrina do cartwheels, stand on her head, and they would try to do what she was doing, but couldn't and would flop around the living room having a good time until they started punching each other.

Winner wants forgiveness for being un-loving towards Sabrina. Children, forgive each other. Hold no resentments nor anger in your mind. Anger produces madness. Your Winner and Sabrina are still married and are more in love today than ever before. No divorce for us, ever. Our marriage is solid. As you grow up you realize everybody makes mistakes. When you make a mistake, admit it, don't cover it up. Our church has confession for you where you can, in private, admit your faults. Go there when you are troubled by your actions. Finally, read the word of God. Jesus will be your Good Shepherd. Follow him.

Holiday Market in Frankford had a delivery service. For two dollars Larry and Curly, the delivery men, would carry your groceries to the Holiday Market van, load up, then deliver your groceries right to your kitchen.

Winner had experience delivering pizza pie, so one day after Larry and Curly had delivered groceries to the sick man's home and received a three dollar tip, he asked Larry, "Do you guys need any help?" Larry replied, "Yes we do." Curly said, "Go down to the store, speak to Ralph or Buck. They are the managers. Tom is another manager. Go talk to them."

"Okay, I'm on my way there right now." Winner jumped on his two-wheeler bike and in ten minutes was speaking to Ralph. "Hi, I'm Charlie Winner. I'm a delivery man who's looking for a job. Do you need any help?" Ralph said, "Yes, we could use a little help. Do you know the Frankford area?" "A little," said Winner. "Okay, fill out this application." Winner filled in the answers to the questions and handed the application to Ralph who conducted a twenty minute interview. "Come in tomorrow, we'll start you training with Larry. Pay is minimum wage." Okay, thanks a lot, see you tomorrow."

Sabrina was happy when she heard the good news. Tony and Ann were also glad. The children could ride along with their Daddy when he learned the area. Larry was the driver. Winner sat looking out the window in crowded Frankford. The route was two miles in all directions with the store at the center. A hundred thousand homes were possible customers. Larry quit. Now Winner and Curly were the delivery men. A month later Curly got himself another full time job but continued to work part-time in the store. Winner worked from 9 in the morning until 4 in the afternoon. Curly started at four and worked until closing. Saturday both drivers worked, splitting tips so there wouldn't be any race for certain customers who tipped more than others.

Winner soon began dropping stories in the bags of customers. People liked the stories and they told their friends; thus business expanded. Another truck went on the streets. One hundred deliveries were made on the best day. The customers enjoyed the delivery men. The delivery man aimed to please by giving the customers a lift home, being friendly and even cutting the grass of the older folks.

The children loved going into neighbors' homes. Winner would give them an extra light bag to carry. One lady tipped Winner but ignored Tony who walked out crying, "She didn't give me a tip Winner." The lady stopped him in his tracks and gave Tony candy. The tears stopped and away we went to the next home.

A.A. meetings continued, as well as Overeater's Anonymous and Narcotic's Anonymous.

Holiday Market's trucks went home with a driver since management feared damage to their vehicle if left on the lot at night because the side door wouldn't lock. Street people would jump into the van, Winner would wake them up in the morning.

Ralph said, "Take the van with you, since Curly has a car." Now the family had transportation. Insurance was paid and the market paid for the gas.

The will often plays the fugitive's part fleeing from discipline, not desiring the disciple that fixed purpose carries. You need to re-establish your purpose quite clearly so the body knows who the master is, the will or the appetite. The appetite wants fulfillment; the will says no.

Sabrina attended A.A. meetings then stopped. Winner was trying to do what couldn't be done—fix himself. Daily, the plan was to wake up, take Tony to Poppe's, make an early morning meeting of A.A. and leave Sabrina at home alone. This was stupid. Priorities were not in order. A.A. was first, writing second, work third, the children fourth, and Sabrina, last. At the end of the day there was no time left for Sabrina. She knew this and grew resentful. Nanny would complain to Winner about *his children's teaching skill.* Winner thought the kids were doing the best they could under the circumstances.

Radman's Real Estate Company sent a letter telling the family they had one month to vacate the premises. Tony had squirted a hose into the neighbors house causing $150.00 dollars worth of damage. The neighbor complained, hence the owner of the rented home wanted possession to sell the property.

The law permits an injured worker collecting Workers Compensation checks to earn a few bucks. He is allowed to earn what he would have made if the injury had not occurred. If the worker goes over the amount allowed, the check is reduced. Each week a check would arrive in the mail. For two weeks the check didn't come.

Summer vacation was about over and the family needed a new home to rent. Four years of accumulated goods were in the house. Winner couldn't lift heavy weights. The groceries at work weighed, at most twenty pounds per bag. He had to be careful, his back was feeling painful.

The best thought men can think should be entertained continually, without interruption, without distraction, without wavering.

Happy, fun-loving Ann looked out the window and shouted, "Winner, Winner, come look out the window. Sabrina has a car, she's driving, let's go for a ride." This explained the two missing checks. Sabrina drove around the block and told Winner she was going to move and live in Kensington, close to her brother Jack. The pressure of eviction along with the pressure of motherhood was pulling her away from responsibility. A home was available for her because the owner of the home was in prison for drug-related crimes. The children went to Poppe's. Winner went to A.A. to moan and complain about back pain, addiction, dealing with mental illness, his disability, eviction and the wife who stole two checks to buy a car.

The next day Sabrina and a strange man arrived at the house. She loaded her car with clothing from the closets. Throughout the day, her car would arrive empty and leave full. This went on for several days. All this time the kids were at Poppe's.

You torture us with selfishness, you torture us with your big ego. Come on down to earth superstar. You torture us with your wild actions, you torture us with your laziness. You torture us with your indifference, you torture us with your vanity. Can you see what's happening? You torture us with your low down ways.

Winner walked down the street to get Tony. As he turned the corner Sabrina pulled up in her car with Tony in the back seat crying. Sabrina had been to Poppe's house. She took Tony and told Nanny she could keep Ann, but she wanted Tony. This was a bad idea in Winner's eyes. He jumped into the Holiday Market van and followed his wife who was in the car with a strange man.

Winner had borrowed $1,500.00 dollars from his boss to use for a new place. He wanted to go to a motel, rent a room, then think of what the next move would be but Sabrina said, "No, it's too much money." One night Sabrina's brother Jack visited Winner at Poppe's house. "Charlie," he said, "my wife's father is in jail, and we need money to get him out on bail. Can you help us?" "No Jack, I can't help you." Sabrina and Jack put together a scheme to rip Winner off. The next day $500.00 dollars *disappeared from Winner's possession.* Jack sold any valuables, Sabrina brought to the house that belonged to Winner.

Mother and the children lived in Kensington until the lady who

34

was in jail was released. She returned to her home, saw Sabrina's things in her living room and asked everyone to leave immediately.

Sabrina's sister Flamingo lived with her husband Woody in a two-bedroom home on Archer Street. An agreement was reached with Sabrina and Winner. They could live in the basement of their home until suitable living arrangements could be made. Woody and Flamingo had two children of their own. Little Woody, the new born, and Star the eight-year-old who played with Ann. They were best friends. The house on Dreamer's Lane was in the hands of the owner.

6

Love Thy Neighbor, Philadelphia Style

Sabrina took to her auto. She loaded up her possessions from the Kensington stop and her man friend unloaded them at Woody's.

A new child started playing with Star and Ann. It was Sally Oldman, a seven-year-old from up the street. The family was together. Yes, we were going to make this marriage work. The kids could sleep upstairs if they wanted, but they didn't want to. They wanted to be with their parents in the basement.

Four people in a basement created a very crowded space that was hard to navigate. The family settled down and tried to be content. It wasn't long before the children asked to go to Poppe's.

Winner had to get to a meeting or he thought he might start drinking, and if he did drink, there wasn't a chance of doing the right thing by anyone.

A common method of brainwashing is to keep repeating a thought over and over until you, the sucker, start to play the parrot's role, repeating bad news to all the other mimics who refuse to drop ego tripping.

The parents of the two sisters lived in Atlantic City. Flamingo, Woody, and their kids went to visit for a day at the shore. Little Sally was in the house playing.

The girls were jumping around, running up stairs, watching TV, coming back to the basement.

Winner shouted. stop! but they kept laughing. Ann shouted, "Daddy show Sally how you and Mommy kiss!" "No" Winner replied, "I think it's time for Sally to go home to her parents" "No!". Sally shouted. "Why can't I stay?" she asked. "Because its time for you to go now, Winner replied in a stern voice. Sally ran upstairs crying. "I want to go roller skating", she ran upstairs with little Ann running behind her. A few minuets later, the kids were gone. Winner left the house, drove to the Stones (Stepping Stones Meeting House) for an afternoon meeting. A.A. teaches honesty. Sally and Ann later became better acquainted with each other. Woody returned from the seashore, life resumed. Winner was looking for a home to rent.

Winner was drinking coffee and listening to a speaker carry the message of recovery at a meeting. A telephone rang. The steward in charge signaled for Winner to come to the phone. "Charlie, you have a call," he said.

Winner went to the telephone and took it from the steward's hand. "Hello?" Sabrina, on the other end with a mild panic and loud voice replied, "Winner, you have to come home right now. The neighbors up the street have been calling here making accusations! They want to see us! Come home, these people aren't kidding!" Winner replied, "Okay, okay, take it easy. I'll be home in fifteen minutes."

Labor Day night, 1989, 9:30 P.M. Winner pulled into the parking place then walked to the house. The family was waiting on the step. Tony, Ann, Sabrina, Woody and Flamingo started speaking at the same time. Winner asked, "What is going on?"

Everyone continued talking until Sabrina shouted, "Be quiet!" Then Sabrina said, "Sally's father has called here making threats to us. Mr. Oldman's wife has called three times wanting to speak to the man of the house. He has spoken to Woody and he thinks that we hurt his daughter. Ann said, "Winner, be careful, you're going to get hurt!" Winner replied, "Ann use your faith honey." Sabrina continued, "Mrs. Oldman told me Sally was talking about french kissing. Before Sabrina could finish Winner jumped in, "What does that have to do with our family?" "I don't know Chal", replied Sabrina. "Okay, let's go up to their house and see what's on their mind." Fifty yards of walking brought the family in front of the Oldman's house. Ann stood across the street, for fear told her to be careful. The Oldmans were strangers. Winner had known little Sally only briefly.

The storm door to the Oldmans stood open exposing the living room. Sally was sitting on the floor in front of the TV. Winner led the way to the top of the concrete steps. Sabrina and Tony stood on the lower step.

Winner was under the impression that this affair would be straightened out. He had no reason to expect harm to his person, after all Mr. Oldman, a neighbor, had invited the family to their home for an explanation.

Knock, knock, knock. Sally looked away from the TV and saw Winner knocking on the door. "Winner, Winner, they are here." Buddy said, "Hello Sally."

Winner was especially pleasant to his children. He offered his better side to both. The kids worshipped him. He found youth hanging out with them, listening to their conversation, enjoying their company, laughing, having fun, singing, teaching, bike riding and walking in the rain.

The Winners stood waiting in the hot summer night. A voice boomed out. "Get my shirt." After that, a big man, maybe six three, around 25 years old slipped his arm through the right sleeve of his short sleeved shirt. He opened the door with his left hand while saying, "Do you have a problem with my daughter, pal?"

"No," Winner said. "I don't" . . . Boom! Mr. Oldman landed a punch right on Winner's jaw knocking him backwards. He fell clear off the step and landed on his back in the grass. Winner couldn't get up. His disability was working in Mr. Oldman's favor.

Mr. Oldman pounced on the visitor. He planted his big feet over Winner's chest, straddled his body and continued the assault. Left, right, boom another left, right.

Sabrina hit the street running. She was scared. The kids ran back to Uncle Woody's house to get help for their Winner. Mr. Oldman was out to injure. He didn't want to talk. He was about to reveal his real intent. Blood gushed down Winner's face and dripped into his mouth. "My daughter doesn't lie to me." That was the second lie! More blows! Winner started kicking his legs into the dark night. His body tumbled down a slight hill onto the sidewalk.

Mr. Oldman said, "I'm going to kill you." Winner couldn't defend himself. This was a planned sneak attack, a well thought out premeditated crime.

Winner lay motionless on the sidewalk taking hard punches to both sides of his head. A few minutes later a lady appeared by Mr. Oldman's side. She held back his swinging arm and said, "He's had enough." Mr. Oldman said, "Get up, get off my property." Mr. Winner struggled to get to his feet. His blood dripped onto the street.

Winner got to his knees, afraid to lift his eyes, expecting another blow. Mr. and Mrs. Oldman watched the injured man. Uncle Woody came running out of his house. The mind started to speak fearful thoughts to the body, "You bet I'll get off your property." Mr. Oldman had one more command. He boomed out, "Now call the police!" Winner started walking home. Uncle Woody passed him on his way to Mr. Oldman who said to Woody, "I don't have a problem with you. He raped my daughter!" Woody replied, "He did not, you're nuts!"

Back at the house, the children were hysterical. Tony was crying, asking Winner if he was okay. Ann was scared. Sabrina was on the phone with the police. Winner looked into the mirror. He was cut up badly and needed to get to the hospital.

Mr. Oldman charged Winner with raping his daughter. After the beating he was kind enough to state why he took the law into his own hands. His daughter never told him that she was raped.

The police arrived and were told the story. One cop went to the Oldmans. He and Mr. Oldman stood on the sidewalk having a conversation. Winner was driven to Frankford Hospital where seven stitches fixed his right eye. The police gave the impression they believed Winner had raped the girl.

Three o'clock in the morning in Frankford, streets are deserted except for the night people. Outside the hospital a hooker walked over to Winner who was walking out of the Hospital. "Honey, honey, what happened to you? Can I help you? Do you want some company?" "No, no, no." The walk home was filled with new thoughts.

This guy Oldman is a madman. First he invites you to his house, then he tries to kill you. You better watch your step, he could be waiting anywhere to finish you off. Get out of Woody's house tonight. You can go up to the Hub Motel. It's $50.00 dollars a night, but that's cheap. *Raped his daughter,* the idiot! . . . Raped his daughter then made a social call! The Hub Motel has air conditioning. The head was running. Couldn't quiet the thoughts. At Woody's house, Winner had to bang on the door for ten minutes because everyone was sleeping. "Sabrina, wake up." "I'm leaving this house tonight. I can't sleep here, I'm going to the Hub Motel."

"Go to sleep, I'm tired. We don't have money for renting motel rooms." "I'll see you." It was out the door, into the night, jump into the truck, speed away, watching out for Oldman who might jump out from behind the bushes. He drove a mile and parked in the Hub's parking lot. He entered, paid and received a key. The air conditioner was on high. What will happen next?

Views of yesterday's experience coupled with the day's enlightenment bring forth new views or different perceptions.

The next day he sneaked over to Woody's house. Sabrina said, "You can't go to work with your eye in that condition!" Buddy replied, "The boss needs me to deliver those groceries, they don't have anybody working that knows where each customer lives." "Look," said Sabrina, "Call Holiday Market, tell your boss how you nearly got murdered on the street in your children's presence. These kids are frightened. Tell Buck what happened, see what he has to say!"

"All right, I'll call. Hello, this is Winner. Listen, last night I got beat up pretty bad by a neighbor. My right eye is shut. It's not a good idea for me to be making deliveries under the influence of heavy pain pills with vision in only one eye. What do you think?"

Buck said, "Come to work, we need you to make deliveries. Nobody knows the neighborhood like you. We'll put a driver with you. You can sit and ride along and tell him which way to go." "Okay, that's a good idea, I'll be at work in a half hour."

Winner purchased the biggest sunglasses he could find and headed for the store. Ralph and Buck were surprised when they saw the wound. Buck made a face and said, "Who did that to you? You can't work! We'll have to take care of the deliveries. What happened?"

The story was retold. Ralph said, "A kid! They believe a kid! Come to work tomorrow." Winner was heavy-hearted. Bad feelings arrive when grown men think you raped a baby.

The family was at the Hub Motel. The kids were running around the halls. They were active children who loved to do anything but keep still. Tony was jumping up and down on the bed with his sister.

Winner said, "I don't know what is going to happen but there are four of us in the family who were in the basement with Sally. You know what happened, you were there. Just tell the truth. We'll be okay."

41

"Who wants to go visit Poppe and Nanny?" "I do," "Me too." The family drove to the elders and again repeated the story.

Sabrina and Buddy went to the police station to file a complaint against Mr. Oldman. The attack was reported, pictures of the injured eye were taken. The detective assured Winner that Mr. Oldman would be arrested and locked up.

7

"Allegations"

Letters from the Department of Human Services started to arrive in Aunt Flamingo's mailbox since the family had moved to the Hub Motel. D.H.S. wanted Winner and Sabrina to come to their Center City Headquarters to file statements. The defendants hired an attorney since they knew nothing of the law or legal matters. The most eye catching advertisement in the yellow pages was the lawyer who won our business. Counsel had explained the need to keep the money coming into *his* hands.

Human Services sent social workers to Poppe's house to investigate. The social worker informed Poppe and Nanny that Buddy was indeed guilty. The lawyer informed his client that there was a strong possibility that both he and his wife would be arrested and charged with rape of a minor. The police at the Sex Crimes Unit wanted to speak to Winner and Sabrina. "Remember this," said counsel, "They are not your friends." Aunt Flamingo was also interviewed by the social workers. Ann told everyone who asked her that no harm was done to Sally in the basement. The social workers didn't want to believe this child. They refused to accept her testimony. They didn't want to believe her. If they did, there would be no case. They wanted a case!

The attorney advised the innocent husband and wife *to remain sugar free* since the hardest part of the experience was likely to occur at the round house, police headquarters, at Eighth and Race streets, where they would be finger printed and have mug shots taken.

The lawyer was waiting outside the Sex Crimes Unit when the

cab pulled in. Winner gave him a check for nine hundred dollars. He looked like he was ready to have a good time over the weekend. He took the check and said, "Wait here."

He walked into the police station and ten minutes later reappeared saying, "They are going to arrest you both." The children were playing at Poppe's house. Sabrina, Winner and the lawyer entered the station where they met Officer Little who arrested them.

"You have the right to remain silent, anything you say can and will be used against you. You have the right to a lawyer. Now empty your pockets!"

Winner pulled out a set of rosary beads. Officer Little said, "Oh, you're getting Religion now."

Col. 3:16 reads, "Let the word of Christ dwell in you abundantly, in all wisdom, teaching and admonishing one another in psalms, hymns and spiritual songs singing in your hearts to God.

Officer Little walked over to the cage that held Sabrina and Winner, unlocked the door and said, "Here is the statement against you, Sally Oldman filed this report against you." "Ann's Winner walked down the basement steps, he saw me, Ann and Tony playing. He told Ann to undress. She did. They had sex. Ann's Sabrina was jumping up and down yelling, "Get it on, get it on. She was pulling her hair while taking pictures with a camera. Tony was grabbing my hiney. Ann's Winner sat down and watched TV. He told me to take off my clothes. I said NO. He grabbed a belt and threatened to hit me. I was scared and did what he told me to do. He raped me while Ann's Sabrina took pictures. When it was over her Winner told me not to tell or he would kill my two week old baby brother."

This statement was placed outside the cell for anybody walking past to read. Police officers would appear in front of the glass window, read the statement and then get one of their friends to join them in reading the charges. Some of the cops seemed to be enjoying the humiliation by casting sinister looks upon the innocent man who was feeling weird.

No more birds in cages, or visits to the zoo, thought Winner when an old first grade classmate opened the cell door saying, "You have one telephone call. Follow me!" This cop was a neighbor who made law his business. He pointed to the phone and said, "Make your call."

The chief of Sex Crimes was a graduate from the same Catholic High School Winner had attended. A reunion was planned. The captain said to Winner by the telephone, "Are you going to the reunion?" He laughed mockingly and walked away.

"Hello mom, Sabrina and I were arrested for rape. We need bail money. The cops are typing up the paperwork. As soon as this is finished, we'll be transferred to police headquarters at Eighth and Race where we will have a bail hearing. Tell dad to be prepared to pay our bail. I'm depending on Jesus for Help." Nanny agreed to cooperate, then hung up.

The cop asked, "What's this Jesus stuff. Are you one of them too?" Winner made no reply.

One arrested for child molestation stands in battle alone. Most people think that to be charged with this crime is a crime. No one takes your side except an attorney who may think you're guilty, even if its his or her job to defend you. The lawyer can't lose. If the defendant goes to jail, the attorney gets another fee for filing an appeal.

Questions without answers brought despair which was beginning to set like wet cement. The mind was full of ugly ideas that spoke. Somebody may kill you right in prison. Big shot Winner, the handsome dude who was going to be a successful writer was, in the eyes of the Commonwealth, a "kiddy rapist."

Mr. Little, for unknown reasons, was convinced that Winner was guilty. Whoever wrote down what Sally reported must have asked leading questions which required yes or no answers since Sally didn't have the slightest idea what she was talking about!

Officer Little called Poppe and asked him to bring Ann and Tony to the police station to be questioned.

Police woman Ms. Rose Ann Freshe, badge number 1614, was busy signing her name to the search warrant, that said, "Being duly sworn (or affirmed) before me according to law, deposes and says that there is probably cause to believe that certain property is evidence of or the fruit of a crime or is contra and or is unlawfully possesses or is otherwise subject to seizure, and is located at particular premises or in the possession of particular persons as described below.

Identify items to be searched for and seized: (be as specific as possible) 1—black belt, 1—black camera, and any photos involving nude males or females or of nude male or female children, or any photo depicting the act of sexual intercourse.

Archer Street, owned by Woody and Sabrina is premises to be

45

searched. White male, early 40's, 6'1", 170 pounds, graying brown hair, first name Charles. Violation: Rape. Probable cause belief is based on the following facts and circumstances.

On September 4, 1989, the complainant Sally Oldman, age 7, white female resident of Archer Street reported to police that on Tuesday, August 29, 1989, she was inside an Archer Street residence with her girlfriend Ann, white female, and they were watching television.

She stated Ann's father came in and that he undressed along with his wife. That Ann then undressed and her father bent down and put his penis in her vagina. The father then told the complainant to undress and he reached into a bureau drawer, took a black belt and threatened to beat her unless she undressed.

The complainant pulled her shorts and underpants down and the father then told the complainant to kiss his birdie. At the same time Ann's mother picked up a black camera to take a picture. The complainant refused and Ann's father came over and bent down and put his penis in the complainant's vagina.

As a result of the above information, I am requesting a search warrant for the above premises to confiscate used items.

They do jump the gun, referring to the basement as the crime scene. Where did Sally get all this sex stuff in her mind? Mr. Winner played no part although the Commonwealth wanted that version to be believed. Who told that child that story? They brought the kids to see Officer Little.

8

Daddy Save Me

A short tine later the D.A. agreed to drop all charges against Oldman for assault. He had the blessing of the law to attack a man and try to kill him. This was okay, after all, look what he did. He is lucky he wasn't killed.

The rights of the Winner family were violated, at this point, by the D.A. who, by dropping all charges against Oldman agreed to prosecute Winner and Sabrina even though Ann's testimony denied what the accuser said. Not a shred of evidence existed against these two citizens of the United States. By dropping the charges against Oldman, the D.A. said it's Okay to attempt to murder a citizen in front of his children. To hell with his rights.

The Commonwealth based its decision on statements that contradicted each other. Ann, according to their prejudicial biased state of mind, was not telling the truth. The authorities had decided to prosecute; now they had to make Ann change her story. The case couldn't go forward until Ann made a statement similar to Sally Oldman's.

This fantasy was born of false conclusions reached prematurely to protect Oldman from the consequence of his violent behavior. Did Little have the right to tell a seven year old child, an eye witness, that she was a liar, that she was holding something back? He made her cry in that office. Who was at the scene? Was Officer Little there? No, Ann Winner was a witness and this officer frightened the child. How did Little know who was speaking truth? There was no evidence except the testimony of Sally Oldman. The Commonwealth via the D.A. and the police then committed themselves to prove the story they wanted to believe was true.

Winner was co-operating with the legal system since truth was on his side. He was anxious to speak his mind but nobody wanted to hear what he had to say. Abuse by the government was picking up speed.

Poppe and Nanny took the children back to their house. Winner and Sabrina sat waiting to be swept into the prison system.

Cease dreaming about yourself to your self. Switch that energy into gratitude. In all things give thanks. Love is not an object chased nor is love a pretty face. Love is God. Fill up with his word that brings healthy healing instead of sickness and disease. You will not complain about experience. Penance is to suffer gladly for one's sin. Trials with tribulations are great gifts. Trounce the trouble with a memory that is attached to God; not the trouble; remember God. Continued attention to virtue is required for successful achievement.

Time, that gift that goes un-noticed, pushed the Winners into the next step; after twenty-four hours of detention, two officers arrived in front of the cell. Sally Oldman's statement was handed to the driver of the van who read the statement, looked at Winner, then passed the papers to his partner. He opened the cell, Winner exited to see Sabrina. "Stand next to your wife and put your right hand out", said he. Sabrina was ordered to do the same. Husband was handcuffed to wife then led to a wagon that transported the couple through the streets they once roamed freely. The back of the paddy wagon was pitch dark. The couple shook then almost were tossed to the floor as the driver turned corners, hit the brakes, stoped the van. The door opened; a cop said, "get out". They were led into the "BUBBLE", where citizens suspected of a crime went before a judge for a bail hearing.

The detention cell at the round house is one large room filled with people. Winner walked by the desk Sergeant who was looking out into the room. He saw the holding cell and thought, "Thank God, I'm not in that cell". The officer who was leading the Winners commanded, "Stop Here". This officer un-locked Sabrina from her husband. A Female jailer led Sabrina to the women's section.

The door to this crowded room was opened. "Okay, get in there", spoke the commanding voice. "In there Sir?", Winner questioned. He didn't want any part of going into that room. "Yes, thats right, I said get in that cell", the commanding voice replied, "Isn't there any other place that you could put me?". Winner stalled, frightened, fearful, charged with sexual abuse on a child. He remembered Woody saying to him, "Don't tell why you were arrested" "Look, don't let me tell you again; in there", the officer said, pushing Winner forward. Winner knew that this jailer was getting upset so he stepped forward through the opened door.

The sight of bodies, mostly non-whites, sitting, standing, lying on the floor, people talking, sick from much drinking, packed together like sardines in a can. This was the next step in the legal system after the arrest procedures.

The Bubble at eight and race is notoriously uncomfortable. You sit and wait til your name is called to get finger printed and have your picture taken for identification purposes. Then, it's more waiting to see the judge.

The fear of God was being put into Winner!

The weekend's crime suspects filled the bubble to a standing room only crowd. Worms in a worm box would be a clear analogy. Bodies jammed together in a single room, stranger's knees touching stranger's knees. A fright broke out between two younger men as conversation mixed with laughter filled the room although at this point the sense of humor didn't exist. Winner was again led to the desk sergeant's space. The police put a plastic bracelet around the wrist of each suspect. The allegation was printed in bold black with a thick pointed magic marker. RAPE.

Winner looked into the glass walls of the bubble filled with fear. Dope addicts were nodding, a white boy was being harassed by a black man. Everyone was out of tobacco. The cop ordered Winner back into this human-being cage. Walking into any room full of complete strangers is difficult but this was intimidation. Fear stood waiting to sit down.

Suspected child abusers are the most unpopular sort of people in this setting. Stress was written all over Winner's face. Your freedom has suddenly been stripped away from you, stigma is branded into consciousness, now, surrounded by suspected criminals who are interested in what you were arrested for!

Charlie Winner's thinking ability had a explosion of mixed emotions. The faith he had been attempting to demonstrate was all but gone. This degrading mental persecution placed severe anxiety into his being as he stood like a statue looking upon the men who looked back at him trying to find enough space to stand without bumping into anyone.

Fear is a horrible emotion that often leads to panic. Winner had to maintain some sense of character since his bearing had much to do with the way people perceived him. He was tense as he glanced down at the plastic wrist bracelet that identified him and the crime he was suspected of Committing. WINNER. large black letters in magic marker ink announced RAPE! like a neon flashing sign. He pulled his shirt sleeve cuff down over the condemnation, hoping that it would stay concealed from the eyes of these strangers surrounding him. "Hail Mary", he silently prayed.

Fear stood waiting to sit down. To obtain a seat, people standing in the crowd had to wait until those detained before them advanced to the top of the waiting list and received their summons to see the judge. When they stood to leave, another person's body quickly assumed their seat. There were a hundred men in this holding tank.

Winner was called out of this cell to have his picture snapped and his fingerprints filed,again, The nasty paperwork proceeded him. In this place a person is treated as guilty. Needless to say, harsh faces with unkind words met Winner from those who knew the charges, in this case the police who led Winner back to the bubble. A seat was available. He sat down. People were on the floor sleeping under his feet. The sign on his wrist slipped into view. A man on the floor opened his eyes and saw the word RAPE on winner's wrist. He wanted to hear the story!

Honesty is not always the best policy. "I didn't do a thing wrong", said Winner as the stranger listened. "The state alleges that I raped a kid, but it is not true; Winner almost pleading to this man. Unknowingly his voice got a bit loud and a crowd instantly turned their attention towards the man who had made his first huge mistake!

Hatred is easily aroused. Winner sat in the middle of this crowd who listened to every word. The prisoners hurled threats. Winner listened to one spanish fellow say, "Oh, you man who like mess with kid". "I am like hell", Winner answered. Another offered. "There was a guy in here yesterday for messing with kids, he went out of here on a stretcher!" Still another said, "You better hope that the gods are with you, I might punch you right in the mouth". The mob was clearly against Winner. What he said was not even heard. He was on trial wherever he happened to be.

Winner looked at the entire cell full of prisoners all looking at him. this might turn into a brawl. Winner was thinking to himself, How did I ever get into this mess? It's a real shame, it's embarrassing to sit here and be treated like this, to have to go through this shit. I don't know what to do but wait and see if anybody wants to try to hurt me".

The guilty verdict was acted out as soon as the charge was mentioned. The cell door opened, a cop shouted, "WINNER". "Yea, right here", as he, stood up and walked over to the open door. "You have to see the bailbondsmen", the officer replied. "OK", said Winner", anything to get out of this cell, he thought to himself as he walked out the door, away from the danger, into a small section that was occupied by the bondsman who said, "Sit down. Can you make bail?". Before he could say another word, Winner took a seat then said, "Hey Mister, I'm innocent of all this crap you people keep saying that I did and now these guys in the bubble are making threats towards my life. I don't want to go back into that cell; my life is in danger!".

"Well there isn't anything that I can do about that! Thats the cell they have designated you to be placed. My job is to see if you have money for bail. Do you?" asked the bondsman. "Yes, I do", said Winner. This man asked a few questions then it was back to the glass cage.

He was too frightened to be angry. Walking with an officer along-side him, Winner scanned the bubble to see the hostile faces he had left there before he went to see the bail bondsman. Miserable troubling thoughts were overcoming Winner as the officer opened the door. Winner took slow steps, all the time, viewing the moods of the men in the bubble. To the surprise of Winner the men who had been giving him the hardest of times were absent and in their place, five white men, arrested for being dead-beat dads who were late with child custody payments shared their story with the crowd. The new men in the bubble had taken the attention off of Winner and the rest went back to minding their own business.

Fifty six hours later, after two nights sleeping on the concrete floor, a heavy growth of grey wiskers produced the derelic appearance. Cheese sandwiches had been lunch and dinner offered by the city to each man. The door opened once more. "WINNER", the officer said. "Come on, lets go; time to see the Judge!."

Winner jumped up from his seat and made his way through the crowd and out the door.

The judge set bail at $10,000 for each defendant. Poppe paid one thousand dollars, 10 percent of bail for Winner and Sabrina who were released and re-united.

Three days in the round house afraid to speak to people makes a man somber. Poppe drove the couple to his house for a reunion with the children who were being subjected to more shock to their underdeveloped minds.

Ann made a comment in Nanny's living room. She said, "Daddy, nobody believes us, we are going to lose this case" "No we are not Ann," replied her Father.

Obsessions, mono-mania, single mindedness, the one track mind, the addiction to thought seemed to be centered on sex abuse. This idea knocked out every other idea. Spiritual thoughts were slow to manifest. Winner remembered one thought from the good book. "My grace is sufficient for you for my power is made perfect in weakness".

Flamingo called and said to Winner on the phone, "The police were in my house last night with a search warrant. They searched the basement, and went through all your things. The police were looking for a black belt, pictures and a camera. They found your camera and took your camera with them as evidence against you and My Sister. No pictures were discovered, nor did they find a black belt". "Flamingo, we had a family camera that we all used for taking happy wholesome pictures, it was one of those twenty-five dollar cameras." "I believe you Winner, I know you didn't do anything like that, the cops came to my house about nine thirty at night. banging on my front door, the neighbors were out on their steps, this is hurting us too." Open up, "they yelled. "We have a search warrant to search this house." Woody let them in since we had no choice. The conversation ended.

Bad reports leaked out into the neighborhood. Enemies were ready to make themselves known. Old friends from years gone by shunned Winner and Sabrina.

Winner was becoming the star he had always wanted to be. He was reaping the fruits of egomania but in the wrong direction. Instead of going to the top of the list, he was heading for the bottom, well below the worst type of felon.

The family was hiding out in the Hub Motel. One long time friend of Winner's said to him under his breath as he passed him on the street, "You're gonna get ten years in prison". He didn't

52

say, "Winner tell me the truth, tell me your side of the story." Slander and gossip were doing what they did best—destroying the tale-bearer and the victim of the slander. Officer Little told Flamingo while inside her house prosecuting the search warrant that he was going to make sure that Winner received a fifteen year prison sentence.

One does not have the slightest desire to tell his fellow man that he has been arrested and charged and is awaiting trial, and out on bail for the alleged rape of a seven-year-old child. No, the virtue called silence was becoming a new experience. What is there to say when the Commonwealth is putting out accusations against you of sexual child abuse?

Winner called Woody to find out if he received any mail. Woody said, "Chal, you didn't get any mail, but I want you to come to my house right now?" "Woody, That maniac is on the lose, Oldman, I ain't coming to that block," replied Winner. "Come tonight, about ten, meet me at my house," countered Woody. "See you tonight". Winner that night cruised slowly down archer street, sounded his horn, Woody walked out of his house, jumped into The Holiday Market van, saying, "Go to the end of the block and park." Woody's car sat under a street light; every window had be smashed; broken glass was all around his car "Look what that bastard Oldman did? I can't prove Oldman did this but who else would?"

Woody didn't have any proof. Days later a court hearing was scheduled. Stay away orders were issued by the court. Mr Winner and Mrs Winner were forbidden to have anything to do with the Oldmans, The Oldmans had to stay away from the Winners, Woody and Flamingo. Star, their daughter lost her friend Sally, they were not allowed to play with each again. Letters began arriving from DHS, demanding that the Winner family come to their office to make formal statements. Winner ignored this request for a time until he decided to submit the following day. Yes, we will file a statement with you. That night, he and his son went for a ride to the river so Tony could play on his brand new scooter.

After a night's sleep, the Winner family was up early getting the children ready for a ride to DHS on the Frankford El. In the train the kids watched people enter and exit the opening and closing doors. The Delaware River was in view looking out the left window. Across the aisle and out the right window, roof tops could be seen as the train cruised along.

In the train, their bodies were shaking and swaying. The sounds of screeching brakes on metal and the whistle blowing told train commuters that they were about to enter the tunnel that burrowed its way underground; avoiding the crowded center city streets above. Winner entertained the children, pointing out sights, asking them to notice more of what they see, "awareness children, pay attention".

"I think you two kids are the greatest children on this earth", said Winner, now listen to me both of you. Our stop is next, 15th. street, get ready. When the doors open move fast. You could get caught in those doors, people have so move quickly, do you both understand?". The children acknowledged that they did. Then the train slowed down, the doors opened. The children bolted into the 15th street station.

"Slow down, come here you two, walk with me, its easy to get lost, Tony, please hold my hand when we get to the street. Is anybody hungry?" asked Winner.

Sabrina said, "I'm hungry. Let's stop and have breakfast before we make our statement."

Center City's activities with high rise buildings fascinated Tony and Ann. This was all new to them. Soon they were eating hamburgers. The waitress took a liking to the children and gave them both their hamburgers free. Once the belly was comfortably full, Winner led the way; his family followed him into the building that served as headquarters for the Department of Human services.

A skinny lady wearing a funny hat approached. Wendy Pathnek, social worker was in charge of this investigation. Ms. Pathnek introduced herself. She was the person about to conduct a interview with Ann while Sabrina and Winner wrote down their statement. Pathnek made it known that she was holding deep suspicions. In other words, she believed that these two people raped Sally Oldman.

Ann again repeated her perceptions of truth, "No. my Mommy and daddy didn't hurt Sally Oldman in the basement". Ms. Pathnek had been abused herself in her childhood so she thought she knew exactly what Ann was going through!

Winner felt the negative vibration from the state worker and wondered to himself why these people refused to believe Ann. The answer came; They had no case if she testified her parents were not guilty as she was no saying to Ms. Pathnek.

False beliefs were creating a dreamed up fanasty. Tony too

stood firm, he was fixed on the truth and said so. Ann stuck to her story which fell on deaf ears.

These employees of DHS had carefully planned out their next move with or without evidence. Sabrina entered an office to write her statement, while Winner kept his eyes on his children. She finished, then it was Winner's turn. He entered the office and began to write his statement, To whom it may concern, I charlie Winner want to say that you people are wrong. This Sally oldman was playing with Ann Winner, have a good time. They ran around laughing, enjoying themselves. At no time, ever or never did any member of the Winner family act out a sexual assault on Sally Oldman. These charges are false, these charges are being created by you people"... an older lady appeared. Winner looked at her walking towards his kids. She was holding a paper in her hand, behind her were two police officers with pistols in their holsters. We have a court order to remove you children from your custody".

Authorities had lured this family into their web like the fly surprised to see the spider making his way towards him. Tony screamed, his face twisted up in painful shock, "Daddy save me. Mommy!"

Winner, Sabrina, both on their feet watched Tony put both his arms around his Father's leg, holding on as tightly as his little arms could hold. "Daddy, Save me!", these words tore at Sabrina's heart. The police moved closer with the older women behind. She grabbed Tony's hands then pulled them from his father's leg. She then pulled Tony away and started to lead the struggling lad down the hallway towards a door. He had never cried this way before. Ann, with tears in her eyes, walked away with more control. No other country in the world would do this except America's sex police. Russia couldn't be this bad.

One last time Winner heard his son plea: "Daddy Mommy, save me". Then it was quiet, the children had passed through the door. Winner was in shock, he yelled out, "Tony, Ann I can't help you."

It was lunchtime, the office workers were heading for their favorite lunch spots. Sabrina said, "I want to go to Atlantic City to see my Mother" "Sure Sabrina' said Winner, "we have to walk over to the bus station". After which no words were spoken as the couple walked in silence to the Greyhound bus terminal.

At the bus station the couple walked through the double glass doors, walked down a few steps, then Winner walked over to the ticket counter to purchase a ticket for Sabrina who was standing a few steps away staring into space. She took the whole incident harder than Winner did.

Winner walked over to his wife and gave her the ticket, he put his arm around her shoulder and said, "Lets take a seat and wait for the bus to arrive". Sabrina said nothing. She walked along side winner. looking for a seat. They spotted two together, sat down for a half a hour without saying a word, then the bus came. Sabrina slowly boarded the bus. Winner saw the hurt in her eyes; he himself was hurting but couldn't bring words out to even say good bye, he shook his head and said, "I love you", the door closed and the bus was pulling out of the station. Winner watched the bus til it turned the corner and was out of sight.

Winner walked alone in the crowded street. Tears fell from his eyes, uncontrolled sorrow had him crying in the street. He cried so hard he could hardly see. People walking by noticed him but said nothing. He walked to the telephone. He needed to speak with his Mother. He removed a quarter from his pocket and put it into the slot, after which he dialed Nanny's number.

The phone rang twice then Nanny picked up the phone. Winner cried into the phone before Nanny could say a word, "They took Tony and Ann, they lied, Mom, told us to come to their office to fill out a statement. All along they were lying and deceiving."

"Charlie", said Nanny, "you come to my house". "Mom, I'm so hurt. Why did this have to happen to us, we didn't hurt anyone, those no good bastards kidnapped my kids". Nanny cautioned, "Don't curse, Winner, say a prayer instead!" Mo more words came from Winner, only sobbing and groaning between Mother and Son.

Walking away from disaster, his mind filled with fears; tears are falling. Sadness rules the heart today; filled with great self pity; dreams keep reappearing, "Daddy, Daddy save me." All is lost and I am weary; death do come and do your thing.

Strangers saying that I hurt my kids, but that's not true. I loved my children and they loved me. We had a happy family.

What will I say to my friends when they ask about the kids? The people at work will want to know: "why don't you bring your kids anymore, where are your children?"

I tell them the truth but they won't believe me. They love to see evil in what they do see; then they put the blame on me; when its them that are blind; them, that can't see.

I'll walk along in silence, like a monk in your big city, an outcast from society, feeling your malice, your hatred; while watching your anger and scorn. Do you care what you're doing to my family?

Winner arrived at his attorney's office crying his eyes out. Inside that office, the receptionist noticed Winner upset and disturbed. She tried to consol him, "Mr winner, please have a seat." The words broke up as they came out of his mouth. Winner said, "Thank You", as he tried to pull himself together.

"Can I get you some tissue?" the receptionist politely asked.

"No thanks". Winner answered, "I'm OK."

Winner asked to see his attorney to which the receptionist replied, "No one is in the office but me, but I will let him know that you were here. Do you want to leave your message with me?."

"Yes! tell him that DHS took my kids and I need to see him as soon as possible."

Winner stood up from his seat and thanked the receptionist for her help. He left his Mother's phone number with her to give to her boss upon his arrival, then he left through the door, out into the streets. His next stop was Nanny's house.

Winner feared a breakdown on the Frankford El. He needed to be alone in his grief, so he decided to walk the ten miles to Nanny's house in Northeast Philadelphia. It was then that the idea arrived that would take him to his Injury Lawyer's office. Al Flame was only a block away from where Winner now stood.

Citizen, when you are forced to have dealings with these people, do not believe one word that they say. They do not speak the truth. They will use any means at all to do what they want to do. The courts permit this type of legal kidnapping. They steal your children and parents have no idea it is happening since they bait their hooks with falsehoods and think that this is all right. The law supports these actions every step of the way. The parents don't have the right to even speak on their own behalf to the court that issues the order to remove the children from the family.

Both children said that nothing happened in the basement. Ann never made a charge against her Mother or Father, nor did Tony. Now, they too were prisoners, held by the state, removed by a mob, who had one purpose, one goal, that is, get these children to say that Winner and Sabrina abused them sexually. The children were forced into the Foster Care system.

9

Anybody Have A Problem?

Ann with Tony were away from their parents and family. Isolated!

The preliminary hearing for the charge of rape against little Sally was a few weeks away. The D.A. didn't have to worry about the defendant's children telling the Judge "nothing happened." The move they made was necessary from their point of view if they were to successfully prosecute the case. A key witness was taken prisoner by the state and sent to "Baby Prison"–Foster Care.

Winner walked in to Al Flame's office, his injury attorney stopped what he was doing and listened to the tale of woe.

Al said, Winner, if I had charges against me like the charges that are against you, I'd want Jerry Humble to represent me. He is an excellent criminal lawyer. I'll call him and explain your case to him if you like."

"Yes, Al, do that. I don't know anything about law or picking attorneys. The fellow we picked out of the phone book was a pot luck yellow pages man." "Winner, I'll call you tonight at your father's house after I speak with Jerry Humble." That night Al called. "I spoke to Mr. Humble, he is interested in your case. Go to his office on Thursday. He has some ideas that he'd like to share with you."

"Thanks Al, I'll do that!" Sabrina came home from visiting her mother Delores in Atlantic City.

Winner thought to himself as he was retelling his story that yes there is a Jesus and yes there is a Satan. The spirit of truth vs. the spirit of evil.

Sabrina distrusted Winner, Nanny, Poppe, Mr. Humble and Al Flame, whereas Winner had all the confidence in the world in Al Flame.

On Thursday, Mr. Humble led the Winners into his office. He was a coatless, bulky man with a mustache, who wore suspenders.

Winner retold the story. Lawyer Humble listened. In the middle of a sentence he picked up the phone and called a representative of the state.

"This is Jerry Humble, I have Mr. and Mrs. Winner in the office and we vehemently deny your accusations." He hung up the phone. This was impressive, after all the Winners hadn't hired him and he was already working on their behalf.

Mr. and Mrs. Winner, these are serious charges. Al Flame tells me that you will have settlement money shortly. I'll represent you for the preliminary hearing for ten thousand dollars, my partner can represent you Mrs. Winner.

"Can you come up with any money now?"

"Yes, my father will lend us money."

"Good, talk to your father, tell him you need ten thousand to get your defense started. I'll need ten thousand now and another ten thousand before the hearing. This fee will cover the preliminary hearing only. We have an ugly case here, this case is going to be ugly for you, ugly for me, ugly for everybody."

Winner had told Mr. Humble about the Yellow Pages Lawyer who didn't know that he was off the case. He asked Mr. Humble to let him know.

We had top notch criminal attorneys on our side who we could have confidence in. Humble picked up the phone, dialed his number and said, "Hi I'm on the case." After a few minutes of conversation, the old was fired, and the new was waiting for money. We needed twenty thousand. Sabrina wanted a divorce. Winner thought that the entire city thought he was a baby raper.

Average Mr. and Mrs. America probably are unaware of the tactics used by prosecutors in the halls of justice. Lawyers, with their superior's approval, hatch hypothetical theoretic possibilities, call conjecture truth, then proceed without restrain to prove what they say is true.

Our conversation ended, we left the office. Sabrina had gone her own way; Winner went to Holiday Market and continued making deliveries. He didn't want the entire store to find out but he did at that period start to write a statement that he intended to send to the authorities.

"Hey dad, the lawyer wants twenty thousand dollars." This news shocked Poppe. He had lost twenty pounds in a month due to the removal of the children. Nobody in the family knew where they were. Reports from the social workers filtered into the home Therapists say both children will need years of psychiatric help and counseling. Tabor Child Care Services have taken responsibility for the children.

The sex abuse expert wanted the children placed in adoption because Nanny and Poppe did not believe the Commonwealth's story. Authority wanted the children taken from the family permanently.

A cult is a system of beliefs, a subject of devoted study. The law is a system of beliefs & a subject of devoted study. Does that make the law a cult?

The monster Frankenstein was put together piece by piece. Likewise the story of false witnesses. To locate truth, a visit to the beginning is required. Truth cannot be found at the end of a lie.

Sabrina was living in a motel outside city limits. She wanted nothing from Winner but money for room and food; other than that responsibility the Winners had little to do with each other.

Poppe withdrew ten thousand from the bank, and Mr. Humble was paid. The defense was, "It never Happened."

Work continued at Holiday Market, the managers knew Winner had good relationships with 300 customers; no complaints were ever brought to their attention. The check-out girl asked where the kids were? Winner replied, "I'm not bringing them to work anymore." The children were prisoners of war totally isolated from the only people that they knew and loved.

The influence of discipline is a mighty weapon in the army of those who want change. The Lord God says in the Bible, not by sword; not by power, but by my spirit. So understand, you read the thoughts of a very sick man who took to recovery with a pen in his hand, to learn, to share, to give, to care; selfishness has always been one great big problem.

Instead of impulsive thought, control the flesh, rebuff, push back, attack the rebellious intruders with your new desire for discipline. You take a good idea and build on this good idea while the belligerent notions clamor for attention. Thought can be your enemy or your friend. Fix firmly on what you'd like to be. Keep that idea as the focus of your attention. Other ideas can come screaming into your mind, pulling you away from discipline, but remember you are now under discipline's influence. This new desire shall strengthen each time you overpower the compulsive idea.

Winner was speaking to Nanny and Poppe inside their home. He said, "Mr. Humble said this was going to be a war, and in a war we don't listen to the enemy while he is trying to destroy us. Those children were doing fine here with us."

Nanny replied, "You and Sabrina caused this to happen with your constant crazy actions!"

"We did not. This just happened. We had nothing at all to do with this. Our biggest mistake was calling the law. I should have taken the beating and left it alone, but couldn't. The cops were the ones who made the mistake. They dropped the charges against Oldman! Is that my fault too? No, it's not. The D.A. wants to believe this happened so she can get a feather in her hat for pressing full steam ahead after us. The conclusions of the Commonwealth are wrong; therefore all that they say cannot be truth."

Don't believe a word they say except when they tell you their name.

Being homeless forced Winner to live in the Holiday Market van. Living with Poppe at his home was out of the question. Visits were made to Poppe's house after ten o'clock at night for fear that neighbors would have something nasty to say. Mr. Winner entered through the back door of their home, not the front, even though he had grown up in this house and lived there thirty years. He was feeling like an outcast.

Life continued. At the Wednesday night prayer meeting, Winner told the brothers and sisters what had happened. They immediately prayed in the spirit. Winner said, "Lung cancer would be better than this."

A brother replied, "No it wouldn't," then Shirley, the leader of the group said, "This is being taken care of by the Lord." Ann often sat next to Winner and Nanny lifting up her hands to the Lord in prayer but now she was under the control of government agents who were determined she was going to tell a judge the story they wanted told and nobody could help her.

The social workers took Ann to a hospital for an examination. Ann told the doctor, "Nothing happened." She was still resisting their suggestions. The D.A. was told by the witness, "Nothing happened." The big time, downtown lawyers know how to torture a person with an attack that greets all who receive these types of charges. The sex police were in business looking for raw material for their product. Business has to grow or it fails. No product, no income. No income, no job. No job, no money. No money, no security. Reasons for trumped up charges are evident. Business.

Mr. Oldman, you might be a bit upset after reading this story. The good news is your little girl has never been touched by anyone in the Winner family. Sorry to say your quick tempered reactions have destroyed a family; but at all times, in every situation there is a good that can be seen with eyes that are wide open.

Count your blessings is the spiritual battle cry of those under the attack of harmful forces that attempt to hurt.

No choice other than writing this book was available. Winner had to keep trying to break into hard hearts in order for them to feel truthful words. This case was started by you, sir. You were the first to mention rape. Your daughter never, ever told you she was raped. You told her she was after you tried to kill me on your front step. Mr. Oldman, you did this as a cover for yourself so that you wouldn't go to prison.

Hard times were no stranger to Winner. He had lived in rescue missions, hitched rides from Alaska to New Orleans, worked the Trans-Alaska pipeline in 75, was outside in 98° below zero. He had worked the oceans in bad storms, stood atop the highest bridges walking the cable. Now he was in a most dangerous environment surrounded by liars out to destroy him. The Justice System!

Winner drove to a safe spot in the van, crawled into the back section and fell asleep. It was chilly outside. During the night he would wake up speaking to nobody but himself saying, "Where are the kids. Tony, Ann, I love you. What's Sabrina doing?" Then he would go back to sleep.

A building in the neighborhood that housed men down on their luck was a possible place to live. Living in the van was just a bit better than the street.

Seventeen men lived in the Mother of Perpetual Help House, which had been founded by a group of alcoholics who wanted to help other alcoholics get back on their feet after drinking their last drink. This was home for those who had no home.

Each person spends many hours becoming aware of his or her

thoughts. Few if any can pinpoint the birthplace of a thought, yet we all know that thoughts do indeed influence all our actions. Thinking words for good or evil. It seems to me we fix our attention firmly on our thoughts and then make corrections.

We as a people need to produce better ideas. Change happens when thoughts change. Our thinking as a group needs to be more focused on the good that we don't see because of the bad that we are in the habit of seeking. It's complex but accurate to assume that our opinions may be wrong *thereby causing the reinvention of error.*

Your enemies grow weaker every second. They fear your faith, your wisdom and your straightforwardness, since they cannot understand the Holy Spirit's power inside you that smashes fear in all its forms. Your understanding of their deceit causes them to plot new strategies which will fail.

Remember, again and again, everyone gets blessed, no one hurt. Forget what the "I" thinks is happening. "I" doesn't know. The Lord has a purpose for this madness.

Our attitudes toward one another are too often filled with condemnations, judgmental explosions, bickerings, and contrary viewpoints.

People let their thoughts work against the common good thereby reinventing strife since all thinking creatures constantly are recreating themselves in the images they form based on their experiences.

One need not travel down a dead end street to know that there is a blockage of progress, a waste of time, a nowhere street, a wrong turn, a halt to forward movements.

Change? That's what reinvention points to, but what to change and how to accomplish change seems a worthy question. Systems that drain the energy of the country need to be fixed but before this reform can possibly occur, politicians as well as ordinary people need to reinvent themselves. That is they need to create that which does not exist. Mass repentance.

Jake Buns was the brother in charge. Winner told Jake the story. Jake wanted to know why a child would lie about something so serious! Winner didn't have the answer. "The decision whether or not you can live here is not for me to make," said Jake ,"I'll call Holy Joe on the telephone and ask him. He is the president and will make that decision. Can you come back in two hours?"

"Yes, I'm on the street."

Two hours passed, Winner again was face to face with Buns who said, "Holy Joe said you can move into our house immediately. Do you have thirty dollars?" "Yes." Winner paid thirty bucks to Mr. Buns who said, "You will be sleeping downstairs on a couch. Four other men will be sleeping downstairs on their couches. The doors are locked at eleven. No drinking or drugs allowed. You drink or use drugs and we will ask you to leave. We have three A.A. meetings per week here in the house. Monday night Holy Joe chairs a step meeting. We want you to be there each Monday night for Holy Joe's step book meeting.

Winner had the responsibility of teaching his children even if the law objected. He had to be true to God, he had to strengthen his family. Children, we may never see one another in this life; then again, we may someday be reunited. You children will be able to learn the truth even with the worldly mob shouting falsehoods. Winner has a job to do and that is to teach you spiritual reality. You are to say your prayers daily, praying always in the name of Jesus.

Winner's story spread like a forest fire through the house. After all, it's not an everyday thing to have an accused kiddy abuser in your company.

The recovery program was tailor-made for situations like this one but pride wouldn't let humility come to the rescue.

10

Keep The Faith, Don't Waiver

Mother was separated from father. Sabrina was doing her own thing. Winner was still sober, attending A.A. meetings and learning what living a spiritual life entailed. No matter what anybody else does, a person should disregard how others effect the self and always do the right thing: help others. This principle or rule must be carried into all affairs.

A new character moved into the Mother house, William Right, a hard core addict looking for recovery. Winner first set eyes on Will as he was getting off a bus. Will stood with a cup in his hand begging quarters from passengers exiting the bus. "Hey buddy," Will said. "Do you have a quarter?" His eye was black, his clothing dirty, and he smelled awful. Winner put some change into his hand saying, "Man, you better get some help quick. Why don't you go to A.A.?" After a brief conversation both went on their separate ways.

A year latter Will walked into the Mother of Perpetual Help house looking for shelter. He was trying to get back on his feet after a severe ass kicking from alcohol. People who suffer seem to be caring when it comes to others. Winner related the entire story to Will who was no stranger to the justice system. He had pulled an armed robbery while drunk and served five years in prison.

Holiday market's business was growing bigger everyday. Another driver was needed to make deliveries. Winner put in a good word for Will and he was hired.

The delivery route went through the section of Philadelphia called Frankford. In this section there were many taverns. Several women had been murdered in this neighborhood during the previous five years and the killer was still at large. Sabrina was hanging out in the very bars where some of these women who were killed, were seen alive for the last time.

Winner would discuss his case with Will constantly while driving through the streets. At times he would see Sabrina walking by herself. She looked hurt but still she didn't want anything to do with Winner. He tried to make amends but the time was not right.

Winner: Will, these city hall people are serious. They got this kid lying her ass off, and she doesn't have the maturity to stand up for her rights. And now Sabrina is taking a chance running around alone at nights in these bars!

Will: Hey Winner, listen man, you can't worry about your wife. She's a big girl, she'll take care of herself. You need to stay close to A.A. Remember what A.A. teaches. You can only hurt yourself by worrying. You don't know what will happen. Remember, if God is for you who can be against you? I can do all things through Christ who strengthens me. It's damn hard to prove a rape case. The D.A. doesn't have evidence. The judge won't find you guilty. Let's go eat at McDonalds. I'm hungry.

Mr. Flame let it be known that he was about to settle the injury lawsuit with one of the major players. He expected $300,000. Workers Compensation had to be paid back for five years of benefits. Mr. Humble was to receive a big bite, and Al Flame was in for forty percent. Winner's share was around $89,000. Al settled because Winner needed money for the criminal case. We waited for the check.

The State separated Ann from Tony the first night of the capture. Tony had never spent one day away from Winner and Sabrina except for trips with Poppe to Cape May. The kid was still drinking a bottle. He cried the first two days until the social workers thought it best to reunite the children and place them with the same foster care parents.

Against her will Ann was being led from social worker to social worker for therapy. Each person who spoke to Ann was told she had been raped by her father and mother. The folks who were doing the investigation were all brain washed themselves so they attempted to have All tell the story that they wanted to hear. Her reply was, "Sabrina and Winner didn't do anything bad to Sally Oldman in the basement."

Hearing day at Family Court. Winner was there early. He was

still afraid of Mr. Oldman. Mr. Winner stood watching Mr. and Mrs. Oldman and Sally walk into the building. Sabrina walked into the park. The Winners were reunited and headed for the court room. This was a tense situation. Undercover police filled the room, looking around like nervous dudes waiting for something to happen.

The lawyers were ready. Sally took the stand. She spoke with conviction and the judge ordered the case to trial. Since Ann and Tony were isolated, they couldn't testify for their parents. It was drama. Mr. Humble made sure the Winners were out on bail. He said to Winner, "You and your wife go. Leave the court room."

Inside the mind thoughts called attention to truth. Remember, you did no wrong to Sally. You have been a truthful witness. Your children have been violated by the state. You will advance and not retreat one inch. Stand fast in Christ, take truth as your weapon and speak up when the Spirit opens up the way.

While the criminal proceedings were beginning, Family Court at 1801 Vine Street had much to say. A court order was issued telling Winner he was not permitted to speak to his children, nor was he permitted to address the kids in any way or by any third party. At a hearing, Mr. Humble told Winner that Social Worker told him Ann was changing her story and that he might get arrested again.

Mr. Humble said, "The social worker has informed me that your daughter is changing her story. Don't be surprised if it happens. Ann has been speaking to an expert on sexual abuse."

"Look at this statement!" Mr. Humble handed Winner a seven-page written statement given by Ann. Winner read the first three lines and shouted out bull-shit, this is bull-shit. The court crier reprimanded Mr. Winner for cursing in the court room. "Forgive me please, I'm sorry," said Winner. He pushed the papers toward Mr. Humble.

All lies, this child couldn't write words like this on her own. She was coached. Someone big told this story.

A master of brainwashing had succeeded in turning the child against her parents. "It's a good thing that I don't have six kids," Winner told Mr. Humble who said, "You and your wife will be arrested for rape."

The Commonwealth kept moving Ann from doctor to therapist to social worker to foster care parents. All worked together to get her to change her story. She held out for a month.

Mr. and Mrs. Oldman sold their home and moved away from the neighborhood. Winner and Will Right went back to making deliveries and attending A.A. meetings. The wife was out there. Nobody knew where she was or what she was doing. She did not know that another arrest was about to take place.

Holiday Market at nine in the morning.

Winner stood outside watching people pass. Officer Little and another cop pulled into the lot, walked into the store and walked by Winner. They didn't look like they were going food shopping.

Minutes later, Buck the manager walked between the two officers heading towards Winner who was drinking a cup of coffee. Office Little said, "You are under arrest." "What for this time?" asked Winner. "You were making kiddy pornography." "I was like hell." "Put down the coffee cup, turn around and put your hands out."

Officer Little searched Winner, then the other cop pulled up in his police car. They put Winner in the back seat.

Sabrina had disappeared. She had missed a hearing. The police had a warrant for her arrest. Poppe was told because she didn't show up for a hearing, he might have to pay here entire bail. Officer Little found her a few days later. She was arrested and sent to prison.

Inside sex crimes unit, Officer Little opened up the cell. He unfolded a chair and in a mean nasty way said, "Look, we can do this the hard way or the easy way. I want to know where the camera is?"

Winner said, "I'm innocent."

Little, "I didn't ask you that, if I don't get that camera, I'm going to your father's house with a search warrant and tear that place to pieces. Then I'm going to your sister-in-law Flamingo's and do the same thing."

Winner replied, "You go do what you have to do, there is no camera and there are no porno movies."

Officer Little finished his interview. He spent no more than two minutes talking to the defendant.

Little couldn't find a movie camera or any kiddy porno so *that porno charge* was changed to rape. Another trip to the police station, this time, right down the street from where Winner had grown up. The same type of condemnation greeted him as he was finger printed and mugged, then put in a cell. Hours later, out on bail, back to Holiday Market to make deliveries.

69

Sabrina had her arraignment, bail was tripled, she needed $3,500 for her freedom. Poppe wouldn't pay since she had failed to show up for her hearing. Winner started to save three hundred a week. It would take at least three months to get her out.

The day before Thanksgiving an old friend came into Holiday Market. Winner told her the story. Mary Jane said, "Charlie, my life was a mess on heroin but I went to a recovery group in South Philadelphia, and asked two people to help me. They did help me. I'm in recovery. It sounds like you should do the same."

Mary Jane gave Winner the address, he went to that group and asked for help. Two ex-addicts stood strong in Winner's corner leading him into an encounter with the twelve steps of A.A.

The hearing before the judge for Ann came. We were all there. Sabrina had lost a lot of weight. She was in handcuffs. The child entered the court room crying so hard that she couldn't speak. The judge postponed the hearing telling the D.A. she had better prepare the witness. This was the second attempt to have her testify.

The D.A. then had the children separated. They couldn't depend on each other any longer. Ann was in a foster care house where the foster care parents told her that she would be helping her parents by testifying against them.

Ann had submitted to her captors and was dependent on them for her ego strokes. The Commonwealth suggested the story to the child and kept reinforcing the lie by putting the child under constant pressure to say it happened.

On the witness stand Ann was articulate and well-spoken as she described being assaulted in the upstairs bedroom on the floor since the age of four. Yes, Winner had sex with me, and Sabrina knew. Yes, Sally's story was true. Winner raped us in the basement.

Mr. Humble didn't want to ask her any questions. He didn't want to give her a victory in her head. We were going to trial with two cases, the charges, rape, two counts, incest and sodomy.

Christmas Dad. Winner had enough money to bail Sabrina out of jail. Will went along. He waited in the truck until Sabrina appeared with the biggest smile on her face that Winner had ever seen.

Al Flame had the money, come down and pick it up. Sabrina was ready for some shopping. A house was purchased to show the court that we were responsible. Two months later it went up in a fire, $38,000 worth of damage. Sabrina put gas into the sink because it was stopped up. She thought gas would clear the drain, but she

70

took a plunger and started plunging. A spark flew off into the gas range. We had more unhappy neighbors who wanted us to leave.

Working the program, going to meetings, staying alive, meeting the bad news with faith and prayer is what held Mr. Winner together.

Pulling the mind away from thinking about the world is the remedy for all strife. Simply go to God and stay there.

Choose God or the world. One brings health, the other all kinds of troubles. This is a demonstration, not mere words but victory in Christ.

What have the child's experience been like since she was removed from her family?

1) The police called her a liar.
2) Social workers ignored her statements of truth.
3) She was separated from her father who she loved by armed police.
4) She was placed in ten foster care homes.
5) Mental health workers didn't believe her.
6) She had been lied to by foster care parents who told her she would be helping her parents by speaking agaisnt them.
7) She is not and has not been permitted by social workers to mention her mother and father when grandparents visit.
8) She saw her father and mother in handcuffs.
9) She was suddenly separated from her brother.
10) She was forced to testify in court since it was not by choice.

I protest in writing, and make a formal complaint, for the record. Ann has lost her will to think for herself because of the impressions left upon her mind. The purpose of this protest is to point out the potential harm that may be inflicted upon the mind and psyche of this child. Please, never forget, the state is not her father yet and never will be.

Ann needs to be deprogrammed. Her thoughts are guilt, worry, fear, anxiety. She sees love as non-existent. Her captors have been ignoring her words unless they match their hidden agenda, which is convict her mother and father.

This printed message is a loving instrument of light, shining hopeful rays of understanding and perhaps will influence the court's judgment, to order the state to cease their heavy handed interference.

The world's system had hit this couple with the hardest blows it could launch. Yet the blows increased Winner's strength. He learned in the A.A. program that he was powerless. So what can powerless men do but turn the situation over to the Higher Power.

Yea, though I walk through the valley of the shadow of death, I will fear no evil; for *YOU ARE WITH ME*, your rod and your staff, they comfort me. Psalm 23:4

I do not count myself to have apprehended; but one thing I do, *FORGETTING THOSE THING WHICH ARE BEHIND AND REACHING FORWARD TO THOSE THINGS AHEAD.* Phil. 3:13

11

"The Massacre"

Nineteen months after the charges were filed all concerned were ready to go to trial. Courtroom 425 started to fill up with people. One hundred potential jurors were led into the courtroom where Judge Henry Herian sat on his bench high above all others. Fourteen from the group would be selected to serve on this jury.

Outside the courtroom two crowds gathered. One group supported Mr. and Mrs. Oldman. It included the police, social workers, experts in child abuse. That group stood close to the entrance to the courtroom.

The second group, Winner's supporters included Nanny, Poppe, Aunt Jane, Will Right, a few people from recovery groups, a couple of ironworkers who came to testify and two people from the Unity Church of Christ.

To meditate on an object of attention is a choice. Charity reminds others that it's possible to pull away from news of the world, the actions of unbelievers, the noise the faithless thunder into the ears, social problems, sickness, health care, abortion, violence and the self and place the attention on truth in God's Kingdom.

To be suspicious is to mistrust, to be guilty, to doubt, to fear something is wrong. Fear is a painful emotion created by danger, dread and terror.

Defending yourself against something that never occurred is downright ridiculous. The mud slinger's strategy is convict by words. Popular opinion was against the state's whipping boy. The children were brainwashed, manipulated into speaking what the commonwealth taught them to say. No crime had been committed.

73

The burden of proof was on the state to prove with evidence that this crime had occurred beyond a reasonable double. Ha, what a joke!

Sabrina stood thirty yards away from both camps with a man friend. She ignored Winner. Mr. Humble made a motion to the court to have Sabrina and Winner tried separately.

Old desires in a new mind equal more of the same stuff. The world solves its crime problems with prison and punishment. Often it is difficult to forgive but always life is more difficult when you don't forgive. Love with forgiveness will work.

Don't dare cause your sister any grief. Your brother needs your unconditional love. Enjoy life, rejoice, that's your Father's will. Take advantage of your pain for gain; be a voice for healing and witness for God's love.

The defense feared Sabrina would act in a way at the trial, in front of the jury, that would harm Winner. Her record of past mental health problems and unpredictable actions could and might cause a disturbance that would influence the jury to view Winner in a negative way. What you see and hear influences how you react! The defendents did not have the advantage of a united defense because he couldn't ask his co-defendant to testify due to her unstable mentality.

Speak to your heart. Tell it to calm down and beat slower. Take it easy, relax, do not worry about the future. Sit at ease in a quiet state of relaxation, calmness, faithfulness and holiness. Be obedient to truth. Choose the present thought you shall entertain. Beat normal heart, steady, neither fast nor slow. Beat heart, perfect in the moment now. No stress is permitted into the awareness. Stay out troubles, stay out memories of the crimes of man, stay out health care drama from political voices. Choose what you will permit into the most sacred place. Enter discipline. Sit on the throne of virtue. Every good deed done in charity for others is directed, controlled, observed, by Lord Discipline, Master Charity, King Unselfishness, Queen Purity. The Holy Spirit is surrounded by these traits, so guard them like your bank account.

The judge ordered Sabrina to be examined by a court doctor who told the court that Sabrina was fit for trial. Judge Herian denied the motion for separate trials. The leading lady, the co-defendant was ruled competent by an incompetent doctor! Father was on trial with a wife not capable of being helpful to the defense.

Sabrina hadn't taken her medicine for months. It was impossible for her to be judged fairly. Doctors told Winner time and time again that if she discontinued her medication she more than likely would have to be hospitalized. On two occasions six months before the trial, Winner signed Sabrina into institutions.

All people have a different view of what is before them. The court made a mistake listening to the incompetent doctor who examined Sabrina. This error helped the D.A. get the conviction. The D.A. and Mr. Humble spent the morning asking questions of the potential jurors. Fourteen were picked and sworn in. We were ready.

After a recess, a court official summoned all concerned into the courtroom. Judge Henry Herian walked into the room. The bailiff cried out, "All rise!" Everybody stood. "The Court of Common Pleas is now in session." The judge sat down, and asked the D.A. a question. "Is the state ready with its case?" Ms. Patricia Vim, Assistant District Attorney responded, "Yes, your honor." "Is the defense ready?" "Yes your honor," said Mr. Humble. "Bailiff bring the jury into the courtroom."

All right Devil, let's rumble! In the name of Jesus, go! Get out, stay out. In the name of the Father, and the Son, and the Holy Spirit. Amen. Jesus falls under his cross but gets back up again.

Winner watched fourteen strangers fill the jury box.

He thought how accused sex offenders are treated like the worst of society. They are disliked, shunned, avoided, treated like lepers.

Abuse. The mere word creates negative reactions in the normal mind.

Once the title of child molestor is branded on a person, trouble follows every step. Homes get burned down, fliers warn residents of the offender's eminent release from prison, angry mobs unite with signs carrying nasty messages. We don't want you in our neighorhood.

The prison protects society by locking up these sometimes innocent people who end up in the court battling legions of professional mental health care professionals. Spirit of fear—out—in the name of Jesus. Spirit of doubt—out—in the name of Jesus. Spirit of worry—out—in the Name of Jesus. Spirit of sin—out—in the Name of Jesus. Spirit of hate—out—in the Name of Jesus. Spirit of pride—out—in the Name of Jesus. Spirit of vanity—out—in the Name of Jesus. Spirit of guilt—out—in the name of Jesus. Spirit of selfishness—out—in the Name of Jesus.

The truth demands full attention. Believe it or not, it happens. Little innocent kids with undeveloped minds are being brainwashed by adults.

The judge made a brief statement to the jury, explaining their responsibility in this case. He said, "Ms. Vim, you may make your opening statement at this time.

Mr. Humble, Mr. Home's, another attorney for Winner, along with Sabrina and Mr. Smith sat at the defense table. The trial was similar to a Broadway play. Judge Herian was the director. The D.A. was the antagonist; Mr. Humble the protagonist. The actors were the witnesses. The jury was the audience who sat fascinated listening to the opening statements.

Start again, forget your failures. This time you can succeed.

II Corinthians 3:4 "Blessed by the God and Father of our Lord Jesus Christ, the Father of compassion, who encourages us in our every affliction so that we may be able to encourage those who are in any affliction with the encouragement with which we ourselves are encouraged by God."

THE PEP TALK

Attention. Listen up. You know exactly what you will do in the game. So, relax, let all worry and stress drift out of your minds. You need to let your confidence take over and work for you. You have been practicing going over your moves again and again. You know when to go forward when to step back. Keep your eyes on your opponent at all times when in competition. Your opponent is scheming his victory just as you are planning his defeat. He wants you to lose your discipline, break down, make a error, do something you shouldn't do so he can bust through your weak point and score.

According to the Commonwealth, this man is the crazy child abuser, married to the off-the-wall crackpot who was driven crazy by her husband. Women were the scourgers; children the victims.

Ms. Vim, was about to begin her startling character assassination. She walked towards the jury. Vim was a beautiful woman about five foot seven, with dark hair. She was slim with not a trace of fat and was dressed in a dark suit. She stopped in front of the jury, paused, looked them over and began to speak.

"Good morning ladies and gentlemen of the jury. As the judge explained to you, this is my opportunity to give you an opening statement, a preview, an overview, a coming attraction of what you are about to see and hear from this witness stand. Unfortunately, I don't have actors to present, I don't have cameras to zoom in to give you the important part of the action. Nor do I have background music to let you distinguish between what is serious and what is light. I have real people. And in this case I have children.''

Winner started squirming in his seat. He taped his fingers rapidly on a wood railing: 1234, 1234, thinking to himself. "Yea, you kidnapped a baby with a court order. You put false suggestions into her undeveloped mind, then you controlled her will to make her do and say what the social workers insisted she say. She is being forced to testify. Ann made no charges against her parents until your demonstrated lopsided powerplay justice scared her into changing her story.

Winner looked at Ms. Vim's back as she continued to speak to the jury. "I have Ann, who is nine years old. I have Sally Oldman who is nine years old and possibly little Tony, who is six years old, real people. real children.

"Use your common sense to understand what it means for them to come into a courtroom, first of all. Them to get on the stand, and talk to you from the stand, in front of a judge, and in front of the parties accused, the defendants, in front of all of you, and any spectators. And then use your common sense to understand and evaluate their words.

As Winner listened, he shook his head from side to side, trying to get the attention of the jury by saying, No, not true.

Common sense is not shared by all. A false story is fantasy, D.A. Vims asked the jury to make common sense out of the Commonwealth's version of a crime. Kids' learn what adults teach! Don't they?

Use common sense continued Ms. Vim, in evaluating what it is like for them to come into a court room and then take it a step further. Use common sense to understand what it is like for them to not only go through that experience of abnormal sex but then to talk about it.

Winner thinking again at the defense table: "What was it like for Ann? She didn't know a thing about normal sex so how could she know about abnormal sex unless someone put ideas into her head. The State refused to believe her for a month when she told all of them nothing happened. She saw her Father get beatup at a man's house, then she was taken from the family, called a liar by the police, told not to change her story by the D.A.

Ms. Vim again challenges the jury to use common sense through out the trial. "Pay close attention to the evidence. You will evaluate that evidence to determine what you, as the fact finders, determine the facts are and you will then apply those facts to the law as the judge will instruct you."

Winner: There is not one piece of evidence that could possibly point to Sabrina or Winner committing this crime.

"Law will describe many things, but law which will include descriptions of charges in this case of rape, of involuntary deviate sexual intercourse, of corrupting morals of a minor, of endangering the welfare of children, and finally of conspiracy. Because we have two defendants who acted in consort and it is these events that you will hear about."

Winner looked at Sabrina who had her back to the jury. She wore a red baseball cap and large sunglasses. She played with a medal that hung around her neck and chewed gum. What a girl!

"Let's get to the facts in this case with those charges in mind."

Winner silently objected. Ms. Vim had no facts in this case. The father is the speaker for his children, not the state. Ms. Vim is repeating words that were spoken to her by therapists. Ann had already proven her will had been destroyed.

Ms. Vim: On August 29, 1989. "You will hear testimony from that little girl Ann. You will hear testimony that at the time she was seven years old. She will tell you she was doing things on that day that you would exect 7-year-olds to do. Running around with her girlfriend, Sally Oldman, watching a movie on TV and jumping on the beds. You will hear things that happened on August 29, that you would not expect a 7-year-old girl and her 7-year-old friend to be doing.

"At that time they were living at Archer Street. When I say they, I mean the defendants, Sabrina and Charles, were living in the basement of Archer Street in Philadelphia. Sally Oldman lived down the street."

"Sally and Tony are playing in the basement. While in the basement the defendants, Charles and Sabrina encourage their child, Tony, who at the time is approximately four or five to take off his clothes and run around nude.

78

"Sabrina encourages Tony to touch tongues with Sally Oldman, the neighbor. She encourages Tony to touch her private area with his penis.

Winner sat shocked at the words he was hearing.

Ms. Vim continued, "While this was going on, you will hear Ann tell you that her father came home."

The defendant shouts, "Not true."

"He came into the basement and engaged in sexual intercourse with his wife, in front of his 7 year-old daughter, a 7-year-old neighbor and a four-year-old boy.

"You will hear that in addition to her father having intercourse with their mother in front of them, he then turned to her, Ann, a 7-year-old, and put his penis in her vagina, and she'll tell you his birdie, that's what she called it, at the time put his . . . Censored! She'll tell you where else he placed it that day. You will hear it from her. She'll tell you that at that point he took a belt. He wasn't finished. First his wife, then his daughter, now the neighbor child.

Mr. Homee, co-counsel to Mr. Humble yells, objection.

Ms. Vim, Sally Oldman.

The Court: Sustained, it is argumentative.

"Ms. Vim, then he turns to Sally Oldman threatening her with a belt and forces Sally Oldman, 7-years-old, the little girl who lives down the street to take off her clothes and proceeds to put his penis in her vagina.

Winner thought to himself, this woman is completely out of her mind. Birdie, yucky, gross, stuff, belts, according to Ms. Vim, Winner was jumping on everything that had life. He kept shaking his head, No, No, No. The jury sat stunned.

Ms. Vim: "You will hear Sally talk to you about his birdie, and she calls her vagina her hiney. At this time she'll tell you that he peed inside of her in her words. While all of this is going on, Mom is still there, the defendant, Sabrina, encouraging the action. Go for it, yee ha, yee ha, like she's at a concert or football game. While things are happening, she grabs a camera and takes pictures. And when the action ended, both defendants told the kids not to tell or they would be hit, not to tell or they would be killed. Keep it a secret. Don't tell.

"Well, unfortunately, the secret wasn't safe this time because. . . .

Mr. Humble: Objection, Your Honor, may we see the court at sidebar please?

The Court: Objection sustained.

Mr. Vim: "Don't tell, but Sally Oldman after having burning urination and after watching a television show with her parents with somebody kissing started talking about kissing, and when her mother asked further questions told what happened, told the secret of what had gone on in the basement, and because Sally told, Ann now is forced to answer the question of what happened in the basement and Ann while with her parents denied all of this happened. She denied it. . . She said, "Yeah, we were in the basement and, my brother Tony was naked in the basement. Yeah, they were encouraging the French kissing. But she denied the oral and vaginal penetration. She denied that while she was with her parents.

Sabrina had her head on the defense table. Winner was destroyed yet he thought, there right there, Ms. Vim admitted that the daughter denied their story. She was kidnapped by the government with the intentions of changing her story. Why else would they remove her from her home? Without her there was no case; there shouldn't have been a case.

Ann should have been with her family at the preliminary hearing but due to the suspicion of the girls in city hall she was removed from her father's protection and put through all kinds of abuse by the government.

The state removed this child after she told them that her parents hadn't hurt her or Sally. They started working her over to make her change her testimony. It should be clear to the most liberal of democrats that this is exactly what occurred!

Ms. Vim: "But Sally Oldman's telling put a crack in the dam that had been built by Ann, because once away from her parents, once in foster care, once in counseling, and asked again, she said yes, it happened on August 29. When you asked me before I lied. I was afraid. I was told not to tell. I was hit in the past. Yes, it happened."

"August 29, ladies and gentlemen of the jury, was just the tip of the iceberg. Ann went on to tell what happened on other days, from the time she was four or five years old, when she was living at another address on Fairy Tale Lane. That she was regularly penetrated by her father, orally, vaginally, anally, and while this was going on, her mom was watching, enjoying, and yelling, yee ha, yee ha, having a good old time and clicking pictures.

Winner: D.A. Vim was back to the yee ha, yee ha, testimony. Bullshit! You crazy idiot. Talk is cheap lady. Let's see those pictures. Produce them. Don't talk about pictures unless you have them. Show the jury. The police didn't find pictures. Not one. A person fitting the description Ms. Vim painted certainly wasn't bright enough to cover his tracks. The jury was told Sabrina had been taking pictures of Winner and the kids in sex photos for five years but no pictures were brought forward.

Ms. Vim: "And in addition to that, she was forced to pose naked with her brother, and in addition to that, she was forced to watch her parents engage in sexual intercourse, and in addition to that she was told she'd be hit if she told or would get in trouble, if she told.

"But Sally Oldman's telling of the incident on August 29, 1989, cracked the dam, and her being taken away from her home environment allowed the crater to gush out and for the secret to come out. That's what we're here about today.

Winner: Ms. Vim is telling two stories as if they were one. She starts telling about Sally and in the next thought brings Ann into the story. The D.A. said it once more, "Her being taking away from her home environment forced it to gush open."

In other words had the state left Ann in her home it wouldn't have gushed open, there would have been no case and the police would have to go after Mr. Oldman for attempted murder. Somebody in government would have to admit that mistakes were made, but most of us know that pride will not admit wrong doing.

"You will in addition to these children, hear evidence from other adults regarding the chronology of what occurred as to what the children told them and when. You will hear from the police that a camera (124 Instatmatic) was confiscated from the basement of Archer Street, the camera that was used by the defendant, Sabrina, while her children and the neighbor child were engaging in sexual acts with her husband.

You will also see as evidence presented by the Commonwealth a letter written by the defendant, Charles which was sent to the social services agency worker for his daughter Ann, "I hereby ask and claim your forgiveness for all of my past wrongs against you in thought, word or deed."

81

Winner: False witnesses, shame on you! These words were written on a 3 by 5 card, addressed to a particular social worker and a similar card was sent to the D.A. Why? Winner attended an abundant life seminar. One of the exercises in that program was writing forgiveness cards to be addressed to ten people against whom we held resentment. The D.A. and the social worker who received the card were two people Winner had no respect for whatsoever. He didn't like these people. This not liking attitude goes against the gospel of Christ. We are commanded to pray for those who persecute us.

Ms. Vim tells the jury this forgiveness note was for Ann! How did she know? Winner wrote the card, addressed the card, mailed the card. Besides, the words from this card came from the mind of the preacher who ran the group. Thirty others filled out similar cards. A Court order was in place commanding Winner to refrain from communicating with his children since Ann was not on the list of ten. The D.A. boldly lied to the jury.

Winner needed to send her a forgiveness note for thinking hatefully toward her. Dear D.A. Vim, "I hereby ask for and claim your forgiveness for all my past wrongs against you in thought, word, and deed. Yes, I'm guilty of thinking unkindly thoughts about you."

Resentment, anger, and hate get alcoholics drunk. This was a spiritual act for good that was being twisted to appear evil. Winner was still working his recovery program; this exercise was part of his spiritual growth effort.

D.A. Vim: "You will finally hear medical evidence regarding Sally Oldman, the neighbor girl: that this 7-year-old's hymen was broken, that she had a green yellow discharge from her vaginal area, that she had a yeast infection. You will hear medical evidence regarding Ann that she had redness and irritation around the walls of her vagina."

Winner's comments: Ms. Vim said nothing about Ann's broken hymen. The girl is a virgin to this day, but the authorities keep her away from those who could upset the apple cart. Sally's broken hymen is part of their fantasy. No doctor saw these kids on Winner's behalf. Why?

"After you hear all this evidence from the children, and relevant professional personnel, remember the children's testimony alone is sufficient to convict, but you will hear other testimony to

82

corroborate what these children said. I am confident at the end of this case you will turn to two defendants, Charles and Sabrina, and say guilty of rape, guilty of involuntary deviate sexual intercourse, guilty of corrupting the morals of a minor, guilty of endangering the welfare of children, and guilty of conspiracy, because they were in it and they were in it together, guilty. *Give Ann and Sally Oldman a chance by saying guilty to these people.*

Mr. Humble: Objection.

The Court: Sustained.

Ms. Vim: Thank you.

The Court: All right, I will see counsel at the sidebar.

Mr. Humble: I move for a mistrial. This opening was so inflammatory and argumentative that there is no way my client can receive a fair trail. To tell the jurors that it is their role to protect the alleged victims by finding defendants guilty, is to misstate the role of the jury. To put them in a position where they are just totally inflamed and prejudiced against the defendants and to lead them to think that if they find the defendants not guilty, or either of them not guilty that they will somehow be endangering children is absolutely **outrageous,** and that's what she just suggested.

The Court: Motion for mistrial is denied. We will recess until tomorrow morning at 9:30.

12

Almost Dead But Still Alive

The following day after a miserable night, it was back inside room 425.

The Court: "Good morning, ladies and gentlemen of the jury. I thank you for your promptness. I know you were here earlier and that we are starting late, and I apologize.

"We wore Ms. Latoo out yesterday, our court reporter, so we have a new reporter with us today, Betty Ge Pardona, and we are ready to proceed.

"While you were waiting, we were looking at a few documents. We are now at the point in the proceeding where I think, Mr. Humble, you may proceed if you wish with your opening statement."

Mr. Humble: "Thank you, Your Honor. With the court's permission, Mr. Homee, Mr. Smith, Miss Vim, good morning. Ladies and gentlemen of the jury, let me introduce myself to you. My name is Jerry Humble. I represent Charlie Winner who is seated right here behind me. (pointing)

You were in this court room yesterday and no doubt noticed that the prosecution has its own table to sit at here (pointing), and the defense, the two defendants, are seated over here at this other table. (pointing).

Please understand that there are two defendants in this case. Each is represented independently by an attorney. That is one attorney representing Sabrina, and Mr. Homee and I represent Charlie. The fact that we are sitting at a table together does not mean we are thoroughly in agreement on everything that is going on as far as the defense is concerned. That is why each defendant has an independent lawyer, and simply because we are seated at one table does not necessarily mean that all the facts you hear or all the testimony that you hear relates equally to each of the two witnesses, or indeed that what I am saying necessarily applies or does not apply to Sabrina. I want to make it crystal clear that each individual is entitled to his or her own defense, and each, more importantly, is entitled to your individual consideration in evaluation the testimony that you hear in this case.

"Now, this is a criminal case, and in a criminal case certain rules apply. First of all, as the Court has explained to you and will undoubtedly do so again, the mere fact that somebody has been accused of a crime or crimes does not suppose guilt. That is an important and fundamental state of principle of criminal law, and possibly even more so in a case where there are individuals who are charged with crimes against children.

Now, each of us, each and everyone of you, naturally feels protective towards children, and in the case where someone is accused of a crime against a child, it is incumbent on each and every one of you to be as objective and as dispassionate as possible in evaluating the evidence that is presented here, because as the Court explained to you and cautioned you yesterday, after the District Attorney's very emotional opening statement, your task is not to protect children. Your task in this court of law is to evaluate the strengths and weaknesses of the evidence that is presented and to determine whether or not a crime or crimes have occurred, and whether or not these individuals charged with those crimes are proven guilty beyond a reasonable doubt.

So, emotional displays are not evidence. Indeed, Ms. Vim was not a witness to any of the critical events that occurred in August of 1989 or prior thereto that you may hear testimony about in this case. She is merely a person who is here to present to you what has been presented to her in a file, and although she is sincere in her efforts to present her case to you in a way that is most favorable to the prosecution, you should understand that emotional displays are not evidence in this case. We must be clear that we are going to examine the evidence to determine what the facts are and what the facts are not.

Now, because there are children involved in this type of a case, it is important to you as people who have experienced it in your

86

every day lives—and maybe you have children or have had occasion to relate to children during the course of your lives—it is important for you to keep in mind that children are easily suggestible; that is, it is easy to suggest things—

Ms. Vim: Objection.

The Court: Sustained.

This is argumentative, Mr. Humble, and please confine yourself to your opening address.

Mr. Humble: Yes.

Ms. Vim: Move to strike, Your Honor.

The Court: All right. Members of the jury, you are asked to disregard those remarks. I direct you to do so.

Mr. Humble: Yesterday, the District Attorney told you she was going to give you a preview of what the case was about. She then went on to say that these witnesses are not actors, they are real people, and that she would be presenting to you real people. I propose to demonstrate through the testimony in this case that a process has gone on in regard to these children who are not actors in an effort to turn them into actors. I intend to demonstrate to you through the evidence in this case that these children have been taken to what is referred to in the files on these children as "court school" to learn how to testify, to learn the most effective way of convincing you of what the Commonwealth is trying to do here. So, referring to these children as not being actors in the sense that they are not professionals, they are not paid to come to court and do this is true—. On the other hand while I am not suggesting that these children are deliberately telling untruths, I am suggesting that they have been put through a process. They have not been brought here without being rehearsed as Ms. Vim attempted to suggest to you yesterday when she said they were not actors. In fact a great amount of time has been spent with each of these children to make them effective as witnesses and to get across the story the prosecution intends to get across.

Miss Vim told you yesterday about Ann and floodgates opening up. You are not going to hear any testimony about floodgates opening up in this case. What you are going to hear is that Ann was taken out of her home and taken away from her parents and family and put into a strange home, and that she resisted suggestions to her that her parents has abused her. You are going to hear about her insistence that she would like to go home to her parents. You are going to hear that it was only after several weeks of isolation away from her family home and parents, that she began to make statements about abuse.

These are issues, ladies and gentlemen, that you will have to evaluate. These are facts that you will have to evaluate to determine how much credence you can give testimony that is obtained under these kinds of circumstances from small children by people who are possible very well meaning people, but nevertheless are obtained from children under circumstances where suggestions are made to them.

Ms. Vim: Objection.

The Court: Overruled.

Mr. Humble: The District Attorney can object to this all she wishes, but just as she is allowed to give you a preview, so am I, so I ask you to listen to the evidence in this case and then decide whether you are hearing what the children are saying or whether you are hearing what has been suggested to them by others, who for whatever reasons they have, and no matter how much they believe in what they are doing, are in essence speaking through the mouths of these children. So, I ask you to take the testimony and listen to it carefully as I am sure you will.

I am not going to get specific about what you are going to hear. I think that will be adequately demonstrated to you through the testimony that you will hear through the witnesses in this case. I think that once you hear everything, ladies and gentlemen, you will believe there is reason to have doubt.

Remember this, the Commonwealth has a burden of proving a case beyond a reasonable doubt. A reasonable doubt simply means this: you must not have any cause to pause or hesitate or be held back from acting in a matter of importance before you can find Charlie guilty here. If you have any reason to hesitate, to pause that is based on the evidence you have heard, or based on the lack of evidence that you have heard, or based on the credibility of the testimony that you have heard, that would constitute a reasonable doubt. Now, we are suggesting to you that there is such a reasonable doubt in this case, that you, in fact, will return here with a verdict of not guilty for Charles. Thank you ladies and gentlemen.

Mr. Humble turns away from the jury, walks to the defense table and sits down.

The Court: Thank you Mr. Humble.

Mr. Smith: (Sabrina's lawyer) Do you wish to make an opening statement at this time?

Answer: "Not at this time, your honor, but I would like the jury to be advised that I am reserving my right to make a statement later."

Court: "I will do that."

So ended the opening statements. Mr. Humble was on record that he thought it was impossible to overcome the bias created by Ms. Vim's asking the jury to save the children. The question yet to be answered was could the DA sell her story to the jury as easily as they sold the story to each other.

Deception was in the air in Courtroom 425!

Ann had been in therapy for 19 months which held up, supported and strengthened the version of the commonwealth. Sabrina and Charles still hadn't spoken one word to each other since the trial started. Four visitors stood up and walked out of the courtroom when they heard what this trial was about.

Winner was looking forward to seeing his daughter whom he had not seen for nineteen months. He sat looking around the courtroom. Paintings of judges hung on the wall. The room was quiet until Ms. Vim announced her intentions: "The State calls Ann to the witness stand."

Father and daughter when together lived a happy life. Winner taught the child to think for herself at an early age because sooner or later, depending on your own thoughts was vital to confidence in one self. He brought her flowers every week, she was his travelling partner. For seven years she was under his roof. He took her to school, picked her up, cooked lunch, took her bike riding, and for walks in the park in the rain.

13

Your Babies May Be Next

Ann entered the court room with an aid of the prosecutor. She was guided to the witness stand. The kid turned her head to look at her parents. Sabrina had her back to the little girl; she was angry. Winner looked at the child, smiled, tossed her a big kiss.

Ms. Vim exclaimed, "Your Honor the defendant is throwing the witness kisses and upsetting her!"

The Judge addressed Winner: "I notice you making gestures and talking to the jury while Ms. Vim made her opening statement. This conduct will not be tolerated by the court. You will not make any signs to the witness! I can be very tough." The judge threatened Winner with severe actions if he continued this conduct.

Would it not be child abuse to ignore your child after not seeing her for almost two years?

Minds sniffing around for child abuse certainly are dedicated. Ideas can create a masterpiece; they can also go off in the wrong direction. History is full of false truth told by wonderful liars who have wreaked havoc.

Mr. Humble ordered Winner to place his chair behind counsel at the defense table so father and daughter couldn't see one another.

Winner had to hide from his daughter who started to answer the questions. Her testimony will not be included, but she was perfect in her performance. Shirley Temple could take lessons from Ann. This child should be a movie star; she knew her lines and played her part. Her brain had been washed clean of all the good experiences she had while living with Mommy and Daddy. She could only recall what never happened as her truth.

90

Unlearning is valuable to thinkers who trust thoughts. Thoughts pop up anytime, speaking what they will without the consent of the thinker which clearly proves the thinker and the thought are separate. One is the thinker, two is the thought. Real being is not thought; being is existing in the simplest of modes.

Ann went from being a Winner's girl—fun-loving, happy, adventurous—to being a perfect witness for his enemies. The manipulation was complete. Whoever was responsible was indeed an expert who must be exposed for the sake of future children who will walk into her office.

Sally was called to the witness stand. Her testimony was halting, full of gestures but short on answers. This witness was not forced to undergo therapy since her parents were able to protect her, while Charles was powerless to protect Ann.

Ms. Vim asked leading questions then waited for an answer like a mother waits to see her child take the first baby steps. The D.A. told the story while the witness nodded her head.

Sally didn't answer questions because she had no answers! It's quite impossible to remember a story you told that was make believe unless the story is pounded into your mind.

Sally sat there listening to the questions but not responding. Mr. Humble found it impossible to cross examine her because Sally wouldn't answer. She shrugged her shoulders and shook her head. More than fifty questions were not answered. The Judge told Sally she was a good witness. Mrs. Oldman was caught lip-synching answers to Sally and was asked to leave the courtroom. Sympathy was on the side of the struggling witness.

You want love; don't want love. You want to be free; don't want to be free. You want respect; don't care about respect. You want protection; don't want protection. You want to quit; don't want to quit. You want to go; don't want to go. You want to receive; don't want to receive. You want to be wise; don't care about being wise. You want to want; stop wanting. What's left? Freedom from want. That's your blessing for today.

Officer Little took the stand to tell the jury that he had told Ann she was lying and holding back the truth from her testimony. He told her she was lying!

During the trial, there were many recesses, many side bar arguments, and many motions for mistrial. Social workers, police women, and Mrs. Oldman testified. The trial continued with a paid-by-the-state professional medical expert witness testifying for the state.

The expert witness wouldn't know Ann if she sat on his lap. He had not examined either child but could have if he desired. According to his testimony Ann had a broken hymen.

Winner know this statement like all the other statements was false.

The doctors who did examine the kids were not called to the witness stand so defense couldn't confront the writer of the medical report.

Mr. Oldman and the sex expert Gloria Mudski were not called to testify. Winner didn't think he could lose the case. He spoke the truth boldly, but the jury thought otherwise.

Winner had sent an eleven page statement of truth to the D.A. In this brief Winner said: "Ann has her heavenly Father's blessing, now she needs her father's blessing.

D.A. Vim held up the manuscript and shouted "Did you say Ann had her heavenly Father's blessing and she now needs her father's blessing?" Answer: "Amen" She asked again! Answer: "Amen" One last time she asked the same question. Answer: "Amen," which means so be it. Nobody liked amen for an answer; not even the judge.

Mr. Humble called two ironworkers, who told the court of their high regard for Winner. Nanny testified. Poppe testified. Cass a neighbor, and friend of 35 years took the stand. The D.A. cried during her testimony because this witness reminded her of her grandmother who had recently passed away. D.A. Vim bolted out of the courtroom in tears and left everyone in the courtroom wondering what she was up to.

Sabrina couldn't be called to testify due to her weak mental health; she was near the breaking point. Woody took the stand. He told the jury that Winner was goofy because he wrote poetry. Then Flamingo was called to the stand. During Flamingo's testimony, Sabrina caused a disturbance. All eyes in the courtroom turned to her. Mr. Smith, Sabrina's lawyer, asked the judge for a recess. Sabrina yelled "My hands are turning black!" The judge asked Sabrina to stop speaking and let her attorney speak for her. The proceedings were halted. Sabrina was taken to the robing room but everyone in the courtroom could still hear her loud wailing and groaning.

The jury was led out of the room, but the damage was done. Sabrina had broken down and it looked bad for the defense. No corrective action by a judge could wipe out this scene from the mind. A two-hour recess was called.

We need a break from the pressures in society. The talking machines are plugged into our life. Habits die hard but what would happen if the entire population pulled the plug, stopped the flow of worldly news from entering the mind. The news would continue but you wouldn't care because ignorance is bliss. Picture this: the six o'clock news is on but not one soul was watching. The great American Protest has begun, a silent rebellion of men and women who decided to stand up for holiness and to silence the communicators who burst into their living rooms to cause damage, trouble, worry, anxiety in the spirit mind.

Mr. Humble approached Winner in the hallway saying, "This is going to hurt you. The Judge wants to continue the case; he doesn't want a mistrial and I have two weeks in on this case." Winner said, "Go for the verdict. You're the lawyer."

Yes, inspiration! Courage calls follow the way of humility, go beyond thought, get acquainted with stupidity, realize how much there is to know; how unimportant vain knowledge used selfishly can be!

Sabrina was ruled incompetent by a doctor. She couldn't go on. Slim Vim pretended Sabrina's mental collapse had just happened and that she had been well until the moment. But the truth was she was sick well before the trial started.

A motion was made for a mistrial but it was denied. Winner testified and argued with Slim Vim and then it was over. We waited for the verdict. Sabrina was ordered to a mental hospital.

New armaments delivered to the hopeless warrior brought the resurrection of the spirit. He was born again, alive, healthy, determined, full of forgiveness so he aimed his loaded weapon fired an explosive charge into the center of a congregation of enemies.

Come O Creator blest, in our souls take up thy rest. Come with your grace and Heavenly aid, fill the hearts which you have made. Winner prayed.

"Has the jury reached a verdict?" "Yes your Honor." "How

does the jury find?" "We find the defendant guilty as charged on all counts."

The judge thanked the jury for doing their patriotic duty, then, single file they marched past Winner out of the courtroom.. Two police officers stood behind the defense table. Slim Vim approached the bench with Mr. Humble.

One police officer guided the convicted child molestor into a chair. Winner said, "I'd rather be sitting right here in this chair than be associated in any way with these liars." The judge informed the defense that a rather lengthy prison sentence was a probability.

Friday night would be spent behind bars. Handcuffs were fastened around Winner's wrist as soon as the judge revoked bail.

"Mr. Humble, will you ask the judge to place me in protective custody," asked Winner. He was well aware that prison life for all was difficult, especially, a convicted kiddy rapist.

Rulers of this present darkness presented false statements dressed as truth. They lied to the jury as well as used car salesmen lie to buyers. They slandered, mocked and abused the Winner family.

We were locked up in a cell to wait for the bus to take us to prison. A hour later, two inmates were handcuffed to each other and led to the bus. The bus took off through the city. After an hour's trip, it pulled off the highway, turned around a bend, drove into the compound, but stopped outside the locked gate where it waited for the door to open. The Sheriff's men drove into the guard area.

Four armed guards watched the inmates in the bus. Two in the front, two in the rear, all armed. The devil is the enemy! Mixing good with evil produces a colorful portrait of two worlds. Keep your spiritual eye open and use the sword of the spirit in your fight.

Citizen, you are now responsible for the well being of the entire Winner family. You are feeding us every day, sending the kids to therapy, paying the salaries of lawyers, mental health care workers, judges, social workers. You are a slave supporting a system that takes but returns nothing. People who work for the state think they can do whatever they want. They think they can take away the rights you were given in the constitution. They judge you guilty without any evidence and then toss you into a tomb to be buried alive.

The bus stopped. The guards left the bus and secured their weapons in a locker. The sheriff's men were not authorized to carry guns into the facility.

The body is not free but the mental movement of ideas knows

not confinement. Life in prison has a certain freedom that freemen can't experience unless they are rich. The world with its changeable realities is not present. The mind simply doesn't respond to news from the world.

The Judge ordered Winner into administrator protective custody which means he was in segregation, kept away from population because his life was in danger if others knew of his conviction for rape, incest and sodomy.

What are you gonna do when the cops tell you that they have a court order to take your children for crimes they think you committed without a hearing and without evidence? Oh sure, I know. It will never happen to you!

A wide sweeping turn, forward, reverse, getting us close as possible to the receiving room steps. The bus went quiet. Three guards waited till the door opened. Prisoners were led into the jail. Their handcuffs were removed and they were ordered into a cell filled with thirty men, waiting to be strip searched. Please, don't ask me about my case thought Winner as he watched the cops look through the inmates' hair, check the bottoms of their feet and look under their arms, in their mouth, and even into the space where the sun don't shine.

The fruit of this tribulation is a fight for freedom that knows not defeat!

"Winner, get up here." The guard looked at the charges and placed the paperwork next to the computer. "Remove your clothing." One inmate kept repeating. The judge gave me ten years, ten years. I can't believe ten years. After Winner was searched, he was issued orange coveralls. "Put these on and follow me." The guard led the way into the institution, past center which is a round glass enclosed headquarters called control. Each block could be seen from center control. Two steel doors stood locked at the entrance of each block.

We walked into the block down a five-foot-wide hallway with a low ceiling. Inmates were all over the place. Every six steps there was a cell. Each cell housed two inmates. Lord help me, I'll never make it here!

A guard looked at Winner and asked, "Are you from Frankford?" "Yes." Small talk was not part of the program. The new inmate was led into the block, toward a certain cell that had been picked for him by authority. The guard stopped and said, "You

95

live here." Winner entered the cell and met his cellmate who said, "I bet your in here for something kinky," Winner replied, "Mister, I'm in here for nothing."

The inside of the cell was lit by a television. On the wall hundreds of roaches were dashing about in all directions. Big ones, little ones, young and old danced around having a grand time. At the same time lines of ants looked for grub while the successful ones returned to their homes with crumbs. Winner looked at the flat steel plate that served as a support for a mattress that was not on the bed. The cellmate said, "You have to tell the CO you need a mattress."

Winner walked into the block looking for the guard., "Hey CO, I need a mattress." The guard said, "Follow me." They walked to the center of the block where another iron gate blocked entrance from "D" block rear where more inmates stood looking at the new man. The guard opened up the locked gate to "D" rear, then walked to an empty cell looked in and saw a mattress. He opened the door and said, "Grab that one." Winner checked out the empty cell and asked, "CO can I live in this here empty cell?" "I don't know. Wait here, I'll call the captain and see." Minutes later he returned saying, "Yes, you will live in D rear by yourself. The captain wants to see you. Follow me." A few moments later Winner was in the captain's office. The Captain who was dressed in a white shirt, said, "Look, for your own protection, don't tell anybody why you are in jail. Lie to them. It's not any of their business. You don't intend to hang up do you? (Kill yourself by hanging.) That's messy." "No, I don't," Winner was finding it hard to hold back the tears. "Captain, I'm gonna speak the truth in here, I'm gonna tell the inmates who ask that I'm in prison for nothing. That's the truth."

D rear was the most dangerous part of the jail. Winner thought it would be safe but prisoners who couldn't get along with the population, inmates with murder charges, child molestors, were assigned housing in D rear.

The neighbors began to welcome the new man in the block, "Hey white boy, white boy on the block! What you in here for whitey?" Winner closed the cell door, the guard locked the door, he breathed a sigh of relief. He was safe for the moment. A mattress less than an inch thick resting on a flat plate of steel makes for a hard night's sleep. Winner cried. Tears fell that couldn't stop. He moaned and wailed. Tony, Ann, Sabrina. His body crumbled to the floor.

An inmate block worker is a prisoner who works on the block. He cleans, serves food that arrives on a food cart, sweeps and mops the floor. He also does chores for the guards. The inmate population was locked down every other day which means we had to stay in our cells all day, every other day, coming out only to eat, and then going back in the cell. Block workers were out of their cell every day.

Country, a block worker appeared in front of Winner's cell door and offered a smoke, "You're the only white man in D rear," he said, "You have to come out of your cell. The food cart comes three times a day. When it arrives, come out, stand in line, get your food and eat. All the brothers will be in line. A lot of brothers don't like the white man. I will work for you for five dollars worth of store bought goods each week and I'll keep the mean brothers from hurting you."

"OK," said Winner. "That cheap enough." The first day in Prison Winner was paying extortion money for protection.

Country walked away. Then a boxer paid a visit to the cell asking if there were any books Winner would like to read since he was alone with nothing but fearful thoughts. "Yes, Could you get me a bible?" "Hey man," he said, "nobody will hurt you here. I have a murder charge. We're all trying to beat our cases!" He left, then came back with a Bible and writing paper.

Winner opened up the word to read. Blessed are they that suffer persecution for justice's sake for theirs is the kingdom of heaven. Blessed are ye when they shall revile you, and persecute you, and speak all that is evil against you, untruly, for my sake: Be glad and rejoice, for your reward is very great in heaven. St. Matthew 5 vs 10–12.

Music, loud rap and television blasted from each cell. Inmates shouted to their friends who may have been fifty yards away. It was nonstop noise.

Winner sat alone in his cell day after day, in pain. Evil memories from the past would appear. Sins he had committed years ago would be seen as plain as day. There were no distractions to help him lose himself. This was the place where repentance was born.

Alone, he thought of the men who looked at him as he passed

97

on the block. Do they know the charges against me? I don't care, let them think what they think. Let them kill me.

Winner fell onto a milk crate and closed his eyes. He was a broken man. Pride, self-confidence, self-esteem, family, goals, ambitions were all gone. All that remained was sinful thoughts and God. He kept repeating God, God, God, then he would have an ugly memory, then back to God, God, God, interrupted by another ugly memory.

Time passed. This type of prayer continued daily, two, three five times a day, calling God, facing sin, repenting. Winner came out of his cell. Men wanted to know why he was in jail. "Nothing. Well tell us about nothing. "Nothing is nothing. Nothing can be said about nothing. As soon as I speak about nothing it becomes a story which I don't care to relive. My case is under appeal. I was set up by the Commonwealth."

This answer satisfied the inmates. Poppe and Nanny came on visiting day. Guards searched inside Nanny's bra which she didn't appreciate. The inmates soon became familiar with Winner. Country was doing his job, keeping the haters away. The price for protection went up, soon country was getting it all and giving Winner enough smokes to keep his addiction fed.

Mr. Humble came to the prison for a visit. No, that's wrong. Humble wanted more money to file post conviction motions. He wanted power of attorney to get at Winner's bank account. He paid himself another ten grand.

In the cell he became afraid of dying. Lord, I don't want to die in prison. Without doubt life is God's gift to be appreciated, to be lived with enthusiasm, excitement, hope, health, trust, love kindness, charity, good will, honesty, and prayer. To believe in what we think we think is to re-invent a recollection. We are spiritual beings united to God without pretense until we fabricate misfortune.

The thought of dying became stronger each day. Suddenly, with no warning death said, "I will be upon you. Use me for your benefit, sin no more. You who fear the Creator will be led by me to him. Terror is for sinners who heed not the call to live a life of holiness. The more you ponder me, death, the better will you live your life. All your anxieties put next to me are vain indeed, empty yourself of the things of the world, walk behind me in confidence. I death take you to your Lord.

The thinker sees an evil thought and cuts down the intruder by refusing permission for the idea to expand. Watch your thoughts as if you were the audience at a picture show.

Think kindly towards all others. See their good and magnify the good. Remember, others are God's children. God loves them. We love what God loves. Keep that in the mind; don't forget!

Mr. Humble drifted out of the picture. Winner lost confidence in his attorney. In prison hours were spent waiting to use the phone. Inmates had the power to give out phone time to whomever they pleased. Winner was last on the list, after standing in line for hours to call Mr. Humble, his secretary would say, "Mr. Humble is talking to a client, and can't come to the phone, please call back in an hour." Winner would hang the phone up disgusted, ready to fire the dude. Humble was out. He had his money. Winner was in jail. The lawyer had lost the case but he benefited while the defendant was jailed.

Tuesday was visiting day. Will Right and another guy called Jim from the neighborhood waited in the visiting room for Winner to come from the block. After some small talk, Will said, "Charlie, Jim worked for a lawyer named Peter Peterson who is one of the best lawyers in the entire state." Jimmy then said, "He's damn good. I could set it up for you so Peterson would represent you." Winner replied, "I heard of him. Philadelphia Magazine recently had a article listing the top twenty attorneys in the area. Peterson was mentioned in the top five. The writer of the article said that when you have to win, Peterson is expensive but is at the top of the list. Peterson was a two-term elected public servant now in private practice. Yeah, I'd like to hire Peterson. I can't even get Mr. Humble on the phone. "He is a fast food lawyer who gets a lot of cases, makes big money, and doesn't spend enough time investigating cases, at least not my case." Jimmy said. "I'll call him for you." The visit ended on a positive note. Maybe the truth will now be told.

Winner walked back to the block, stood in the phone line, called Poppe and told him about the new development. Poppe arranged to meet with Mr. Peterson who was hired. Mr. Peterson told Poppe to have Winner call him after five o'clock any time he wished. He was there and would accept all calls.

Winner now had two high-priced attorneys on his payroll. A few days later, Will's friend Jimmy sent a bill. Jimmy wanted ten thousand dollars for helping retain Mr. Peterson. Will Right and

Jimmy believed that Winner had money from his settlement and were after their share.

A man by the name of Bear was a leader of the inmates. Strong inmates controlled the weaker inmates while the guards kept watch on the surface. Bear came to Winner's cell and said, "Hey Man, we were talking to the guard and he told us why you're in jail. You raped two little girls. Some of the brothers want to go *upside* your head. I told them that we have to forgive you! Nobody will mess with you. You tell them Bear is looking out for you."

Winner said, "Bear, I don't need your forgiveness! I need you to pray. Your prayers are what I need. I have been telling the courts that they are wrong. It's all a mistake; nothing more.

To be weak among the strong is better than being strong among the weak. The L.A. riots had the inmates watching and cheering those who were rioting. These men wanted LA destroyed. They didn't have a trace of sympathy for the white man.

One young buck tossed a plate full of food into Winner's cell. Leaders of the Muslim faith would warn Winner when somebody was going to get messed up on the block. "Stay in your cell." The leaders of the Muslims soon were friendly with Winner because they believed he was innocent and treated him justly. Black men were familiar with the justice system. Winner was getting educated in this system which is not fair or just and needs to be reformed.

Proverb 7 vs 23 says, For as he thinketh in his heart, so is he.

Sabrina was in the mental hospital going through her torture. She spent a few months in treatment, was released, and set free on bail. Then she had her trial.

A fellow on the block introduced himself. "Hi, my name is Jesse, I'm a Christian. We are going to start a prayer meeting in one of the cells. Would you like to attend our church behind the wall?" Yes, I would! Each night we would get together, about ten men, sing and read the word. Friendships were formed, the pressure was being lifted. Study of God's word became the most important aspect of life. This word held Winner firmly on truth's foundation.

The Lord Jesus gives his children powerful desires which urge the soul to seek the virtues. Winner asked God to make him one of his saints. Great sinners become great saints. Saints act like saints; talk like saints; live like saints; forgive like saints; love like saints. Most important saints overcome the terror of un-friendly thoughts in the name of Jesus!

100

Little Ann and Tony were yoked with non-believers against their will. The pagans were teaching them the ways of the world. Dead ends were before them but they couldn't be seen by their leaders, yet they claimed it was the crazy christians who were destroying man's rights.

Winner called Flamingo on the telephone. Flamingo said, "Winner, Sabrina had her trial. Judge Herian found her innocent of all charges against Sally Oldman. The Judge couldn't find any evidence against Sabrina. She was innocent of taking pictures. Winner replied, "Wonderful news. But if Sabrina was innocent of taking pictures, how could I be guilty of having pictures taken by Sabrina of sexual acts. What about all those lies that are in the notes of testimony at my trial? This was a joke but not funny. Sabrina was found to be guilty of all charges against her daughter Ann and she was sentenced to seven and a half years in State Prison.

The secret was out on the block. All the inmates knew Winner was a convicted child molestor, a booty bandit!

14

Good; Not Good Enough!

The court would set a date to hear the post verdict motions then postpone the hearing upon request of lawyers who may have been in other courtrooms on that date. Mr. Humble couldn't be fired or dismissed until after trial motions were heard and the court's decision rendered by Judge Herian on the record. He, Humble was a lame duck fired for incompetence. Mr. Peterson was on the sidelines waiting for the call to action but he couldn't get involved until after the appeal to the judge was heard. He studied the notes of testimony and prepared to write his brief to the State Superior Court.

Forget ego. Just exist, be alive, remember death. The ego receives all types of "whatchamacallits" that fill the mind with useless notions depicted as truthful reality which are in fact false.

You have faith, un-shake-able trust in the Holy Spirit. Your faith is in God's word that brings great joy. Happiness surrounds your being. You are blessed, holy, perfect, saved, in Christ not in "Ego I."

You have doubts in the flesh, in the ego, in the self. Sins, abuse, hate, strife, worry, pain, fear, corruption, news, gossip, selfishness; troubles without solutions could make anyone sick!

Look out for your brother's interest. Keep your thoughts pure and clean in the company of women.

Received suggestions are called advice. Experience teaches that while the world begs you to conform, liberated voices shout follow me, this way. Do wonder where you are being led!

God's word says clearly, "We walk by faith, not sight. What

we see is always changing. Be happy that you don't know since what the Lord wants done will be done with or without your knowing. Faith often walks blindly towards an unknown destination.

Mr. Humble made his motions for a new trial and or arrest of judgment and sent Winner a copy while he was locked up in Holmesburg.

Listing: Courtroom 425.   Gerald P. Humble, identification number 21365, attorney for defendant from 104 West Penn Square Building in Philadelphia submits to the Commonwealth Court of Appeals, trial division these motions.

TO THE HONORABLE, THE JUDGES OF THE SAID COURT:

The petition of defendant in the above captioned matter, by his attorney, GERALD P. HUMBLE, Esquire, respectfully moves the Court for arrest of judgment, or in lieu thereof, to grant a new trial for these reasons:

1. The verdict was against the evidence.
2. The verdict was contrary to the law.
3. The verdict was against the weight of the evidence.
4. Permission is respectfully requested to be allowed to file additional reasons in support of these motions within a reasonable time after receipt of the notes of testimony as such reasons shall appear after a reading of the notes of testimony.

SUPPLEMENTAL REASONS IN SUPPORT OF MOTION
FOR NEW TRIAL/OR ARREST OF JUDGMENT:

5. The Trial Court erred in failing to grant defendant's motion for mistrial where the co-defendant's disruptive behavior and later psychotic episode during the course of the trial resulted in prejudice to the defendant.

6. The prosecutor's opening statements were prejudicial; inflammatory and mischaracterized the role of the jury. The Trial Court erred in not granting a mistrial.

7. The Trial Court erred in denying defendant's motion to suppress.

(a) There was insufficient evidence to establish probable cause necessary to support the issuance of search warrant.

(b) The search warrant failed to state with particularity the place to be searched.

(c) Information that allegedly supported the Magistrate's finding of probable cause was stale.

8. The Trial Court erred in finding a nine-year-old common-wealth witness competent to testify.

9. The Trial Court erred in failing to strike an expert witness' testimony, which was based on extraneous factors and outside the parameters of the offer of proof.

10. The prosecutor abused her discretion by arguing with witnesses on cross-examination, by asking prejudicial questions and improperly commenting on the defendant's religious beliefs.

11. The Trial Court erred when it denied defense counsel's request for mistrial when the prosecutor engaged in a pattern of conduct during closing arguments that was designed to prejudice the defendant and deprive him of a fair trial.

12. There was insufficient evidence to prove guilt beyond a reasonable doubt.

Respectfully submitted,

Gerald P. Humble, Esquire
Attorney for Defendant

MEMORANDUM OF LAW IN SUPPORT OF POST-VERDICT MOTIONS:

I. THE TRIAL COURT ERRED IN FAILING TO GRANT DEFENDANT'S MOTION FOR MISTRIAL WHEN THE CO-DEFENDANT'S DISRUPTIVE BEHAVIOR AND LATER PSYCHOTIC EPISODE DURING THE COURSE OF THE TRIAL RESULTED IN PREJUDICE TO THE DEFENDANT.

A trial court is required to grant a motion for mistrial when an event which prejudices the defendant deprives him of a fair and impartial trial. *Commonwealth vs. Brinkley,* 480 A.2d 980, 505 Pa. 442 (1984).

During the course of the trial, the co-defendant, Mrs. Winner, the wife of the defendant, acted in a bizarre and disruptive manner. She repeatedly put on and removed her sunglasses; she inappropriately fidgeted and constantly rubbed her sweater and a medallion around her neck. Additionally, Mrs. Winner put her head down on the table for extended periods of time, apparently asleep (N.T. April 10, 1991, pp.75–77). All this was in the presence of the jury.

As the defense proceeded with its case in chief, Mrs. Winner's disruptive behavior escalated to the point where she had to be removed from the courtroom. Specifically, she announced, "I feel

105

like I'm going black'' (N.T. April 10, 1991, p.68), and was escorted from the courtroom by her attorney. While in the judge's chambers, Mrs. Winner's moans were audible throughout the courtroom, Mrs. Winner was examined and was found to have experienced a "psychotic episode" (N.T. April 10, 1991, p.70). The court severed her case from her husband's case. Defense counsel made an appropriate motion for a mistrial. The motion was denied. (N.T. April 10, 1991, p.78).

The decision to grant or deny a mistrial depends on whether improper evidence was admitted at trial that would so prejudice the fact-finder that it would be unable to remain impartial and prejudice the defendant beyond a reasonable doubt. *Commonwealth vs. Larkins,* 340 Pa. Super. 56, 63, 489 A.2d 837 (1985).

The events described above clearly resulted in prejudice to the defendant and deprived him of the fair trial to which he is entitled.

The nature of the charges brought against the two defendants involves the entire family unit. As both defendants were charged with conspiracy, it would be difficult, if not impossible, for the jury to view them as separate, distinct entities. The result being, quite naturally, for Mrs. Winner's actions to reflect unfavorably on her husband.

The unavoidable was to have a deleterious effect on the right of the defendant to a fair trial. Therefore, the motion for mistrial should have been granted.

II. THE PROSECUTOR'S OPENING STATEMENTS WERE PREJUDICIAL, INFLAMMATORY, AND MISCHARACTERIZED THE ROLE OF THE JURY. THE TRIAL COURT ERRED IN NOT GRANTING A MISTRIAL.

The role of the prosecutor is that of advocate and minister of justice. Rules of Professional Conduct 3.8. The prosecutor has a responsibility to not be vindictive or attempt to influence the passions or bias of the jury. *Commonwealth vs. Gilman,* 470 Pa. 179, 368, A.2d 253, 257 (1977).

While the Commonwealth is permitted some latitude in presenting its version of the case to the jury, the test to determine whether a new trial is warranted based on the prosecutor's comments is the "unavoidable prejudice test."

Where the language of the district attorney is intemperate,

uncalled for and improper, a new trial is not necessarily required. The language must be such that it's "unavoidable effect would be to prejudice the jury, forming in their minds fixed bias and hostility toward the defendant, so that they could not weigh the evidence and render a true verdict."

Commonwealth v. Stern, 393 Pa. 152, 573 a.2d 1132, 1137 (1990) citing
Commonwealth v. Johnson, 516 Pa. 27, 532–533, 533 A.2d 994,. 997 (1987).

Prejudice resulted from the prosecutor's opening statement, which also required balance and fairness.

The purpose of the opening statements is to tell the jury how a case will develop, its background, and what the parties will try to prove. *Commonwealth v. Nelson,* 311 Pa. Super. 1, 456 A.2d 1383, 1389 (1983). The prosecutor is allowed to make a fair deduction from the evidence of what is to be presented during testimony. *Commonwealth v. Stevens,* 276 Pa. Super. 428, 419 A.2d 533, 534 (1980). But those comments must be made in food faith and cannot be mere assertions intended to inflame the passions of the jury. *Commonwealth v. Galloway,* 302 Pa. Super. 145, 448 A.2d 568, 576 (1982).

For the defendant to obtain judicial relief, the prosecutor's language in the opening statement must be such that it's unavoidable effect is to so prejudice the jury against the accused and prevent the finding of a true verdict. *Id.*

In the instant case, the prosecutor exceeded all bounds of fairness.

In the first instance, the prosecutor made comments that suggested that child abuse was rampant.

You will hear Sally Oldman talk to you about his birdie and she calls her vagina her hiney. At the time she'll tell you that he peed inside of her in her words.

She'll tell you that she was wet in her words. While all of this is going on, mom is still there, the defendant, Sabrina Winner, encouraging the action, go for it. Yee-ha, Yee-ha, like she's at a concert or a football game. Grabbing a camera, click, click, while things are happening. And when the action ended, the defendants both of them told the kids not to tell or they would be hit, not to tell or they would be killed.

Keep it a secret. Don't tell.

Well, unfortunately, the secret wasn't safe this time, because—

(N.T. April 10, 1991, p.85).

After counsel objected, the Court sustained the objection.

In the second instance, the prosecutor mischaracterized the role of the jury. The prosecutor suggested that not only must the jury determine, guilt or innocence, but also whether these children can be saved.

> After you hear all of this evidence from the children and the personnel, remember the children's testimony alone is sufficient to convict, but you will hear other testimony to corroborate what these children said. I am confident at the end of this case you will turn to these defendants, Charles and Sabrina Winner, say guilty, guilty, guilty of rape, guilty of involuntary deviate sexual intercourse, guilty of corrupt morals of a minor, guilty of endanger the welfare of children, guilty of conspiracy, because they were in it and they were in it together, guilty. *Give Ann Winner and Sally Oldman a chance by saying guilty to these people.* (N.T. April 10, 1991, pp.88–89);

> (Emphasis added).

Defense counsel moved for a mistrial. The motion was denied (N.T. April 10, 1991, p.90).

The prosecutor's statement mischaracterized the role of the jury–as protectors against abuse of children. The statements suggested that if the defendants were not found guilty, the children would be harmed.

The effects of these comments prejudiced the defendant. Although the trial court gave a curative instruction, the instruction came too late. It had already left an indelible impression on the jury. No curative instruction could negate the suggestiveness and prejudice.

"It is only when the jurors are asked to place themselves in the unfortunate circumstances of the victim or are otherwise encouraged to divert their attention from the evidence before them in favor of their own sympathies or fears, that the argument exceeds the bounds of propriety." *Commonwealth v. Youngkin,* 285 Pa. Super. 417, 427 A.2d 1356, 1365 (1981).

The prosecutor's statement diverted the jury's attention away from its function of determining guilt or innocence. The prosecutor gave the jury an additional task—to save the children from harm. These comments played to the emotions of the jury and prejudiced the defendant. A mistrial was warranted.

III. THE TRIAL COURT ERRED IN DENYING DEFENDANT'S MOTION TO SUPPRESS.

A. These was insufficient evidence to establish probable cause necessary to support the issuance of a search warrant.

Pennsylvania Rules of Criminal Procedure 2003 (a) states that a search warrant shall not be issued but upon probable cause supported by one or more affidavits before an issuing authority.

The standard for determining probable cause is a practical, common sense approach to determine whether, given all the circumstances set forth in the affidavit, there is a fair probability that contraband or evidence will be found in a particular place. Veracity and basis of knowledge of persons supplying the information is included in the determination. *Commonwealth v. Healey,* 331 Pa. Super. 199, 480 A.2d 313, 316 (1984).

While an unknown informant's information may not by itself support a search warrant, where the supplied information can be corroborated, a search warrant may be issued. *Commonwealth v. Corleto,* 328 Pa. Super. 522, 477 A.2d 863, 865 (1984).

To establish probable cause, the magistrate must be informed of underlying circumstances from which the informer concluded that suspects possessed fruits or evidence of a crime. The tip cannot simply be rumor. *Commonwealth v. Prokopchak,* 279. Pa. Super. 284, 240 A.2d 1335, 1338 (1980).

In the instant case, police relied on the information from a 7-year-old child to apply for a search warrant. The information provided was not corroborated or verified by the police (N.T. April 10, 1991, p.40). The police did not investigate who owned the house to be searched, if there was more than one party living there or if the defendant had moved out. All that the police did was to drive by the house. "We went by the area and it appeared to be a one—a single family dwelling." (N.T. April 10, 1991, p.40). Nowhere in the search warrant are the Winners named.

Mere suspicion is insufficient to establish probable cause, *Corleto, supra* at 866. In this case, the information from a 7-year-old child who claimed she had been in the house 10 days earlier was insufficient, without more, to establish probable cause.

When a child under 14 is called to testify in a *trial*, the minor's competency must be independently established by showing that the minor is conscious of the duty to tell the truth. *Commonwealth v. Bailey,* 322 Pa. Super. 249, 469 A.2d 604, 609 (1983).

The same criteria should have been applied when determining if what the child said was sufficient to establish probable cause issue a search warrant.

All that was relied upon was the child's statement, without regard to whether she was competent to give accurate information. The information was not confirmed or verified by the police.

Based on the "totality of circumstances" standard that is required in the probable cause section of a search warrant, *Healey, supra* at 316, there was insufficient probable cause to issue a search warrant, based upon only on the information of a 7-year-old minor. The Trial Court erred in denying defendant's motion to suppress.

B. The search warrant failed to state with particularity the place to be searched.

Rule 2005 of the Pennsylvania Rules of Criminal Procedure outlines specifically what a search warrant should contain.

A search warrant shall:

    (a) specify the date and time of issuance;

    (b) Identify specifically the property to be seized;

and   (c) Name or describe with particularity the person or place to be searched.

The search warrant in this case stated that the premises of Archer Street were to be searched. There was no mention of the basement in the premises section of the search warrant (N.T. April 10, 1991, p.25). The search warrant was for the entire home, although the officer's intent was to search only the basement (N.T. April 10, 1991, pp.27–28), and in fact only searched the basement.

The general rule is that a search warrant directed against an apartment house or other multiple-unit structure will be held invalid for lack of specificity if it fails to describe the particular room or unit to be searched with sufficient definiteness to preclude a search of other units. 68 Am. Jur. 2d *Searches and Seizures* Section 77 (1973) cited in *Commonwealth v. Carlisle,* 517 Pa. 36, 534 A.2d 469, 471 (1987).

The purpose of such a rule is to prevent general, exploratory searches by police and to prevent police from searching other apartments or rooms where there is no legal basis for police intrusion.

In *Commonwealth v. Kaplan*, 234 Pa. Super. 102, 339 A.2d 86 (1975), the court held that separate living units in multiple tenant building must be treated as if they were separate dwellings and that probable cause to search each one must be shown.

But in *Commonwealth v. Yucknevage*, 257 Pa. Super. 19, 390 A.2d 225 (1978), the Superior Court held that a search warrant was not valid because it authorized a search of an entire house that was made up of two separate dwelling units without further evidence that the house's outside feature would indicate two separate units.

In the instant case, although the search warrant was for the entire premises, the police knew that the alleged incident had occurred in the basement. The police were "under the impression" that the defendants had access to the entire house (N.T. April 10, 1991, p.26).

Once police learned that there was a separate dwelling unit that was occupied by the defendants, the police were required to obtain a separate search warrant. The police only learned of the separate dwelling unit once they arrived at Archer Street (N.T. April 10, 1991, p.28).

The owners of the property, Flamingo and Woody, cooperated with police (N.T. April 10, 1991, p.23). But the owners were unable to give valid consent.

A landlord may not consent to a search of his tenant's premises as compared to areas of common usage. This is so, even though the landlord may have some right of entry for cleaning or inspecting purposes. *Chapman v. United States*, 365 U.S. 610, 81 S.Ct. 776, 5 L.Ed. 2d 828 (1961).

The police were informed by the property owners that the defendant occupied the basement. The defendant was not present, but his things were still in the basement. In fact, the police were told that the defendants had moved (N.T. April 10, 1991, p.38).

In *Commonwealth v. Brundidge*,—Pa. Super.—, 590 A.2d 302 (1991), the Superior Court held that the police entry and search of a motel room after check-out time did not infringe on the defendant's Fourth Amendment rights, but any additional intrusion into the defendant's personal effects violated his constitutionally safeguard expectation of privacy.

The Winners had not abandoned the basement. Although they were not at home, their personal effects were still inside.

Even if the first floor was a common area, once police learned that the Winners occupied the basement, the police should have obtained another search warrant. There was no exigency to verify a warrantless search. The Winners were not at home. There was no danger that the evidence would be destroyed nor was there a danger to police or the owners of the property. The items to be seized—a black belt, camera and photos—were unlike drugs that would be quickly distributed.

Under the Pennsylvania Constitution, there is no good faith exception to the exclusionary rule. *Commonwealth v. Edmunds,*—Pa.—, 586 A.2d 887 (1991). " . . . Our constitution has historically been interpreted to incorporated a strong right to privacy, and an equally strong adherence to the requirement of probable cause under Article I, Section 8. . . . To adopt a "good faith" exception to the exclusionary rule, we believe, would virtually emasculate those clever safeguards which have been carefully developed under the Pennsylvania Constitution over the past 200 years." *Id.* at 899.

The police in this case failed to strictly adhere to the probable cause or particularity requirement of the search warrant. The Trial Court erred in not granting the motion to suppress.

C. Information that allegedly supported the Magistrate's finding of probable cause was stale.

As a general rule, probable cause cannot be based on stale or temporarily remote information. *Commonwealth v. Weidenmoyer,* 518 Pa. 1, 539 A.2d 1291 (1980).

If a magistrate is presented with evidence of a criminal activity at an earlier time, it must also be established that criminal activity continued up to the time of the request for a warrant. *Commonwealth v. Burkholder,* 388 Pa. Super. 252, 565 A.2d 472 (1989); *Commonwealth v. Hagen,* 240 Pa. Super, 444, 368 A. 2d 318 (1976).

While the courts have been reluctant to establish a "Hard and fast rule" as to what is staleness, such a determination is made on a case-by-case basis. *Id.* at 474.

In *Commonwealth v. Klimkowicz,* 331 Pa. Super. 75, 479 A.2d 1086 (1984), the Superior Court set forth guidelines for deciding whether information in a search warrant is stale. They include: the nature and quantity of the items to be seized; the time lapse involved; and the ease which the items may be disposed. The standard for determining time limits for search warrants is reasonableness. *Id.* at 1089.

The incident in this case allegedly occurred on August 29,1989. It was reported to police on September 4, 1989. The search warrant was executed on September 8, 1989.

The search warrant failed to allege any continuing activity. It only stated that there was an isolated incident 10 days earlier. Additionally, the information in the search warrant did not lead to the conclusion that on September 8, 1989, the police would find the items they were seeking.

In *Commonwealth v. Alewine,* 384 Pa. Super. 283, 558 A.2d 542, (1989), a search warrant for gambling devices was not stale even though the warrant was not issued until 21 days after police had played the machines in a bar. The court based its decision on the fact that poker machines are large and were a fixture in the bar.

But in this case, the police sought a camera, a belt and photographs. There was no reason to believe that these items would still be on the premises 10 days after the incident, especially after the Winners moved out.

In *Commonwealth v. Macolino,* 336 Pa. Super. 386, 485 A.2d 1134, 1138 n. 2 (1984), a search warrant was issued one week after possible drug activity. The court held there was sufficient indication of continuing criminal activity when the defendant used the telephone in an ongoing drug network.

There was no continuing activity in this case. Police had only a report of one incident 10 days earlier. There was no indication that this criminal activity was continuing.

It is the criminal activity that must continue to or about the time of the warrant, and not the investigation. *Commonwealth v. Shaw,* 444 Pa. 110, 281 A.2d 897 (1971).

Based on the insufficient probable cause, the lack of particularity and the staleness of the warrant, the trial court erred in denying defendant's motion to suppress.

IV. THE TRIAL COURT ERRED IN FINDING A NINE-YEAR-OLD COMMONWEALTH WITNESS COMPETENT TO TESTIFY.

When a witness is under 14 years old, there must be an inquiry into her mental capacity before she can testify. This competency inquiry should determine whether the witness has the capacity to observe or perceive the occurrence with a substantial degree of accuracy; the ability to remember the event; the ability to understand questions and to communicate intelligent answers about the occurrence; and the consciousness of the duty to speak the truth. *Commonwealth v. Anderson,* 311 Pa. Super. 1, 552 A.2d 1064, 1067–1068 (1988). Such an inquiry is required because children are "peculiarly susceptible to the world of make believe and of suggestions." *Rusche v. McCoy,* 397 Pa. 615, 621, 156 A.2d 307, 310 (1959) cited in *Anderson, id,* at 1067–1068.

In the instant case, the trial judge held a competency hearing to determine if Sally Oldman, a nine-year-old Commonwealth witness, was competent to testify. Throughout the inquiry, the witness continually shrugged her shoulders, failed to answer questions and failed to respond in any coherent way to many of the questions.

The witness failed to recall events about what she discussed with the Assistant District Attorney, and failed to recall when she discussed those events. These were events that happened only days or weeks before the trial. This was troublesome because the witness was being asked to recall an event that occurred more than a year and a half earlier.

Additionally, the witness' notion of truth and lie clearly showed she was incompetent to testify.

Question: (By Assistant District Attorney Pat Vim).

In your own words, what is the difference between telling the truth and a lie?

Answer: The truth is when you say something that happens that really happens and a lie is when you say that something really didn't happen.

(N.T. October 16, 1990, pp.7–8).

This was insufficient to show that the witness was capable of knowing the difference between truth and lie. The court itself was concerned with the witness' answer and allowed for further questioning.

The witness also failed to communicate in a coherent manner. Many of the questions asked were either disregarded or she simply failed to respond.

The trial court ruled that the witness was competent to testify (N.T. October 16, 1990, pp.17–18). The court, however, noted that there was some hesitancy in her

114

ability to tell the difference between truth and a lie. Rather, the court found the witness hesitant in her ability to recall.

After the trial court held the witness was competent to testify, it became clear throughout her testimony that she was incompetent to testify. Her testimony is full of shrugs and no response.

At one point during a sidebar discussion about photographs, the Court said:

Mr. Humble is correct in that this witness is not, on many occasions, responding to questions. She is shrugging her shoulders and simply not responding to many questions. It is a very difficult proceeding for her, obviously. (N.T. October 16, 1990, pp.71–72).

At that point, when it was evident to the trail court that the witness was incompetent to testify, her testimony should have been stricken.

The trial judge has considerable discretion in ruling on the competency of an infant witness. *Commonwealth v. Fultz,* 316 Pa. Super. 260, 462 A.2d 1340 (1983). But that discretion should be predicated on qualification testimony. *Kaufman v. Carlisle Cement Products Co.,* 227 Pa. Super, 320, 323 A.2d 750, 752–732 (1974).

In the instant case, it was clear, especially to the trial court, that the witness was incompetent to testify. The trial judge erred in ruling otherwise,

v. *THE TRIAL COURT ERRED IN FAILING TO STRIKE AN EXPERT WITNESS' TESTIMONY, WHICH WAS BASED ON EXTRANEOUS FACTORS AND OUTSIDE THE PARAMETERS OF THE OFFER OF PROOF*

Dr. Art Mojong, a Commonwealth witness, was present to testify about the physical findings of the case. But Dr. Mojong did not personally examine the children in this case. He was simply used as an expert to testify about the physical findings based on the medical records.

The Commonwealth's offer of proof was that the doctor was to testify regarding physical findings in an alleged sexual abuse case (N.T. April 18, 1991, p.15). The Commonwealth clearly went beyond this. At one point, the doctor admitted that his testimony was based on other than the particular findings of the case.

Cross examination by Mr. Humble:

> Q.   You have made a—you have drawn a conclusion here that there has been penetration of the vagina consistent with the hypothetical that was described to you and the physical findings. You have stated a conclusion to this jury, is that right?
>
> A.   Yes.
>
> Q.   Is your opinion that has been stated to this jury based on something other than the particular hypothetical that was proposed to you and the particular physical findings in this case, yes or no?
>
> A.   Yes.

Mr. Humble: Could we see the Court at sidebar?

The Court: It is about that time for a recess.

(N.T. April 18, 1991, pp.80–81). After an in-camera hearing in which the doctor was questioned, the Court ruled that his testimony was admissible (N.T. April 18, 1991, p.87).

In *Commonwealth v. Dunkle*, 385 Pa. Super. 317, 516 A.2d 5 (1989), alloc. granted, 524 Pa. 625, 574 A.2d 67 (1990), the Court held that if expert testimony was offered solely to sustain the credibility of the victim, the testimony should not be admitted.

Here, the purpose of Dr. Mojong's testimony was offered to bolster the witness' testimony. It had no other purpose. During the in-camera hearing, Dr. Mojong testified that he was unable to make a determination solely based on a hypothetical and the medical chart. "I have to process that information using my experience. And so that when I said yes, I don't only use what is given to me as the hypothetical and what is written down. That—I use my knowledge as well. And that's why I answered yes to that." (N.T. April 18, 1991, p.81). The doctor said his answer was based on his knowledge, the literature in the field, but not based on "behavioral patterns per se" (N.T. April 18, 1991, p.81). The court was satisfied with the doctor's answer and denied the defense motion (N.T. April 18, 1991, p.81).

In *Commonwealth v. Emge,* 381 Pa. Super. 139, 553 A.2d 74, (1988), the court held that an expert need not place the alleged victim in a class of known victims for his testimony to be inadmissible and an infringement on the province of the jury. The Court said that testimony that matches the behavior of known victims of child sexual abuse with that of an alleged victim can serve no purpose other than to bolster the credibility of the alleged victim, and so is prohibited.

The doctor's admission that his answer was based on his clinical experience *and* reading of the literature meant that his testimony was based on the general behavior of victims, and was an invasion of the province of the jury and, therefore, inadmissible.

VI. THE PROSECUTOR ABUSED HER DISCRETION BY ARGUING WITH WITNESSES ON CROSS EXAMINATION, BY ASKING PREJUDICIAL QUESTIONS AND IMPROPERLY COMMENTING ON THE DEFENDANT'S RELIGIOUS BELIEFS.

Throughout her cross examination of witnesses, the prosecutor constantly asked prejudicial and argumentative questions. She also improperly made reference to the defendant's religious beliefs.

The Court admonished the prosecutor about this, outside the presence of the jury.

The Court: Well, let me direct you in no uncertain terms at this point of the following: Your references to going to a Hub Motel and your suggestion that that is an unhealthy environment for children is irrelevant to this case and it could be prejudicial. It is that kind of characterization in your questioning that I think trespasses on fairness. You must stop those kinds of questions and the argumentative nature as well. I cautioned you about the argumentative nature of your questions, I have cautioned you previously about the content of your questions. Now, especially with reference to the book and to religious affiliations and to his religious beliefs, are my third subject of cautioning you. Please, please, please think of the kinds of questions that you are asking on cross examination. I cannot understand, I have heard at least twice this reference to a Hub Motel and the argumentative question is, Do you think that that is a proper environment to raise children? That kind of questioning is simply improper and I won't allow it.

(N.T. April 19, 1991, pp. 129–130). Defense counsel requested a mistrial based on the prosecutor's comment on religious beliefs. The

117

Court said he would caution the jurors and denied the motion (N.T. April 19, 1991, p. 129).

In *Commonwealth v. Eubanks*, 511 Pa. 201, 512 A.2d 619 (1986), the Supreme Court held that prosecutorial remarks amounting to a sarcastic commentary on what the prosecutor perceived as defendant's attempt to clothe himself in innocence by asserting affiliation with religion were irrelevant to any issue in the case. Even after the Court sustained the objections, gave an instruction and ordered the remarks stricken from the record, the Court held the remarks still violated the defendant's right to a fair trial and required vacating the judgment and a new trial.

Notwithstanding a prosecutor's intentions, questions about religious beliefs are not permitted. 42 Pa.C.S.A. Section 5902 (b) states:

> No witness shall be questioned, in any judicial proceeding, concerning his religious belief; nor shall any evidence be heard upon the subject, for the purpose of affecting either his competency or credibility.

Any religious affiliation of the defendant were irrelevant to any issue at trial. The prosecutor's argumentative questioning on this subject, coupled with similarly argumentative questioning on other matters, required a mistrial. Despite the Court's cautioning the jury, the prejudice had already occurred. A new trial is warranted.

VII. THE TRIAL COURT ERRED WHEN IT DENIED DEFENSE COUNSEL'S REQUEST FOR MISTRIAL WHEN THE PROSECUTOR ENGAGED IN A PATTERN OF CONDUCT DURING CLOSING ARGUMENTS THAT WAS DESIGNED TO PREJUDICE THE DEFENDANT AND DEPRIVE HIM OF A FAIR TRIAL.

In her closing arguments, the prosecutor mischaracterized the evidence and the stipulations and make several prejudicial comments.

The prosecutor's closing argument must present facts in a way that will lead the jury to a dispassionate and objective evaluation of the facts. *Commonwealth v. Davis,* 363 Pa. Super. 562, 563, 526 A.2d 1205, 1216 (1987); *Commonwealth v. Clark,* 280 Pa. Super. 1, 421 A.2d 374 (1980).

Several times in this case, the prosecutor blatantly mischaracterized the evidence. She also mischaracterized the stipulations on which both sides had agreed. Despite the Court's sustaining the argument, the prosecutor continued to mischaracterize the stipulations.

> DISTRICT ATTORNEY PAT VIM:
>
> The Children's Hospital report indicates one centimeter opening.
>
> Mr. Humble stipulated to that recording of the stipulation—that's a fact in evidence—
>
> Mr. Humble: Objection.
>
> The Court: Sustained. That's not the stipulation.
>
> It is the stipulation that those reports are true.
>
> Ms. Vim: True and accurate reports.
>
> Mr. Humble: I object this.
>
> The Court: Sustained. The stipulation is that they are authentic, not that the measurement is accurate. There is a difference.

(N.T. April 22, 1991, p. 62).

The prosecutor also mischaracterized her own witness' testimony.

> DISTRICT ATTORNEY PAT VIM:
>
> Also Dr. Mojong talks about the other signs found, the redness in Ann. Let's talk about Ann first. The redness and the acne of her buttocks. Yes, it could be consistent with sexual intercourse or sexual assault and, not, it could also—
>
> Mr. Humble: Objection.
>
> The Court: Sustained.
>
> Ms. Vim: I'm characterizing Dr. Mojong's testimony.
>
> Mr. Humble: Objection.
>
> The Court: It is a mischaracterization of his testimony.
>
> Ms. Vim: Doctor Mojong said that those findings were non-specific. That they could go either way.
>
> Mr. Humble: Objection.
>
> The Court: In as much as the argument now relates to the acne on the buttocks sustained.

(N.T. April 22, 1991, p. 63).

Even the Court acknowledged the prosecutor's abuse of the testimony, but the prosecutor continued:

> Ms. Vim: He could not say whether or not the redness was definitely from sexual assault or was not, but do

you think it is coincidence that she also has another symptom that could be consistent with sexual assault? I say not. What about Sally Oldman—

Mr. Humble: Objection.

The Court: Sustained.

Ms. Vim: Discharge. Yellow, green discharge, a yeast infection—

Mr. Humble: Objection. He never testified to that.

The Court: Sustained.

Ms. Vim: Doctor Mojong when asked specifically by me about a yeast infection and discharge and the color of the discharge said that those findings were, again, were non-specific. He couldn't say one way or the other. It could be sexual assault. It may not be. Again, do you think that those findings are coincidence in this case? I say not. Most important about those reports is Sally Oldman's report on 9–6, he put his bird in her and peed. Same thing she testified to on the stand a year and eight months later.

(N.T. April 22, 1991, p. 64).

In another instance, the prosecutor attacked the defense attorney's performance on failing to comment on certain evidence. It was a blatant attempt by the prosecutor to diminish counsel's position in the eyes of the jury.

DISTRICT ATTORNEY PAT VIM:

Next, detail and description. You know Mr. Humble on behalf of the defendant went through a lot of evidence, thought it was a blatant omission that he never assaulted the kids. Detail and description about the actual penetration. Never talked to you about Sally Oldman saying a birdie in behind when she meant her vagina. A birdie means penis. Never commented on the detail of sticking, of being wet, never once commented, because those things indicate truthfulness, because kids don't make that up—

Mr. Humble: Objection.

The Court: Overruled.

Ms. Vim: Because 7 year olds don't know that—

Mr. Humble: Objection.

Ms. Vim: It is not common in a 7 year olds experience to know what happens when a penis and a vagina—it

120

is not common in a 7 year olds experience to know that something comes out and that it is wet—

Mr. Humble: Objection.

The Court: Overruled.

Ms. Vim: Yet he doesn't talk about that detail. No. He will stay on peripheral issues. He will talk about the Dirty Dancing picture. He will talk about things that you don't remember.

(N.T. April 22, 1991, pp. 56–57).

The Pennsylvania Supreme Court has held that a prosecutor's argument during summation, in which he talked of counsel's failure to call witnesses improper. The Court said that no adverse inferences may be drawn merely because the accused failed to call individuals as character witnesses. *Commonwealth v. Lipscomb,* 455 Pa. 525, 317 A.2d 205, 208 (1974).

Although the prosecutor's comments in this instance do not deal with character witnesses, the same argument can be applied. The prosecutor's comments on defense counsel's performance were inappropriate and unwarranted.

On their own, these isolated incidents may not be enough to prejudice the jury, but the cumulative effect deprived the defendant of a fair trial. "When the cumulative effect of improper remarks so prejudice the jury as to prevent a fair trial, a motion for mistrial must be granted." *Commonwealth v. Baranyai,* 296 Pa. Super. 342, 348, 442 A.2d 800, 803 (1983).

The jury may give special weight to the comments by the prosecutor due to her position. This has been recognized by the American Bar Association:

In determining whether the established bounds of propriety have been exceeded in closing argument, we must be every mindful of the weight to the prosecutor's arguments, not only because of the prestige associated with his office, but also because of the fact finding facilities presumable to him. (ABA Standards, Section 5.8, Commentary at 126–27).

Because of the prejudicial comments to the jury, and the weight which may have been accorded by the jury, defense counsel's motion for mistrial should have been granted.

VIII. THERE WAS INSUFFICIENT EVIDENCE TO PROVE GUILT BEYOND
A REASONABLE DOUBT.

The Commonwealth has the burden of establishing that each element of each offense charged is supported by the evidence and inference sufficient in law to prove guilt beyond a reasonable doubt. In determining whether the Commonwealth has met its burden, a reviewing court must determine whether "accepting as true all of the evidence reviewed in light more favorable to the Commonwealth, together with all reasonable inference therefrom, the trier of fact could have found that each element of the offenses charged was supported by evidence and inferences sufficient in law to prove guilt beyond a reasonable doubt." *Commonwealth v. Lovette,* 498 Pa. 665, 669, 450 A.2d 975, 977, (1982), cert. denied, 459 U.S. 1178, 103 S.Ct. 830, 74 L.Ed.2d 1025 (1983), quoted in *Commonwealth v. Robach,* 496 A.2d 768, 770 (Pa. Super. 1985).

The defense requested a demurrer, which was denied by the trial court. The test to be applied in ruling on demurrer is whether, accepting as true all of the prosecution's evidence and all reasonable inferences therefrom, it is sufficient to support a finding by the factfinder that the defendant is guilty beyond a reasonable doubt. *Commonwealth v. Duncan,* 473 Pa. 62, 65, n. 2, 373 A.2d 1051, 1052, n.2, (1977), cited in *Commonwealth v. Turner,* 491 Pa. 620, 421, A.2d 1057 (1980).

In the instant case, the Commonwealth failed to sufficiently prove involuntary sexual intercourse. There was insufficient evidence of such relating to Sally Oldman.

Additionally, there was insufficient evidence of any criminal conspiracy regarding Sabrina Winner. The testimony revealed that Mrs. Winner made football crowd sounds to Tony Winner, but there was no evidence that Charles Winner was in the room at the time. There also was insufficient evidence of an agreement between the two. Therefore, a new trial should be granted.

Respectfully submitted,
Gerald P. Humble, Esquire
Attorney for defendant.

Fourteen months after the post verdict motions where submitted to the court another hearing date was scheduled. All participants were in the courtroom which was packed with watchers. All the

122

people from the Commonwealth who had anything to do with the case were waiting for the final blow—the sentence.

Mr. Humble made a weak plea to the Court: "Your Honor, Mr. Winner has never been arrested, he has worked most of his life. He was a sergeant in the Marine Corps. Herian listened. Then he asked Winner if he had anything to say? "Yes, I do. You have only heard half the story and the half you heard was false." The judge then said, "I don't see any repentance." Well your honor how can a person repent of crimes that never happened?

The judge then started reading out his sentence. Mr. Winner broke into his reading on several occasions to inform the court that it was in error. Mr. Humble pulled at Winner's shirttails in an effort to silence the convicted man but he would not be quiet.

It was finished. He was sentenced to 16 to 60 years and was quickly rushed out of the county jail to begin his sentence up state.

15

Be Patient, Fear Not. Courage.

THE JUDGE RESPONDED WITH HIS OPINION:

IN THE COURT OF COMMON PLEAS OF PHILADELPHIA
FIRST JUDICIAL DISTRICT OF PENNSYLVANIA
CRIMINAL TRIAL DIVISION

— — —

COMMONWEALTH OF PENN-   V.
SYLVANIA
CHARLES WINNER

                       : JANUARY TERM, 1989

   : NO. 120-126   :
: DECEMBER TERM, 1989   : NO. 1416–2141

— — —*OPINION*

Herian, Henry   August 1992

I. PROCEDURAL HISTORY

    This sad case stems from the systematic and repeated sexual abuse defendant forced upon his daughter beginning when she was four years old. On or about August 29, 1989, defendant in the basement of his residence had forcible oral, anal, and vaginal intercourse with his daughter, then seven years old. Defendant also had forcible oral, anal, and vaginal intercourse with a friend and neighbor of his daughter, Sally Oldman, then seven years old.

    Following a hearing on his motion to suppress evidence which was denied on April 10, 1992, defendant was tried before this court and a jury in a trial which began on April 10. On April 19, 1992, defendant's wife and co-defendant, Sabrina Winner became distraught and had to be taken out of the courtroom. A court appointed doctor, after examining Mrs. Winner, determined that she was unable to participate in her defense; consequently the cases were severed. On April 22, 1992, the jury returned verdicts of guilty against defendant on all bills of information. Defendant filed timely post-trial motions which were denied after a hearing held on June 18, 1993. On that same date, the Court sentenced defendant to serve not less than one nor more than five years in the state correctional institution and to pay $140 costs on Bill No. 120 (corruption of minors, victim Sally Oldman). On Bill No. 136 (rape, victim Sally Oldman), he was sentenced to serve not less than six nor more than 20 years in the state correctional institution consecutive to Bill No. 120. On Bill of Information No. 2391 (rape, victim Ann Winner), defendant was sentenced to serve not less than six nor more than 20 years imprisonment consecutive to Bill No. 128. On Bill of Information No. 2383, (involuntary deviate sexual intercourse, victim Ann Winner), he was sentenced to serve six to 20 years imprisonment concurrent with Bill. No. 2391. On Bill No. 2382 (corruption of minors, victim Ann Winner), defendant was sentenced to serve not less than one nor more than five years imprisonment consecutive to Bill No. 2391 and to pay $145 costs. On Bill No. 2387 (criminal conspiracy, victim Ann Winner), he was sentenced to serve two to ten years consecutive to Bill No. 2382. No sentence was imposed on either Bill No. 124 or Bill No. 2388. On appeal, defendant raises six claims of error.

II. DISCUSSION.

A. *Sufficiency of Evidence*

Defendant first claim that the evidence presented at trial was insufficient to prove him guilty of committing involuntary deviate sexual intercourse and criminal conspiracy. Specifically, in his memorandum of Law in Support of Post-Verdict Motions, defendant contends that the evidence presented in support of IDSI was insufficient with regard to "Ann Oldman." The victims in the instant case are Sally Oldman and Ann Winner. The Court is unable to determine which victim is referred to by "Ann Oldman" but must assume

Ann Winner is the victim referred to since she is the victim listed on the sole ISDI Bill of Information (No. 2383).

Evidence is sufficient if, accepting as true all reasonable inferences arising therefrom, the fact finder could have found the defendant guilty of each element of the crime charged beyond a reasonable double. *Commonwealth v. Hughes,* 521 Pa. 423, 430, 555 A.2d 1264, 1267 (1989); *Commonwealth v. Caldwell,* 516 Pa. 441, 532 A.2d 813 (1987); *Commonwealth v. Sabharwal,* 373 Pa. Super. 241, 243, 540 A.2d 957, 958 (1988), quoting *Commonwealth v. Jackson,* 506 Pa. 469, 473–474, 485 A.2d 1102, 1103 (1984). A review of the relevant statute, 18 Pa. C.S. 3123, and the pertinent notes of testimony (April 11, 1991, pages 62–63, 68–69) prove beyond a reasonable doubt that all elements of the charges were proved beyond a reasonable doubt.

Similarly the evidence proving a conspiracy beyond a reasonable doubt may be found at pages 64–66, 71–73, of the April 11, 1991, notes of testimony. The pertinent statute is found at 18 Pa. C.S. 903. *See Commonwealth v. Anderson,* 381 Pa. Super. 1, 552 A.2d 1064 (1988) (direct proof of corrupt agreement not necessary to convict defendant of conspiracy, existence of common agreement between co-conspirators may be inferred from circumstantial evidence surrounding alleged conspiratorial activities, and from relationship between and the conduct of the parties).

B. *Search Warrant*

Defendant next claims the Court erred in failing to suppress evidence seized from the basement area of Archer Street in Philadelphia, the residence where all of defendant's sexual misconduct occurred. The Court makes the following findings of fact:

1. Beginning on September 4, 1989 and on subsequent days afterward, Sally Oldman was interviewed by a detective and other members of the Philadelphia Police Department.

2. Sally Oldman told the police that she had been witness to and victim of a sexual assault committed by Charles Winner inside of Archer Street in Philadelphia on August 29, 1989.

3. Sally Oldman also related to police that Charles Winner had threatened to beat her with a black belt if she didn't comply with his demands and also that Sabrina Winner, Charles' wife, had taken photographs of the sexual assaults committed on August 29.

4. As a result of what Sally told her and other police officers,

detectives prepared and presented to a magistrate, Search and Seizure Warrant #11463 which the magistrate signed on September 7, 1989.

5. On the evening of September 8, 1989, a detective accompanied by three additional police officers traveled to Archer Street in order to search the premises.

6. When the police officers knocked at the above address, it was answered by the property owners and residents, Flamingo and Woody.

7. The police officers identified themselves as law enforcement officers and told the residents that they had a search warrant for the premises.

8. The residents invited the police into the residence where they searched the basement and seized one Kodak Electrolight Instamatic Camera and some photographs. (Lies—no photos were found.)

9. The residents told the police on September 8, that the Winners had, previous to that date, vacated the premises.

Conclusion of Law

1. The search warrant stated sufficient probable cause. The police were entitled to rely on the uncorroborated statement of Sally Oldman, a minor, a victim and an eyewitness. Ms. Oldman was not an unidentified or anonymous informant whose reliability or track record needed to be proved. *See Commonwealth v. Schilling,* 312 Pa. Super. 43, 458 A.2d 226 (1983) (where informants on whose information affidavit for search warrant is prepared are not paid, unknown tipsters, but actual identified eyewitness to transaction, their trustworthiness is presumed).

2. The warrant is not overly broad. It specified the dwelling to be searched and the probable cause contained within the four corners of the warrant was sufficient to support the magistrate's signing the warrant allowing a search of the entire dwelling. Moreover, the residents, owners of the dwelling, consented to the search and informed the officers that the Winners had moved, and therefore, had abandoned the premises.

3. The information contained within the affidavit of probable cause was not stale. The sexual assault occurred on August 29, it was reported to police on September 7 of the same year, the warrant was signed by a magistrate on the same date and executed on September 8 of the same year. Thus, slightly more than a week elapsed between the incident and the execution of the warrant. The items

sought and recovered were not of the type (i. stolen items, controlled substances) which move quickly through the stream of commerce and would not be likely to be found unless immediate action was taken. *See Commonwealth v. Yocum,* 274 Pa. Super. 533, 418 A.2d 534 (1980) lapse of eight days between burglary of durable goods and search of defendant's apartment was not so great as to render search warrant stale.

c. *Competency of Nine Year Old Witness*

Defendant next complains that the Court "erred in finding a nine year old Commonwealth witness competent to testify" against him. *Defendant's Concise Statement of Matters Complained of on Appeal.* In his Memorandum of Law in Support of Post Verdict Motions, defendant discusses the same claim and identifies Sally Oldman as the nine year old witness whose competency he challenges. Defendant quotes testimony in his memorandum from an October 16, 1990 hearing. The Court is confused by this reference since it has found no notes of testimony for that date in the record. Sally Oldman did testify at defendant's trial; however, she did so on April 16, 1991. This witness knew the difference between truth and a lie and recognized it was wrong to tell a lie. (N.T. 4/16/91 competency hearing, pp. 19–22). She clearly understood that she would be punished ("spanked") and God would be "sad" as consequences of telling a lie. (N.T. 4/16/91 competency hearing, p.8). It is clear that this child had a sufficiently developed consciousness of her duty to speak the truth. Her testimony as a whole during the competency hearing evidences no fantasizing about events. She demonstrated an ability to remember events, to thoughtfully listen and respond to questions and communicate. The Court properly found this witness competent.

To the extent that the defendant raises a claim challenging the competency of his daughter, Ann Winner, to testify at trial, that claim must fail as well. A trial court is vested with considerable discretion in adjudging a child witness' consciousness of duty to tell the truth and is required only to find that the child is sincere, understands the importance of truth telling and feels that lying is wrong and may have adverse consequences. *Commonwealth v. Trudell,* 371 Pa. Super. 353, 538, A.2d 53 (1988). A review of the testimony from Ann Winner's April 11, 1991, competency hearing, pages 16–35, establishes that this court correctly found her competent to testify. See *Commonwealth v. McEachin,* 371 Pa. Super. 188, 537 A.2d 883 (1988) (trial court in child sexual abuse case did not abuse its discretions finding victims who were aged five, five and three and one half competent to testify where each knew his or her name, age, and where he or she went to school; each could distinguish colors; and each knew difference between truth and lie and consequences of telling a lie); *Commonwealth v. Stohr,* 361 Pa. Super. 293, 552 A.2d 589 (1987) (trial court did not abuse its discretion in finding that defendant's four and one half year old daughter was competent to testify at trial concerning prosecution of indecent exposure, indecent assault and corruption of the morals of a minor).

D. CO-DEFENDANT'S BEHAVIOR/DENIAL OF MISTRIAL

Defendant next claims that the Court erred in failing to grant a requested mistrial following an exclamation by his wife and co-defendant, Sabrina Winner. On April 29, 1991, the seventh day of trial, during cross examination of a defense witness, Flamingo, the following took place:

A. The detective already had them by then.

Q. (By the prosecutor): I'm not talking about the detectives; I'm talking about Tony and Ann.

(By Defense counsel for Charles Winner): Objection.

(By Defense witness Flamingo): I don't know what you are talking about.

The Court: Sustained.

Ms. Vim: I'm sorry, you are well beyond the direct examination. This witness did not testify on direct to these areas and thus, you are prohibited from pursuing them on cross examination.

(By the Prosecutor): Judge, it goes to her credibility.

The Court: You may not offer that comment. Members of the jury, you are directed to strike that. You did not hear it. It is improper for you to offer that comment. I'm sorry. I'm sorry.

(By Counsel for Sabrina Winner): Your Honor, can we have a moment?

(By Defendant Sabrina Winner): I feel like I'm going black.

(By Co-Defense Counsel for Sabrina Winner): The defendant feels like she is going to black out.

The Court: Excuse me. Would you please not speak aloud. Talk to your lawyer.

(By Counsel for Sabrina Winner): Your Honor, this is a request just for temporary—

The Court: We will take a five minute recess.

(By Mr. Smith, Counsel for Sabrina Winner): Thank You, Your Honor.

The Court: Hold on for a moment. If you will, you may take her through the back way. That is fine.

(Mr. Smith and Ms. Winner exit the courtroom).

The Court: Okay.

The Court Crier: Jurors, do you want to follow me, please. Everybody please remain seated while the jury leaves the room.

(The jury leaves the courtroom at 11:34 a.m.

The Court: All right. Can I see counsel briefly at sidebar?

(N.T. 4/19/91, 67–68).

The Court immediately ordered that Sabrina Winner be examined by a doctor who reported to the Court that Mrs. Winner was incapable of cooperating in her defense. The Court denied counsel's request for a mistrial and after consultation with defense counsel instructed the jury as follows:

(The Jury enters the courtroom at 2:38 p.m.).

The Court: Good afternoon, members of the jury.

The Jury: Good afternoon.

The Court: I hope you enjoyed your lunch. Mrs. Winner has become physically ill and is unable to continue with these proceedings. Her condition has been verified by court physicians. Accordingly, this Court is severing the charges involving her and you should not allow and you must not allow this occurrence involving Mrs. Winner to in any way affect this your consideration of the charges involving Mr. Winner.

And we shall proceed. I understand that there is one witness remaining. Ms. Vim, having completed her questions of the last witness, Mr. Humble, please proceed.

(By Counsel for Defendant Charles Winner): We call Charles Winner.

(N.T. 4/19/91, 82).

In determining whether to grant a mistrial, the necessary inquiry is whether the alleged occurrence is prejudicial to defendant, that is, whether it was of such a nature that it may reasonably be

130

said to have deprived defendant of a fair and impartial trial. *Commonwealth v. Farrell,* 265 Pa. super. 41, 401 A.2d 790 (1979), *accord Commonwealth v. Chestnut,* 511 Pa. 169, 512 A.2d 603 (1986). In the instant case; co-defendant Sabrina Winner's exclamation that she was blacking out was not of such a nature as to have deprive defendant of a fair and impartial trial. Even assuming as counsel contends, Mrs. Winner was gesticulating and exhibiting otherwise odd behavior at various times throughout the trial, the Court's explanation to the jury was sufficient to satisfy any curiosity they may have had about her behavior. Defendant argues that due to their marital relationship and the nature of the charges against them, any abberational behavior on the part of Mrs. Winner would unavoidably reflect unfavorably on him. This Court is unconvinced by this argument in part because it is wholly speculative, and based on an antiquated view of marriage. Accordingly, the Court granted defendant no relief on this claim. *See Commonwealth v. Hoffman,* 301 Pa. Super. 312, 447 A.2d 983 (1982) (motion for mistrial rests within sound discretion of trial court and, when prompt curative actions are taken by trial court, an abuse of discretion will not be readily found); *Commonwealth v. Gibson,* 230 Pa. Super. 340, 326 A.2d 471 (1974) (that co-defendant mentioned that he had been arrested on an unrelated charge did not entitle defendant to mistrial in view of fact that such utterance was spontaneously volunteered in response to question which was natural development of facts in evidence and that any prejudice would be solely toward co-defendant).

E. Prosecutorial Misconduct During Opening, Closing Argument and Cross Examination of Witness During Trial.

Defendant next claims that the Court erred in failing to grant appropriate relief requested when the prosecutor allegedly engaged in misconduct during her opening and closing arguments to the jury as well as during her examination of witness during trial. In his Memorandum of Law in Support of Post-Verdict Motions, defendant discusses only allegations of misconduct during the prosecutor's opening statement to the jury. The Court will, therefore, confine itself to addressing that claim.

Defense counsel made two objections during the prosecutor's opening argument (N.T. 4/10/91, 85, 88–89) which are both sustained. Following defense counsel's motion for a mistrial, the Court denied the same after argument (N.T. 4/10/91, 91–92) which was sufficient to cure any possibly improper suggestion made by the prosecutor. *See Commonwealth v. D'Amato,* 514 Pa. 471, 526 A.2d 300 (1987) (a mistrial is not warranted unless the unavoidable effect of the prosecutor's questions or comments is to so bias and prejudice a jury against the defendant as to render it incapable of objectively weighing evidence and delivering a true verdict).

F. Expert Witness' Testimony

Defendant finally claims the Court erred in failing to strike the testimony of an expert witness. Defendant seeks to equate the testimony of the witness, Art Mojong, with the type that has been proscribed by the Superior Court in *Commonwealth v. Dunkle,* 385 Pa. Super. 317, 561 A.2d 5 (1989) modified in *Commonwealth v. Dunkle,* — Pa. —, 602 A.2d 830 (1992). The Court in *Dunkle* held that expert testimony offering an opinion regarding the credibility of a child witness in a sex abuse case is not permissible. In the instant case, Dr. Mojong's testimony was confined solely to responding to a hypothetical question posed by the prosecutor which sought the doctor's expert opinion regarding whether the *physical* findings of examinations performed upon the two complaints were consistent with the complaints made by the child victims here. The doctors expressed no opinions nor made any comment about the credibility of either complainant. The Court, in Consultation with all attorneys in the instant case, was very careful to confine the doctor's testimony to permissible areas (N.T. 4-18-91, 29–48, 81–87). The Court, therefore, can grant no relief to defendant on this claim.

BY THE COURT _____ Henry Herian.

16

Charge! Into the Battle.

A point that needs to be resolved in this case is the medical records. In the courtroom no mention was made of Ann's hymen being broken. Winner didn't hear one word from anyone stating that her hymen was broken. The testimony was she had redness, pimples and a yeast infection. This point was brought to Attorney Peterson who replied: Dear Mr. Winner,

I got your latest letter.

My conclusion that your daughter suffered a broken hymen is based upon the testimony that was adduced at your trial. I am not in any way agreeing with that nor should you. There was, however, medical testimony that such was the case. Sincerely.

The medical report said nothing about Ann's broken hymen. Fathers would hear statements like that if made.

Child,you played no part in this outrage! You were perfect in your father's sight. Never did your father think unkindly towards you for your actions. You were used by others so they could get what they wanted. You couldn't fight them so you had to do as they wished. Tony, please, never ever cause your sister any grief over this affair. As you mature you will be able to see the hardships your sister was forced to undergo at the tender age of seven. You both have the right to be angry but not at each other. Drop the anger! That's not good. Know Sabrina and Winner love you with no conditions on this love.

Innocent people can't be guilty no matter what the court proclaims. The question is will justice continue to err?

NOTICE
re: COMMONWEALTH V WINNER,

THIS IS TO ADVISE THAT THE ABOVE CAPTIONED AP-
PEAL HAS BEEN LISTED FOR ARGUMENT BEFORE PANEL
NO A08, DAILY LIST NO. 13 OF THIS COURT SITTING IN
SUPERIOR COURT COURTROOM
530 WALNUT STREET
THIRD FLOOR
PHILADELPHIA, PA.
On FEBRUARY 19, 1993.
COUNSEL ARE REQUESTED TO NOTE THE FOL-
LOWING:

1. COURT CONVENES AT 9:30 A.M.; ALL COUNSEL
   ARE REQUESTED TO BE PRESENT AT THAT TIME.
   THIS OFFICE WILL NOT BE ABLE TO INFORM
   COUNSEL OF THE PROGRESS OF CASES BEING AR-
   GUED BEFORE THE PANEL.
2. THIS OFFICE WILL NOT KNOW IN ADVANCE THE
   COMPOSITON OF THE PANEL AND REQUESTS
   THAT COUNSEL NOT CALL TO INQUIRE ABOUT
   SAME.
3. THE ABOVE ARGUMENT DATE IS FIRM AND THIS
   OFFICE WILL NOT ENTERTAIN REQUESTS FOR RE-
   SCHEDULING.

The date was set. Mr. Peterson was ready. He sent Winner a
copy of his appeal which stated: In the Superior Court of Pennsylvania, Philadelphia County No 01144PHL92. Commonwealth of
Pennsylvania, Appelle v Charles Winner. Appellant appeal from the
judgement of sentence of the Court of Common Pleas of Philadelphia County, the Honorable Henry Herian, June 15, 1991.
BRIEF OF APPELLANT
Peter Pete Peterson
Attorney for Appellant

STATEMENT OF JURISDICTION

The jurisdiction of this Court is found at 41.Pa.C.S.A. 742. This is an appeal from judgment and sentence of the Court of Common Pleas on a criminal charge involving corrupting the morals of a minor, involuntary deviate sexual intercourse, conspiracy and rape.

ORDER IN QUESTION

The Order of the Court of Common Pleas dated June 16, 1992, denying Post-Verdict Motions and imposing a prison sentence of 16 to sixty years.

STATEMENT OF THE QUESTIONS

I. Were The Juvenile Witnesses Competent And Credible?
II. Did The Court Improperly Allow Expert Testimony?
III. Did The Co-Defendant's Bizarre Behavior Deprive The Defendant Of A Fair Trial?
IV. Did The Prosecutorial Misconduct During Trial And In Argument Deprive The Defendant Of A Fair Trial?

STATEMENT OF THE CASE

On Labor Day night, September 4, 1989, Sally Oldman, who was then seven years old and in the second grade, was watching a movie with her mother and expressed a verbal interest in "french kissing." Under questioning, she told her mother that the previous Tuesday, August 29th, she had seen Ann Winner, age seven, and her brother, Tony, age three or four, (93a), french kissing while they were watching a TV movie called "Dirty Dancing" on a VCR at the place that the Winners were then living. Mrs. Oldman recalled that a day or two after August 29th, Sally complained of a burning sensation when she urinated. (422a). She acted mopey and tired, (425a), but Mrs. Oldman did not think there was anything seriously wrong with her at that time. Sally acted normally after that. (435a).

Mrs. Oldman further recalled that on August 29th, Sally came home for dinner, ate dinner with her family and then went back to play with the Winner children at the place they were then staying. (424a, 425a). Mrs. Oldman satisfied herself that the burning that

Sally complained of was not unusual, (422a, 439a), but spoke to Mrs. Winner about the incident on the telephone. Mrs. Winner denied that anything untoward had happened. (423a). Shortly after that, Mrs. Winner received a telephone that the Oldmans wanted to see Mr. Winner immediately. She called him at AA, he came home and together, they went to the Oldmans where Mr. Winner was viciously attacked by Mr. Oldman. (815a–817a). Mrs. Winner called the police to complain that her husband had been assaulted. (438a).

Mrs. Oldman testified that her daughter told her things a little bit at a time. (434a). The story that she told on the second day was completely different than the story she had told the previous day. (440a). The interviewing police officer stated that when first interviewed, Sally said that her clothing remained on during the entire incident and that the defendant placed his birdie against her clothed vaginal area. (669a).

As a result of these disclosures, the Police Department obtained a search warrant for the basement apartment being occupied by the Winners during this period of time. They were looking for a black camera which allegedly was used to take photos of these sex acts, a black belt allegedly used by the defendant to threaten the children, and photos taken of the sex acts themselves. They found a camera with no film. (41a). No one could testify to whether or not the camera worked. (446a). They did not find a black belt nor any other evidence. (467a). There was no attempt made to analyze any of the material in this basement apartment for semen stains or anything else. This, in spite of the fact that an expert testified that semen could be detected as long as years later. (683a). There was no further corroboration of the story told by either of the juvenile witnesses.

Eventually, after a period of intense manipulation, Sally Oldman and Ann Winner testified that on August 29th, the defendant, Charles Winner, placed his penis at or in their mouths, butt, or heinie. While Sally claims she left crying, her mother testified that she appeared normal, came home and ate dinner then went back to play with Ann. Ann eventually was to testify that her father had been doing this to her ever since she was four or five on an unknown number of occasions in various locations.

The defendant testified on his own behalf and denied that he ever committed any of these acts with either his daughter or Sally Oldman. He admitted that he returned home that day, as he said he did on many occasions during the day, kissed his wife and saw his

136

son running around naked. He didn't see his son try to touch anybody nor did he touch either Sally or ann nor threaten anyone. (813a, 814a). The Commonwealth introduced a written message from the defendant to a social worker active in the case and the District Attorney. The Commonwealth contended that these were an admission of guilt. Two independent witnesses testified that they were part of a workshop group with Mr. Winner that was trained to send out these "forgiveness cards" with a dime attached to make peace within themselves and that the cards were not an admission that Mr. Winner had done anything improper. (723a, et seq., 732a, et seq.).

SUMMARY OF ARGUMENT

Both the competence and credibility of Ann Winner and Sally Oldman was so undermined by the collective manipulation of the Commonwealth that their testimony should be stricken in its entirety.

The Court improperly permitted a medical doctor to give testimony that was neither required nor expert in an attempt to bolster the testimony of Ann Winner and Sally Oldman.

The co-defendant's bizarre behavior throughout the trial and during a psychotic episode in full view of the jury deprived the defendant of a fair trial.

The prosecutor's conduct in both arguing and questioning witnesses deprived the defendant of a fair trial.

TABLE OF CONTENTS

ARGUMENT

I. THE JUVENILE WITNESSES WERE NEITHER COMPETENT NOR CREDIBLE.

Sally Oldman testified with an intern from the District Attorney's Office standing at her side. She regularly refused to answer questions and would do no more than shrug her shoulders. She testified that she could not remember obvious recent things like whether or not she was with the Assistant District Attorney last Friday. (261a). She constantly interrupted her testimony with a request for recess and didn't even remember the names of Ann Winner, her brother Tony or their father. (280a, 281a). She said she forgot whether or not Tony even touched her, (229a), and refused to tell the Court why she pushed Tony away. (294a). She first claims she didn't tell anyone about these events, then admitted that she told her mom and dad, then said she told Tracy but she did not know who Tracy was and that it happened a long time ago. (298a). She didn't remember what she told the police or what she told her mother. (300a). She said that she did not know what the defendant had done to his daughter Ann in her presence. (306a). She claims she couldn't remember any of the details about what the defendant did with his daughter or with her. (308a–313a). She claimed that she didn't tell her mom anything until "a couple of weeks later." (333a).

Under cross-examination, she didn't remember testifying before at the preliminary hearing and never remembered being in court. (350a, 351a). During her testimony, the defense objected because the Assistant District Attorney was indicating anger to the witness over some answers and the Court instructed the prosecutor not to display facial feelings to the witness during her testimony. (362a, 363a). She didn't remember telling the police that she was fully clothed when the defendant put his "bird" next to her. (373a). She didn't remember testifying at the preliminary hearing that all Mr. and Mrs. Winner were doing was kissing and didn't remember whether or not they were lying down while they were kissing. (378a, 380a). She didn't remember testifying at the preliminary hearing that Mrs. Winner did nothing with a camera. (391a).

At the beginning of her testimony, her grandmother was observed coaching her from the audience, admitted that she was doing it and was excluded from the courtroom. (260a, 261a). During the cross-examination, she refused to continue testifying and asked for her mother. (398a).

Flamingo was the sister of Mrs. Winner. It was in their basement that the Winners were living at the time of the alleged incident. She had a daughter about two years older than Ann and Sally and they all played together. She testified that her daughter stayed with the Winners on many occasions and had never made any complaint

139

at all about any sexual improprieties on the part of Mr. and Mrs. Winner or their children. She recalled that the first telephone call from Mrs. Oldman was inquiring about whether or not Tony, the brother of Ann Winner and the son of the defendants, Mr. and Mrs. Winner, was french kissing Sally. Mrs. Oldman made no complaint about anyone else in the house touching her daughter. In this telephone conversation, Mrs. Oldman said Sally complained that Tony had grabbed her private parts. It was Flamingo's firm impression that Mrs. Oldman was uncertain what it was that Sally told her went on when Sally first spoke with her mother about this incident.

Although Sally testified that on the day in question she was watching "Dirty Dancing" in the basement, Woody, the owner of the premises, testified under oath that there were two TV's in the basement that did not work but that there was no VCR.

While Mrs. Oldman now recalls that Sally complained of some burning in the vaginal area around this period of time, she examined her and concluded that there was nothing wrong. She did admit, however, that her daughter's stories, once she began to discuss this incident, differed completely from day to day.

Ann Winner was first interviewed by Police Officer Little on September 9, 1989. She had been brought in by her grandparents at the police's request and indicated that there was absolutely nothing wrong. The second time she was interviewed was October 7, 1989, almost a month later and she had already been taken away from her parents and placed in a foster home. During these interviews, Officer Little told Ann that she wasn't telling the truth. Ann also refused to make a complaint to Wendy Pathnek, a social worker. At her request, Mr. and Mrs. Winner brought the children into the Department of Human Services Office where they were physically removed from their custody on September 13th and placed in foster homes. In an attempt to get Ann to repeat the story told by Sally, Ms. Pathnek told Ann that she had experienced a similar incident when she was young. While everyone had denied that anyone had ever told Ann what Sally had said, the best that she could remember was Ann said whatever Sally told you is what happened.

On September 28th, Ms. Pathnek arranged for Ann to be interviewed by Gloria Mudski, who Ann understood to be a psychiatrist. Ms. Mudski was the first person who spoke with her about getting in trouble as a result of this incident. Ms. Mudski never testified about that interview but social worker Pathnek corrected the misimpression about her training and expertise and identified her as a "sexual abuse expert" with a masters degree in social work. It was on that day, after Ann had been removed from her parent's home for more than two weeks and interviewed by her "psychiatrist" that she first told of the many incidents of prior sexual abuse.

Ann admitted being very susceptible to the opinions of others. Besides the interviewing officer telling her that she was a liar and her "psychiatrist" telling her that she could get in trouble, she told the trial assistant that "her parents didn't do anything." The trial assistant got mad at her. This, of course, caused her to change her story in an attempt to tell what she now calls the truth. Not only did she first tell the Assistant District Attorney that nothing happened, when she went to the hospital to be examined, she told the doctor that nothing happened. She was assured by both the Assistant District Attorney, her social worker and her foster parents that she would be helping her parents by testifying against them and saying that things did happen. She told both Officer Little and her psychiatrist that Sally was lying about her story. She told the Assistant District Attorney that the first time she spoke with her also. She was told by her psychiatrist that the defense lawyer would scare her and try to confuse her. She also told another social worker that her parents did nothing wrong.

In addition, both Ann and Sally attended "court school" in City Hall. During this school, she and Sally were taught songs such as "I'm Going To Tell The Truth, Ruth" and they played roles and learned certain hand motions. It was here that Ann learned to tell the truth. She went to court school two times. Her psychiatrist, however, had to help her with the words to use in court. Ann believed that her first disclosure about these incidents did not occur until five months afterwards when she was in foster care. She admitted, however, that she had seen "stuff like this on TV."

The point of this argument is that these two young girls were rendered both incompetent and uncredible as witnesses as a result of the combined manipulative efforts they were subjected to by various Commonwealth agencies. The hesitant, reluctant story told by Sally Oldman was accepted as the polestar of truth and a continuing displeasure was visited upon anyone who tried to change that story or who told a different story. The Winner children were uprooted from their home and removed from their parents' custody without any form of judicial hearing based solely upon the story told by Ms. Oldman. There was absolutely no corroborating evidence. While there was talk of pictures being taken, no pictures were found. No chemical tests were even attempted to be done to determine whether or not semen stains were present in the basement. After they were removed from their home, the Winner children were subjected to a series of interviews with various people and led to believe that they would help their parents by testifying against them. The lower court, in its Opinion, believes it fulfilled its function by getting the children to admit that they know the difference between right and wrong, a truth and a lie and an ability to distinguish colors. Responses to these questions, of course, are part of the continuing program that these children were put through.

It is noted that these children were not prepared for trial after they gave a credible corroborated story. What might otherwise be legitimate methods of preparing a juvenile witness for trial became an oppressive training program to get them to change or to stick to a story which the authorities represented as truth.

The law has always treated the testimony of young children as suspect and required that the individual proposing their testimony first must show they are competent to testify. The methods used by the Commonwealth in this case, in order to obtain a specific line of testimony from these children, became more oppressive than any attempts to obtain a confession from a defendant. Completely neglected is the fact that neither of these two girls exhibited any signs of physical or mental discomfort as a result of the trauma that had recently been visited upon them. Sally went home and ate dinner with her family. Her mother observed nothing unusual about her demeanor and after dinner she went back and played with Ann. For over a month, Ann maintained that her parents did absolutely nothing and that the story told by Sally for some reason was untrue. After she was removed from her home, subjected to all kinds of interviews and placed in a foster home, she then said whatever Sally said was true.

A witness is presumed competent to testify unless proven otherwise. Commonwealth v. Riley, 326 A.2d 384 (Pa.1974). When a proposed witness is under 14 years of age, there must be a searching judicial inquiry as to mental capacity. Commonwealth v. Short, 420 A.2d 694 (Super.1980). This inquiry must probe the capacity to communicate, observe, and remember, and a consciousness of the

142

duty to speak the truth in proportion to the witness' chronological immaturity. Rosche v. McCoy, 156 A.2d 307 (Pa.1959). It is respectfully urged that the potential for manipulation is indeed, one of those factors which must be examined in proportion to the witness's chronological immaturity. In the present case, each witness admitted that she had, indeed, lied in the past and Ann Winner's testimony showed quite clearly that even once she had given a story, she had tried on several occasions to change it to say that her parents did nothing wrong.

The trial court, in its Opinion, quoted Commonwealth v. Trudell, 538 A.2d 53 (Super.1988), in commenting upon its duty to determine the competency of a witness. That case did not involve a juvenile witness. It held that an underworld informant who had admitted committing perjury was still qualified to testify. The Court, however, did comment upon the qualification of young witnesses. It notes that courts have recognized what every parent will recognize, that children are particularly susceptible to "make believe" and, therefore, are often not sufficiently aware of or able to fulfill their duty to tell the truth. It is this concern which led to the rule requiring the court to make a specific special ruling upon the competency of a child witness. Courts are required to find "a consciousness of the duty to tell the truth." It is exactly this characteristic which it is respectfully submitted has been shown to be totally lacking in the testimony of these two young girls.

II. THE COURT IMPROPERLY ALLOWED EXPERT TESTIMONY

The Commonwealth presented as an expert witness Dr. Art Mojong, the Chief of Pediatric Medicine at Washington University. After lengthy argument, the Court overruled objections to Dr. Mojong's proposed testimony, and he was permitted to review the records of medical examinations of Ann Winner and Sally Oldman. He was then permitted to opine that the physical findings of the examining physicians were consistent with the history given by someone to those physicians at the time of examination. He based his opinion upon the facts that both of these young girls had a broken hymen which he claimed was a result of injury. He also noted that each of them had an enlarged introits. His opinion to the average size of the introits was based upon statistics published in medical literature. The enlarged introits, he stated, went along with penetration through the hymen itself.

Dr. Mojong never examined either of these girls, although they were certainly available to him if he chose to do so. He admitted that he did not know the physicians who did perform the examinations and, therefore, did not know the extent of their experience. He did not know what instrument was used to measure the size of the introits and was not able to say whether any instrument at all was used or whether the recorded measurements were determined without the benefit of instruments. The broken hymen, he admitted, was consistent with an accident of any kind and did not necessarily indicate sexual penetration. There was no abnormal physical findings on examination of the rectal area or the mouth. He noted, however, that the intrusion of a penis does not necessarily leave injuries in either of these areas. The physical examinations generally were within normal limits and he could say that there was no fresh injuries found on either girl. While he admitted that the measurement of the introits could be influenced by the position the young girl was placed in before the measurement was made or estimated, he did not know what position either child was in when those measurements were taken. He further went on to admit that while indications of anal molestations were often observed, non were present in either of these two girls.

The opinion that Mojong gave was that the history given by someone on behalf of these young girls at the date of examination was consistent with the medical findings. The only medical findings, however, were related to the vaginal area and showed that at some point in time, an injury had occurred sufficient to tear the hymen. Whatever the injury was, it had long since healed at the time of the examination in September.

Dr. Mojong was introduced to the jury as an expert in research on child abuse and one who lectured rather extensively regarding the subject of child abuse. His opinion was based upon something more than the hypothetical case that he was supplied. It was based upon his past findings in his research projects and his interpretation of the physical findings of the doctors. While he was never really asked for a formal opinion, specific questions clearly established that he was saying that the lack of specific medical findings which are often observed in molestation victims did not mean that neither of these girls had been molested at one time or another.

The basis of Dr. Mojong's opinions were the medical records of the examination of these two girls. Setting aside for a moment any attack upon the accuracy of measurements which formed the entire basis of Dr. Mojong's opinion, medical history is nothing more than a hearsay statement and very often in the case of children, is supplied not only by the child itself but by someone accompanying the child. There was no attempt made by the Commonwealth to show the circumstances under which these histories were supplied or even that they were supplied by the girls themselves. As such, they are hearsay and cannot form the basis of Dr. Mojong's opinion. Arnold v. Zangrilli, 566 A.2d 865 (Super.1989); Commonwealth v. Haber, 505 A.2d 273 (Super.1986).

Hospital records are admitted for a very limited purpose in Pennsylvania. Commonwealth v. Garcia, 387 A.2d 48 (Pa.1978)(; Commonwealth v. DiGiacomo, 345 A.2d 605 (Pa.1975). These two cases do not allow even a diagnosis let alone medical history. The hospital record which contains the opinion of a social worker is not admissible. Williams v. McClain, 520 A.2d 1374 (Pa.1987). The admission of a medical report regarding the abuse of a 10 year old girl without producing the author or showing the author's unavailability violated the defendant's right to confrontation. Pickett v. Bowen, 798 F.2d 1385 (11th Cir.1986). This Court has ruled inadmissible a statement in a medical report that the defendant was run over by a truck where it was not made contemporaneously nor was the maker known. Isaacson v. Mobile, 461 A.2d 625 (Super.1983). This is exactly the factual situation in the present case.

In a very recent case, this Court examined the right of a testifying expert to rely upon medical reports compiled by others who did not testify. Primavera v. Celotex Corp., 608 a. 2d 515 (Super 1992). The Court noted that this rule has been in effect in Pennsylvania since 1971. In revisiting the history and rational behind the rule, this Court made it quite clear that what an expert was entitled to rely upon were the opinions and findings of other experts and certainly not an unsubstantiated medical history supplied by an unknown source.

Beyond the examination of the manner in which Dr. Mojong reached his opinion is the unresolved question of why he testified at all. While the colloquy regarding objections of his testimony when he was presented as an expert clearly show that all parties agreed that Dr. Mojong could not testify about the credibility of

145

these two young girls, that is exactly what he did. He was introduced to the jury as an expert on child abuse and a man who spent considerable time investigating specific instances, reading the literature and lecturing about this subject. Yet the only opinion he was asked to give was whether or not the physical findings were consistent with the history which was presumably given by the girls themselves. What he said was yes it was and thus, the sole import of his expert testimony was that these girls had told the truth in September when they received examinations from two different physicians. As such, it clearly violated the law of Pennsylvania. Commonwealth v. Sees, 605 A.2d 307 (Pa.1992). The result was nothing more than a thinly disguised attempt to bolster the credibility of the victims and, as such, was inadmissible. Commonwealth v. Higby, 938 A.2d 939 (Super.1989). The question of a witness's credibility is reserved exclusively for the jury. Commonwealth v. Davis, 541 A.2d 315 (Pa. 1988).

The credibility of these two victims was, indeed, the entire issue in this case. Unlike many of the cases presented to this Court, the defendant took the witness stand and denied that he ever molested either one of these victims. He did admit that his son, then four years of age, had a habit of running around without clothes and of licking tongues with his mother but noted that he disapproved of such practices and did his best to discourage them. He admitted being in the basement that day and kissing his wife in a proper manner. He explained that he moved from the basement apartment shortly after his confrontation with Mr. Oldman because he was afraid Mr. Oldman would beat him further and he healed better in an air conditioned room. He and others told the jury that he had worked as an iron worker and was injured on the job and unable to work again. When confronted with the accusation from Sally Oldman, he went immediately to Mr. Oldman's house as he was asked by the Oldman's to do and was severely beaten. His character testimony established that he had no prior record and witnesses testified that while they had children the age of the Winner children, who played constantly with the Winner children and even stayed with them on occasion, there was never a complaint of any improper sexual conduct.

When the court considers that the Commonwealth's evidence falls in even the slightest way to corroborate the testimony of the two victims and further considers the lengths to which the Common-wealth has gone in order to manipulate these children into telling what the Commonwealth undoubtedly believes is a version of what happened, it cannot be said that the presentation of Dr. Mojong's testimony was in any way harmless error. He was presented by the Commonwealth. He was described to be an expert in the field of child abuse and he testified that the children involved in this told the truth to someone at the time they were medically examined. The admission of this testimony requires a new trial.

III. THE CO-DEFENDANT'S BIZARRE BEHAVIOR DEPRIVED THE DE-PENDANT OF A FAIR TRIAL.

Charles Winner was indicted along with his wife, Sabrina, on various sexual changes arising out of incidents on August 29, 1989. in advance of trial, there was an application for severance filed alleging that Mrs. Winner was mentally unbalanced, had a history of mental instability and her actions during trial were likely to severely prejudice her husband. This motion was based upon the fact that the defendants were husband and wife and were jointly responsible for raising one of the victims and, of course, protecting the other while she was playing within their home. The behavior they were accused of violates the accepted code of almost every society and is often regarded as the product of only a demented mind. If the jury believed that Mrs. Winner was in some way mentally deranged, it was very easy for them to come to the conclusion that Mr. Winner knew it and since he did nothing about it, cooperated in some way with his wife's bizarre behavior.

The Court rejected this based upon a psychiatric evaluation that concluded that Mrs. Winner was capable of undergoing a trial. The Court's ruling was never based upon a determination by it or anyone else that she would not act in a bizarre manner throughout the trial. On April 19th, the last day of trial testimony, during the testimony of her sister Flamingo, Mrs. Winner under went a psy-chotic episode in front of the jury. (789a, 797a). Throughout the trial, she sat in a position where she was directly facing the jury and, according to counsel, was constantly putting on and taking off extremely dark sunglasses and putting her head down on the table. The episode in the presence of the jury showed that she stood up and exclaimed out loud that her hands were turning black. She was removed to a robing room where she continued to exclaim in a loud voice, complain about her hands turning black and cry out loud. These incidents were heard by those people who remained in the courtroom as did the jury. An examination by a court psychiatrist showed that she, indeed, suffered a psychotic episode, she was incapable of cooperating in any way and she was committed to an institution for in-patient treatment. The jury was told that she was sick and removed from the trial. Mr. Winner's trial attorney properly requested a mistrial, (791a), which the Court denied. (797a).

Each of these victims related factual circumstances regarding the occurrence of charged events which were contradicted by the defendant. They both testified they were watching a tape called "Dirty Dancing" on a VCR in the basement. The owner of the property testified without equivocation that there was no VCR in the basement and that neither of the TV sets down there worked. (762a). Ann was permitted to describe a series of prior offenses involving sexual contact with her father that she claimed occurred in the second floor bedroom. Several defense witnesses, including the defendant himself, testified that as a result of an incident in 1986, he was unable to go up and down steps and used to sleep the living room of his home. (803a, 809a). With corroboration completely lacking and with no medical substantiation of any of these charges, it is respectfully submitted that the jury's view of this psychotic incident and their overhearing the rantings of Mrs. Winner shortly thereafter, deprived the defendant of a fair trial.

IV. THE PROSECUTORIAL MISCONDUCT DURING THE TRIAL AND IN ARGUMENT DEPRIVED THE DEFENDANT OF A FAIR TRIAL.

During her opening argument, the Assistant District Attorney exhorted the jury to find both defendants guilty. She said, "give Ann Winner and Sally Oldman a chance by saying guilty to these people." (51a). An immediate objection and a motion for mistrial was made because of these specific remarks and the inflammatory nature of the opening argument. The motion was denied.

Ann Winner testified that once she changed her story that she was telling to the Assistant District Attorney and that the Assistant District Attorney became angry at her. She said the Assistant District Attorney told her "not to change the story." (73a, 74a).

In her examination before the jury, the prosecutor questioned

Ann about interviews with her in the prosecutor's office. Ann testified that she told the prosecutor that her parents didn't do anything and the prosecutor got mad, gave her hot chocolate, allowed her to play and draw things and then things got better and she told the prosecutor "the truth" (150a). The truth, of course, as viewed by the prosecutor, was that her father sexually molested her.

The night before her testimony, the prosecutor spoke with her on the phone about watching a tape called "Dirty Dancing" and she recalled for the first time that she did, thus corroborating the testimony of Sally Oldman. (186a).

The prosecutor tried to enter the entire notes of testimony at the preliminary hearing in order to show the prior consistent statement of Ann Winner. The Court rejected this offer in spite of continued argument. (229a–242a). In spite of this ruling, the prosecutor proceeded directly to suggest to the witness that she had told the judge at the preliminary hearing that her father put his penis in her mouth, vagina, and butt. An objection was sustained and the jurors were instructed to disregard it.

During the testimony of Sally Oldman, the prosecutor repeatedly asked leading questions. While this was an extremely reluctant and difficult witness, the prosecutor was clearly attempting to supply testimony on the witness's behalf. The clear testimony from this witness was that she observed Mr. Winner touch his daughter's butt with his private part. The prosecutor then put the rabbit in the hat and said, "Now you said Mr. Winner put his private part in Ann's butt." Answer: "Yes." There was an objection and a motion to strike and the Court properly observed that the testimony was "touched." (311a). During this testimony of this witness, the witness was observed looking at the Assistant District Attorney before answering a question. The Court indicated that there was a concern about her communicating answers to the witness and instructed her to either look down, away or blank. (363a, 364a). Before trial, the Assistant District Attorney went to the house of Ms. Oldman and spoke with her together with the intern who was permitted to stand by the witness while she was testifying. (388a). In an obvious disagreement with the Court's earlier ruling, the prosecutor once again attempted to introduce the entire notes of the preliminary hearing testimony of this witness. The Court restated its earlier ruling. (409a, 410a).

During the cross-examination of the defendant, Charles Winner, the Court found it necessary to caution the prosecutor because of suggestions that a motel is an unhealthy environment for children and because of the argumentative nature of her questions. Objection was made to her ridiculing the defendant's religious beliefs and she claimed that that was proper because she did not initiate it. (848a, 849a). Defense counsel found it necessary to make a motion for mistrial based upon the cross-examination. The motion was denied.

In closing argument, the Assistant District Attorney misstated the nature of a stipulation by defense counsel by telling the jury that defense counsel stipulated to medical measurements. The Court found it necessary to sustain an objection and to inform the jury that the stipulation was that the reports were authentic, not that the measurement was accurate and to note that there was a difference. (873a). Almost immediately thereafter, the Court sustained an objection because she mischaracterized the testimony of Dr. Mojong not once but twice. (874a, 875a).

In her continuing attempt to corroborate her witness, she misstated the evidence by claiming before the jury that Sally Oldman told Wendy Pathnek everything that she testified to in the courtroom. The Court sustained an objection. At one point she supplied the jury with the question and answer that even the Court could not recall. (884a). She mischaracterized testimony about the defendant and his daughter, (888a), and admittedly mischaracterized what the defendant said in his "forgiveness note." (889a).

Throughout the trial the prosecutor never ceased her efforts to impress upon the jury that she believed that the two girls were telling the truth. It was clear from the testimony of Ann Winner that she tried to change her story and the prosecutor, herself, got mad at Ann. This testimony was elicited by the prosecution's questioning of Ann. Through the use of support personnel and the examination of witnesses, it became apparent to the jury that more individuals in the prosecutor's office than just this prosecutor herself believed that these two girls were telling the truth. This was even true as to the investigating officer who Ann said got mad when she tried to change her story. This was nothing more than improper vouching for the credibility of two witnesses and clearly established prosecutorial misconduct. United States v. DiLoreto, 888 F.2d 996 (3rd. Cir.1989). The reason for the ban on such activity is that the jury could clearly infer that there is information known to the prosecutor but unknown to the jury which supports the veracity of a witness. United States v. Wallace, 848 F.2d 1464 (9th Cir.1988).

The mere fact that a prosecutor, in closing argument, comments on facts which are not in evidence required a reversal. Commonwealth v. Brooks, 523 A.2d 1189 (Super.1987). It has even held by our Supreme Court that repeated instances of misconduct permeated the entire proceedings and denied the defendant a fair trial. Commonwealth v. Bricker, 487 A.2d 348 (Pa.1985); Commonwealth v. Hickman, 466 A.2d 148 (Super.1983).

It has for some time in this Commonwealth been the law that the prosecution may not bolster the credibility of their witness. In this case, the Commonwealth did nothing but. The direct and repeated intervention of the prosecuting attorney with both of the young girls, who were her main and exclusive witnesses regarding sexual molestation, while it might be regarded in other instances as proper trial preparation, became nothing more than blatant bolstering when its existence was made know to the jury. The fact that both the prosecuting attorney and the investigating officer got mad at a seven year old juvenile witness when she tried to "change her story" and convinced her to "tell the truth," carries the clear implication that both the prosecutor and the police officer knew what the truth was. Whether such a policy is necessary and exists in child abuse cases is not the point. The point is that, in this instance, it was made known to the jury. The truth is that, in this case, neither the prosecutor nor the investigating police officer had any credible corroborative testimony to lead them to believe what the truth was. Ann Winner's earlier protestations that her parents had done nothing were dismissed summarily, even in the absence of any physical evidence or any of the photographs that were supposed to exist or any medical findings. The highlight of this bolstering was the testimony of Dr. Mojong which amounted to nothing more than a professed expert in child abuse saying that these children told the truth when they told someone that they were molested because the medical findings were consistent with that story. Such expert bolstering is clearly improper. United States v. Candoli, 870 F.2d 496 (9th Cir.1989).

The resolution of the credibility of juvenile witnesses is one of the most compelling and one of the most pressing problems faced by our present system of justice. For years it has been argued with some degree of truth that young people are subject to manipulation by their parents. It is established beyond dispute that, although young in age, they possess fertile imaginations, and with the availability of television fiction and documentaries dealing with child abuse and sexual blackmail, they certainly possess the necessary elements to fabricate serious charges for their own reasons. But, if these children may, indeed, be manipulated by parents or persons with evil motives, they are just as susceptible to manipulation by representatives of the prosecution. A well-meaning person who believes, for any one of a number of reasons, that the charges of abuse be true is just as much a manipulator as the evil doer. This case clearly indicates that exact situation. It is respectfully submitted that constitutional protection against conviction by manipulative witnesses lies in our appellate courts and this Court is urged, in this case, to find that, indeed, such manipulation did take place and to order a new trial as free of manipulative influences as possible. This Court has recently held that an attempt to bolster the credibility of a child sexual assault victim by the use of prior consistent statements was an error of law. Commonwealth v. Jubilee, 589 A.2d 1112 (Super.1991.).

CONCLUSION

WHEREFORE, it is respectfully requested that this Court grant the defendant a new trial based upon the errors committed at trial.

Respectfully submitted,

Peter Pete Peterson.

Finally after waiting eight months Winner received a thick envelope from Mr. Peterson.

The Superior Court had affirmed the lower courts blunder. The appeal was denied. Winner experienced depression, sadness, despair, anger and pain.

On "E" block there was a jail house lawyer called Paul who asked to see the decision and the appeal. A few days later Paul said, "Charlie, you were sold down the river. Your lawyer, Peterson, made a huge mistake. Your motion for mis-trial due to your wife's mental instability at time of trial was waived by the court because he didn't back his argument with law. It's a gross mistake and you have to fire him and hire a new lawyer. I know an attorney named Dwight Goodman. He'll rumble for you. He is a hard hitter. Here is his address. Write to him. Get you mother and father to get in touch with Goodman. He is expensive but worth the money.

"I don't understand why Peterson didn't quote precedent law for the court to study, but he didn't and the court dismissed your entire motion concerning Sabrina's incompetence due to her poor mental health." Here, read the decision again." Paul placed the verdict in Winner's hand and walked away.

The battle continued and there was little time for weakness or doubt in the truth.

Amen, amen I say to you, unless the grain of wheat falling into the ground die, itself remaineth alone. But if it die, it bringeth forth much fruit. He that loveth his life shall lose it; and he that hateth his life in this world, keepeth it unto life eternal. John 12 v 24–25.

I trust in the Blood of Jesus.

Winner read the decision from the court and made notes.

17

The Error Continues

KGB09047/93
COMMONWEALTH OF PENNSYLVANIA: IN THE SUPERIOR COURT OF

                     : PENNSYLVANIA

           v.   :

CHARLES WINNER   : NO. 2055 Philadelphia 1992

     Appellant   :

Appeal from the Judgement of Sentence, June 16, 1992, in the Court of Common Pleas of Philadelphia County, Criminal Division, No. 7910-0126-0127, 7912-3381-1472

BEFORE: Sandmeyer, Mouse, and Prendergast.

JUDGMENT

On Consideration Whereof, it is now here ordered and adjudged by this Court that the judgment of the Court of Common Pleas of Philadelphia County be, and the same is hereby AFFIRMED. JURISDICTION RELINQUISHED.

                     By the Court:

                     Prothonotary

Dated: May 24, 1993

Superior Court denied the appeal and wrote their opinion.

KGB09047/93
COMMONWEALTH OF PENNSYLVANIA: IN THE SUPERIOR COURT OF

                     : PENNSYLVANIA

           v.   :

CHARLES WINNER   : No. 2055 Philadelphia 1992

     Appellant   :

Appeal from the Judgment of Sentence, June 16, 1992, in the Court of Common Pleas of Philadelphia County, Criminal Division, No. 7910-0126-0127, 7912-3381-1472

BEFORE: Sandmeyer, Mouse, and Prendergast, JJ.

MEMORANDUM:

Court: Charles Winner ("appellant") appeals from the judgment of sentence following his jury convictions for two counts each of rape, corrupting the morals of a minor, and indecent sexual assault, and one count each of involuntary deviate sexual intercourse and criminal conspiracy. Following a jury trial, appellant was convicted of the aforementioned crimes and the Honorable Henry Herian imposed a total sentence of incarceration for twenty-three to twenty-eight years. We affirm.

Well la-de-da, thought Winner, three more system hangmen unable to separate truth from fantasy. Your honor, writers of this verdict take notice of the defendant's rejection of your decision. You did not take one second to suppose the defendant's appeal was truthful. This never entered your mind. Had it entered, the truth would have forced you to reverse injustice.

You refuse to go back to the beginning where the fantasy was born. The entire story is false. The sentence is not real; it's dream stuff that pretenders are calling reality. The truth is I am in prison because of your blindness. Ann is a virgin right now. Get her to a neutral doctor. Let's see some evidence. Words are not evidence and what you are presenting is mere words, just like the rest of the mob!

Bad news for the innocent man and woman. Superior Court agreed to believe the fantasy story told by the false misguided conceptions of well-meaning people. Slander folks, watch what you say about another.

Court: These convictions stem from the events that transpired on August 29, 1989. On this date, appellant engaged in vaginal and anal sexual intercourse with his wife (did not) in the presence of his four-year-old son, Tony, his then seven-year-old daughter Ann, and her seven-year-old playmate, Sally Oldman. His wife then took photographs and shouted encouragements to her husband as he raped their daughter vaginally, anally, and orally, ejaculating into her mouth. Ann Winner testified that she and her father had engaged in vaginal, oral, and anal intercourse on many previous occasions, starting when she was approximately four or five years old. If Ann

155

refused to submit to intercourse, her father would hit her with his belt.

We are seeing words not reality. We are looking at pictures based on the belief system of the judges who refuse to investigate. One more time: the wife who the judges say was taking pictures of these acts was found to be innocent of taking pictures in the basement. Doesn't that destroy your decision? The Superior Court is presenting a version that they cherish. They want to believe these children were raped and that's the reason they affirmed the sentence of the lower court. What are all those lies doing in the transcript of Mr. Winner. The jury heard all those false facts. In Pennsylvania a husband can be found guilty of having his picture taken by his wife who was found innocent of taking pictures. Who took the pictures if Mrs. Winner was declared innocent by Judge Herian. Who?

The Superior Court refers to the notes of testimony. Clearly from the above stated conclusions uttered by the Superior Court they did not know Mrs. Winner was innocent in Sally's case. Or did they know? If they knew Mr. Winner did not have pictures taken by his wife, could they in fairness refer back to the notes of testimony?

The wife was found innocent of all charges filed against her in connection with Sally Oldman. Each word that accuses her in the transcripts from Winner's trial is not true. How can you Judge ignore these truths. Nobody is pretending, or making clever remarks in order to stroke the ego.

Court: On August 29, 1989, after he had intercourse with his wife and raped his young daughter, appellant then turned to his daughter's friend who had been in the room the entire time. Appellant instructed seven-year-old Sally Oldman to take her clothes off or he would hit her with his belt. He then vaginally raped Sally Oldman and ejaculated inside of her. Appellant warned the girl that if she told anyone that he would hurt her and her little sister.

Court: Appellant raises several issues for our review: (a) whether the juvenile witnesses were competent and credible; (2) whether the court improperly allowed expert testimony; (3) whether the co-defendant's bizarre behavior deprived appellant of a fair trial; (4) whether the alleged prosecutorial misconduct during trial and in argument deprived appellant of a fair trial. We will address these issues *seriatim.*

Appellant contends that the juvenile witnesses, Ann Winner

156

and Sally Oldman, were neither competent nor credible witnesses. We cannot agree. The standards for determining the competency of a child to testify are quite clear:

[t]here must be (1) such capacity to communicate, including as it does both an ability to understand questions and to frame and express intelligent answers, (2) mental capacity to observe the occurrence itself and the capacity of remembering what it is that [she] is called to testify about and (3) a consciousness of the duty to speak the truth.

Commonwealth v. Penn, 497 Pa. 232, —, 439, A.2d 1154, 1158, *cert. denied sub non, Penn v. Pennsylvania,* 456 U.S. 980 (1982), *quoting Rosche v. McCoy,* 397 Pa. 615, 620–621, 156 A.2d 307, 310 (1959).

Furthermore, in determining whether the trial court properly exercised its discretion, this court must examine not only the victim's testimony during the respective competency examinations, but their entire testimony at trial. *Commonwealth v. Trimble,* Pa. Super. —, 6155 A.2d 48 (1992).

Winner: The children were competent only to the incompetent observer. Questions were asked which were not answered. This witness made charges, yet she couldn't verbally respond to questions concerning the alleged incident. Is that competent? Yes, but only to the incompetent. Sally knew she was lying, that's why she had no testimony. Calm down Winner, remember you have to win friends and influence people. Forgive me, judge, for being honest.

Court: In the instant case, the trial court properly exercised its discretion and determined that both Ann Winner and Sally Oldman were competent and credible witnesses. The court held a competency hearing for each girl. During her hearing, Ann Winner was articulate and gave responsive answers to the questions. Furthermore, she specifically stated that she understood the difference between truth and falsehood. At trial, she recounted in graphic detail the events as they unfolded on August 29th, and she remembered specific facts including the fact that the children were permitted to watch "Dirty Dancing" on T.V. before the rapes occurred. The trial court declared her competent to testify based upon her demeanor, thoughtfulness, sincerity, and her obvious understanding of the difference between truth and falsehood. A determination of competency will not be disturbed on appeal absent a clear abuse of discretion. *Penn, supra.* Because the record reveals no such abuse, appellant's claim that Ann Winner is incompetent cannot prevail.

Winner: Judge you are blinded by your opinions. "Dirty Danc-ing" is irrelevant to the subject of rape. The court inserted its preju-dices. Ann understood fear, she knew the prosecutor expected her to condemn her father and mother. She was forced against her will to be on the witness stand. The abuse of discretion was the court totally ignored the evidence. To dwell in truth one must go back to the beginning. What did the child say when first interviewed by authorities? How did her story change. Why did Officer Little tell the child she was a liar? Why did she tell the DA nothing happened? Why did she say that Sally Oldman was lying? Why is the only evidence her words? The answers to these questions are the truth the court ignored. You can not look at what is not real and expect to find what is real. Early on the judgment of the Superior Court was favorable to the Commonwealth.

Court: In addition, the trial court also properly concluded that Sally Oldman was a competent and credible witness. Although Sally was a bit more nervous and timid than her friend, her testimony as a whole supported her competency. She gave responsive answers to most questions; (lie) and while these answers were often communi-cated by nodding her head yes or no, the affirmative or negative response was noted in the record. We acknowledge that at trial the little girl experienced some embarrassment in discussing the traumatic event (lie). She took a few breaks in order to get a glass of water and shrugged in response to several questions. However, Sally ultimately testified that appellant inserted his penis in her "hei-nie" and "peed" (ejaculated).

Furthermore, Sally demonstrated an understanding of the dif-ference between truth and falsehood. She stated that "[t]he truth is when you say that something happened that really happened and a lie is when you say that something really didn't happen." When appellant objected that this statement did not demonstrate her ap-preciation of the difference between the truth and a lie, the Common-wealth asked Sally a few more questions.

Winner: Sally was not an honest witness. Mr. Humble could not cross-examine her because her story was false and Sally knew it was false. The traumatic event Sally was experiencing was the trial, not the dream that she couldn't remember because her words demon-strated that the DA was the story teller and the child sat there not being a witness but a head nodder. If the DA had asked Sally what happened, the child wouldn't have spoken. The fantasy was pulled out of her by the spokesperson for the lie—the prosecutor!

Court: [Ms. Patricia Vim:]

If I told you that it was pouring rain outside would
that be the truth or a lie?

[Sally Oldman:]

A lie.

[Ms. Vim:]

What is it like outside today?

[Sally Oldman:]

Nice. Nice.

[Ms. Vim:]

Is the sun out?

[Sally Oldman:]

Yes.

This additional testimony sufficiently established Sally Oldman's knowledge of the difference between truth and falsehood, and the trial court correctly determined that Sally Oldman was competent to testify. Her ability to distinguish between the truth and a lie reflected an understanding of the difference between the two. With regard to her memory, she demonstrated an ability to recall certain events but stated at times that she could not recall others. However, we agree with the trial court that her ability to communicate and differentiate between the two indicated that she was competent to testify. A thorough review of the victim's testimony establishes that the lower court properly exercised its discretion in finding Sally Oldman competent to testify.

Appellant further alleges with regard to this issue that the victim's were "rehearsed" by various individuals prior to trial and thereby subjected to undue influence. This claim lacks merit. Both victims state that the police and the social workers asked only open-ended, non-leading questions and never encouraged the children to testify in a particular fashion. Ann Winner admitted that she tried to change her story the first time that she met with Ms. Vim, the Assistant District Attorney. She "lied" and Ms. Vim stopped and told her not to change the story. Although *this may have been an inappropriate instruction of the part of the Assistant District Attorney, it did not impermissible taint the child's testimony.* Ann Winner

159

explained that she did not want to implicate appellant at first, because, notwithstanding his sexual assaults, she loved her parents and did not want to get them into trouble.

Winner: If you believe that the social workers did not ask leading questions you're really naive. That's all they did, that's all they could do. Why didn't they believe Ann when she was being led from social worker to doctor, to police officers, to the sex experts? Who suggested to Ann that she would get her parents in trouble? The Superior Court admitted that the DA tampered with the testimony of the witness, but said it was OK with them. That didn't violate fairness since the verdict was guilty exactly what the Superior Court was attempting to justify. A truthful story does not change. A false story must change. A story untrue cannot be mixed with truth and be called reality.

Court: Moreover, appellant's argument that the children's participation in ''court school'' somehow influenced their testimony is tenuous at best. Court school is a program run by non-law enforcement personnel. It is designed to teach young children about the function and procedure of a trial, without any discussion of a particular criminal case. There is absolutely nothing in the record to support the allegation that the children somehow changed their testimony because they participated in ''court school.'' Indeed, if anything, the experience probably helped them to feel more comfortable during a stressful and unfamiliar proceeding.

Appellant next contends that the trial court erred in admitting the testimony of an expert witness, Dr. Art Mojong, regarding the empirical findings of the physical examinations of the victims. This is despite the fact that Dr. Mojong did not testify regarding the victims' credibility. This court recently dealt with a similar issue involving the same expert in *Commonwealth v. Hernandez*, _____ Pa. Super. _____, *615 A.2d 1337 (1992).*

At trial in the Hernandez case, Dr. Mojong compared the medical records resulting from the examination of the victim at Washington University's Hospital for Children with a hypothetical question which contained the victim's history of the assault and subsequent events up to the time of the examination. Dr. Mojong testified that he found the physical facts, as stated in the medical record, consistent with the child's allegation. Dr. Mojong went on to describe several other possible methods not involving sexual contact which would also be consistent with the medical findings. *Id.* at ——, A.2d at 1343.

This court observed:

> It follows that a pediatrician such as Mojong, qualified as a medical expert, may testify that the physical facts observed and reported by the treating physicians were consistent with the allegation of anal sodomy set forth in the history of the child. The medical history of a patient is customarily relied upon in practicing medicine. Consequently, it is not error for the expert to testify on cross-examination that his opinion assumes the truthfulness of the history supplied by the victim. We conclude that the testimony of Mojong is admissible, and there is no merit to the underlying issue in this ineffective assistance of counsel claim.

Id.

The *Hernandez* court also distinguished *Commonwealth v. Garcia*, 403 Pa. Super, 280, 588 A.2d 951 (1991), *appeal denied*, 529 Pa. 656, 604 A.2d 248 (1992), a case relied upon by the appellant in the instant case as well. According to the court, *Garcia* prohibits expert testimony regarding the behavior patterns of the victims of child assault when it is solely offered to explain the conduct of the victim. *Id.* at 16, *citing Garcia*, 403 Pa. Super. at 288, 588 A.2d at 954. Reliance upon *Garcia* was misplaced where a medical expert testified that the physical findings of the medical exam were consistent with the victim's allegations and anal intercourse. Further, the *Hernandez* court was unable to conclude that Dr. Mojong's testimony improperly bolstered the victim's credibility or withdraw the issue of witness credibility from the jury. *Id.*

Hernandez controls the instant case, and *Garcia* is factually in opposite. In this case Dr. Mojong reviewed the medical records that were admitted into evidence by stipulation. He testified that those records revealed that each victim had an enlarged introits (vaginal opening of one centimeter, over two times the normal size for a seven-year-old girl. Ann Winner also had mild vaginal erythema (redness), and multiple erythemous papules (pimples) on her buttocks. Sally Oldman also had a broken hymen and a slight yellow-green discharge.

As in *Hernandez,* Dr. Mojong compared the medical records resulting from the examination of the victims with hypothetical

161

questions which contained the victim's histories of the rapes. Dr. Mojong testified that he found the physical facts, as stated in the medical records, consistent with the children's allegations that appellant had raped them. Furthermore, the expert's testimony was not offered solely for the purpose of "bolstering" the testimony of Ann Winner and Sally Oldman and as a result reliance upon *Garcia* is misplaced. Accordingly, appellant is not entitled to relief based upon the expert's testimony.

Winner: This sex expert had nothing at all to do with the children. He couldn't answer questions that were important to the defense. He couldn't know what the doctors who performed the exams thought. Defense wanted to ask the doctors questions but the right to confront accusers was denied. Ann is a virgin with a hymen. Sally Oldman has a hymen. The evidence is false if they say Mr. Winner broke their hymens.

Court: Appellant next argues that the trial court erred in denying motion for a mistrial after the codefendant exhibited "bizarre" behavior before the jury. During the course of her sister's testimony, Mrs. Winner stated that she thought she was going to black out. The court immediately recessed the trial, and the co-defendant was removed from the courtroom. Before the trial resumed, a court-appointed expert examined Mrs. Winner and concluded that she had suffered a psychotic episode and that she was no longer competent to stand trial. The Court declared a mistrial with respect to the charges against her and instructed the jury that she could no longer participate in the trial because she had become "physically ill." The court further advised the jurors that they could not in any way consider the co-defendant's behavior or condition in resolving the charges against appellant. Appellant now contends that if the jury believed that Mrs. Winner was mentally deranged that they could easily conclude that he knew it and since he did nothing about it, cooperated in some way with his wife's bizarre behavior.

Winner: Before trial, a motion was presented to the court asking for a separation of defendant's case from co-defendant's case due to her mental health which was poor. A doctor/expert said she was able to stand trial. This expert was proven to be wrong. It was medical malpractice, incompetence by a doctor. He couldn't see what Mr. Winner knew. His wife was mentally sick, and in need of medicine. The court erred because Mrs. Winner couldn't function

162

properly. The jury heard her loud moanings and wailing but the notes of testimony don't show the hysteria.

Court: As the Commonwealth correctly points out, appellant cites absolutely no case law in support of this proposition. As a result, appellant's failure to provide any legal support for the claim gives us reason enough to summarily reject it. *Commonwealth v. Jones,* 418. Pa. Super. 93, 613 A.2d 587 (1992) (claim without legal support in appellate brief is waived). Furthermore, even addressing the issue on the merits, the argument is tenuous at best. Before the trial, appellant moved to sever based upon the fact that Mrs. Winner had a history of mental instability. The Honorable Henry Herian followed proper procedure and, on two separate occasions, two different psychiatrists examined Mrs. Winner and both concluded that she was competent to stand trial. Unfortunately, during the course of the trial Mrs. Winner's mental condition deteriorated, and she suffered the psychotic episode. However, the judge gave appropriate cautionary instructions to the jury and the jury was well aware that Mrs. Winner had become ill and could no longer participate in the trial.

The motion for a mistrial was properly denied and appellant did not suffer prejudice by association because of the statements made by his wife. The average juror could see that he was not responsible nor did he encourage his wife's outbursts. (court denied mistrial where appellant attached one of the prosecution witnesses in the presence of the jury); *Commonwealth v. Savage,* 529 Pa. 108, 602 A.2d 309 (1992) (mistrial denied and curative instruction sufficient despite outburst by victim's mother where she shouted that victim was the second child that appellant had murdered). The trial court in the instant case properly denied appellant's motion for a mistrial based upon the conduct of the co-defendant at trial.

Appellant's final argument that the trial court erred in denying his mistrial motion because of prosecutorial misconduct during the opening statement, the examination of witnesses, and the summation. However, as the trial court correctly observed, in his Memorandum of Law in Support of Post-Verdict Motions, appellant discussed only allegations of misconduct occurring during the prosecutor's opening statement to the jury. As a result, the other arguments have been waived. Pa. R.A.P. 302 (a).

J. A09047/93

The Assistant District Attorney made three questionable statements during her opening argument. First, she referred to appellant's intercourse with his wife, daughter and his daughter's playmate as a "triathalon" [sic]. The prosecutor stated that appellant instructed both girls not to tell anyone or they would be hit. She then added, "[w]ell, unfortunately, the secret wasn't safe this time, Because —— . . . " The prosecutor concluded her statement and encouraged the jury to "[g]ive Ann Winner and Sally Oldman a chance by saying guilty to these people." (Notes of testimony, 04/10/91 at 80–89). Counsel for appellant objected to these statements and Judge Herian sustained the objections. Appellant then moved for a mistrial and argued that the opening statement was so inflammatory and argumentative that appellant was deprived of the right to a fair trial. (Notes of testimony, 04/10/91 at 89). The trial court denied the motion for a mistrial and gave an immediate curative instruction, advising the jury to disregard any comments made by the prosecutor that might have been argumentative. Furthermore, he reminded the jury that its role was to determine whether the Commonwealth proved appellant guilty beyond a reasonable doubt and not to give the children a "chance." (Notes of testimony, 4–10–91 at 91–92).

We agree with the trial court and conclude that a mistrial was not warranted because of the prosecutor's comments were not so inflammatory as to prejudice the jury and render it incapable of objectively weighing evidence and delivering a true verdict. *SEE COMMONWEALTH V D'AMATO.* 514 PA 471, 526 A.2d 300 1987 (prosecutor's improper comments regarding inadmissible evidence did not warrant reversal of convictions where defense objected and court gave immediate instruction) As a result, the trial court properly exercised its discretion in denying appellant's mistrial motion.

Accordingly, judgement of sentence is affirmed. Jurisdiction relinquished.

Mr. Peterson was dismissed, the case was going to the Supreme Court of Pennsylvania.

18

The State Supreme Court

Dear Mr. Goodman, please help! A great injustice is well under way in the courtroom. I need a lawyer to take an appeal to the Supreme Court. Poppe and Nanny Winner will be in touch with you to explain the case. Please take this case. A miscarriage of justice has put two people in prison due to the opinions of misguided thinkers within the commonwealth.

The reader will have to understand that the Gospel of Jesus is the way we Christians respond to the world so it will be plentiful.

How are they to call on one in whom they do not believe? How are they to believe in one of whom they have never heard? How do they hear without a preacher? How can they preach unless they are sent? Romans 10–14.

Three years in prison had quickly passed. Life is short. I learned that in a cell. The world had hit with blows that increased the faith. God sends trials as blessings while the world attempts to hurt, destroy and cause grief. Sabrina and Winner had patched up their tumultuous relationship. Never again would Winner look at his wife in a negative way. Sabrina wrote a letter and said, "Dear Buddy Boy, how are things? Fine, I hope. Miss ya! When is the next date for court with Peterson? Do you know? Well, I guess he is getting all ready to get you out of there. It's real hot here in Muncy Prison for women. I hate this place.

I don't hear much from you. How is Nanny and Poppe? I can't wait til they come up to see me. I love them so much and miss them. In here, there's not much to write about my hands are all callused and I sweat continually. I need to have them healed from the Lord.

I had two hot dogs for supper. It's back to work tomorrow. I'm glad cause it's nice to motivate myself around here to stop from getting upset over things. I wear brown clothes, uniforms, and work six and a half hours per day.

There are five flys in my room flying all around and they are nerve racking cause I can't catch them.

Outside, in the mountains, a lot of grass, bee's, trees and dirt, mud, acres of paths, cows and orchards, about 500 cows, fenced wire keeps the moo cows off the paths, and large corn grows all over in the fields. There are deer out there, I can't believe . . . they run over the path, babies, cute.

Send me some money. I want to buy new clothes.

You keep in touch, take care, be good, stay out of trouble. Love Sabrina.

The real child abusers receive their pay from the citizens of the state.

In his letter Mr. Peterson said it would take one year to hear from the Supreme Court. This court could refuse to hear the case and let the Superior Court's ruling stand, or it could hear the case. The appeal filed by Mr. Goodman asked the court for a hearing. In case the Supreme Court continued the mistake, the case will then go out of the state into the Federal courts seeking justice for a violation of rights.

Winner had been healed of fear. He continued to study, pray his rosary, go to confession weekly, attend mass, receive Holy Communion, read the saints, and prepare for death. Death is not to be feared with a good conscience.

Nanny and Poppe went through their own hell. One day Nanny also wrote a letter.

Dear Buddy, it's not all roses here, between visiting family court, paying lawyers, and going to court hearings, fighting to get the children home; something I didn't plan on; not to mention traveling 400 miles every month to visit you and Sabrina in Prison and our children in Foster care, we're tired, not young anymore.

Its 100 in the shade and that hell hole you're in won't let you have a fan. Do they think you don't need a fan or just don't care. I guess thats too much to ask for, besides, all they do is blow hot air around.

Someday, maybe, when and if Ann starts to think for herself

the commonwealth will get a surprise. All the brainwashing is one sided. The children know nothing of our position.

I was shopping for your children and bought both of them two outfits and some toys for Tony, a flashlight, caps along with a top you throw on the ground that spins. I got Ann a necklace, a hair blower, shorts, pants, tops and underclothing.

I hear from Anthony weekly. He is a cub scout, a member of the wolves. He doesn't speak much on the phone. His Foster mom tells him not to stay on the phone too long. The case workers tells me that Tony doesn't like to come to Phila for visits. I don't blame him since Family Court makes little preparations for the children on visiting day. You visit in a crowded lobby.

Put the Judges who will decide your case under intensive prayer. "Soaking Prayer," ask the faithful in jail to pray for a just decision, don't neglect to pray for the court one day. Keep on praying for victory in the appeal. Pray for vindication, be not shy. Jesus said, "What would you have me do?" Be specific! Recall the women asking for scraps from the table. Recall the women who had the dead son, and the women who only needed to touch his garment. All Gospel. You can be sure that the Lord is among his people where he promised to be.

You should be doing something positive like attending school for improvement of your knowledge. Remember what you are charged with! Will you? The day you where released on bail the police passed the charges around to each other just in case one didn't know. It may be the same where you are.

Social worker's inform me that Tony has "Attention disorder" A.D. is the current Buzz word when the experts can't explain what causes high spirits with youthful exhilaration. For instance. Why can't Tony sit quietly for two hours in a visiting room eight feet by ten feet. The social workers forget kids are not born quiet and docile.

Mr. Goodman should be your only defender, not you,nor me, and not a jail house lawyer. Sabrina is thinking parole, not proving innocence. Sabrina signed the papers giving the state permission to have Tony in one to one therapy since you refused to sign they went to your wife for her OK.

Tony has been hounded for four years and if he isn't hyper, he'd be nuts. Four years of age and this mess. He should be loved and cared for by his own family. Its a wonder Tony is as good as he is considering the number of females he has called Sabrina. He

167

gets a new Sabrina about every year, within two weeks he is calling foster Sabrina. "My Sabrina." Ann has had five. Tony has all A's and B's except for social studies while Ann is on the Honor Role.

I am trying to make the best of a bad situation. Tony, being ninety five miles from home makes us travel that much more. Tony doesn't see Ann like he should. The state should bring them together or better still send them home. The state makes indifferent parents. Your children are numbers just like you and Sabrina. Its called Social engineering. Kids are the big losers.

Being devoted to the Blessed Virgin Mary is a sure relationship with the real Jesus: not the Jesus created by Men. Our Lord is serious about saving the world from sin! Did you ever stop to think that each time you went to court, it was on the Blessed Mother's Feast day? Well, it was and did you know your appeal went before the Court on February 11th, this is the date Mary appeared at Lourdes. She is a Miracle worker through her son.

A friend from our Prayer Group called me to say that she is claiming a miracle for you Bud. Ginny was listening to a preacher on TV who said, "I have a strong anointing from the Lord. There is a man in Prison and he is coming out. You will be released." Ginny said to me, "You claim this for Buddy and don't doubt for a second."

The Blessed Mother is appearing all over the world. My friends are praying for us everyday and they are prayer warriors. Be of good cheer. Keep your chin up and know God is with you every step of the way, especially when its hard, but always and forever. . . . He doesn't abandon us, thats his promise, remember, Faith moves mountains, thats the word of the Lord, and aren't we lucky the Holy Spirit gives to us faith and the Lord dwells in us? How can we lose? Love Nanny

Mr. Goodman filed the appeal to the High court. This is what the appeal said:
June, 1993
Mr. Charles Winner
Drawer "K"
BW 0618, Dallas, PA.
18612

Dear Mr. Winner

168

Enclosed is a copy of a petition for Allowance of Appeal which I filed in the Supreme Court June, 1993. Now we must wait for the Supreme Court to decide whether or not to take your case. I will communicate with you shortly regarding your case.

Very truly yours,
Dwight Goodman

DG . . . sde
Enclosure
copy to: Mr and Mrs Charles Winner Sr.

IN THE SUPREME COURT OF PENNSYLVANIA

No. 336 E.D. Allocatur Docket 1993

Commonwealth of Pennsylvania
v.
Charles Winner, Jr.

Petitioner.

Petitioner for Allowance of Appeal

Petition for Allowance of Appeal from the Order of the Superior Court of Pennsylvania Dated May 25, 1993 (No. 2055 Philadelphia 1992), Affirming the Judgment of Sentence of the Court of Common Pleas of Philadelphia County, Information October Term, 1989 Nos. 131–126, December Term, 1982, Nos. 2482–2692 June 16, 1992.

Dwight Goodman, Esquire
Suite 1641, Moo Goo Ho Building
36 South 14th Street
Philadelphia, PA 19104
(215) 416-4253
Attorney for Petitioner,
CHARLES WINNER, JR.

ORDER FROM WHICH APPEAL IS SOUGHT

This is a Petition for Allowance of Appeal from the Order of the Superior Court of Pennsylvania entered on May 25, 1993, reading as follows:

JUDGMENT

ON CONSIDERATION WHEREOF, it is not here ordered and adjudged by this court that the Judgment of the Court of Common

Pleas of PHILADELPHIA COUNTY, be, and is hereby AF-
FIRMED. JURISDICTION RELINQUISHED.
——STATEMENT OF QUESTIONS PRESENTED

A. DID NOT THE TRIAL COURT ABUSE ITS DISCRETION IN RULING
THAT THE CHILD WITNESSES ANN AND OLDMAN WERE COMPE-
TENT TO TESTIFY.

B. DID NOT THE TRIAL COURT ERR IN ALLOWING AN EXPERT WIT-
NESS TO TESTIFY WHERE THAT TESTIMONY WAS NOTHING MORE
THAN A VEILED ATTEMPT TO ESTABLISH THE CREDIBILITY OF
THE COMPLAINTS.

STATEMENT OF THE CASE

Procedural History

On September 9, 1989, petitional Charles Winner, Jr. (hereinafter "Winner") and his wife Sabrina Winner (hereinafter "Sabrina") were arrested (Winner–M.C. 89–09–0807) (Sabrina–M.C.
89–09–0808) and charged with Rape, Indecent Exposure, Terroristic
Threats, Criminal Conspiracy, Unlawful Restrain, Indecent Assault,
Simple Assault, Criminal Solicitation, Corruption of Minor, False
Imprisonment, and Endangering the Welfare of a Child in connection with allegations of crimes committed on August 29, 1989, upon
seven (7) year old victim Sally Oldman (hereinafter "Sally Oldman"). On September, 20, 1989, the Honorable Tootsie Larkson
conducted a preliminary hearing and held all charges for court. On
October 11, 1989, Winner was arraigned on bills of information
October Term, 1989, Nos. 0121–0128.

On October 10, 1989, Winner was arrested (M.C.–89-10-1053)
and charged with Rape, Indecent Exposure, Statutory Rape, Endangering Welfare of Children, Sexual Abuse of Children–Photo, Criminal Conspiracy, Indecent Assault, Simple Assault, Incest,
Involuntary Deviate Sexual Intercourse, Indecent Exposure, and
Corrupting Morals of a Minor in connection with allegations of
crimes committed on August 29, 1989, upon his seven (7) year
old daughter Ann Winner (hereinafter "Ann") from approximately
January 1989 until August 29, 1989. On December 8, 1989, the
Honorable Tootsie Larkson conducted a preliminary hearing and
held all charges for court. On December 29, 1989, Winner was
arraigned on bills of information December Term 1989 Nos.
2382–2892.

On March 2, 1990, Winner's case was consolidated for trial both together and with the cases against Sabrina (C.P. October 1989 Nos. 129–136 and December Term 1989 Nos. 2393–2403). Trial commenced on April 10, 1991, Sabrina underwent a psychotic episode in the courtroom in front of the jury, and was subsequently declared incompetent to proceed with trial. Winner's request for a mistrial of his case was denied. On April 22, 1991, the jury adjudicated Winner guilty of Corruption of Minor (No. 2382, victim—Ann); Involuntary Deviate Sexual Intercourse (No. 2383, victim—Ann); Rape (No. 2391, victim—Ann); Criminal Conspiracy (No. 2387, victim—Ann); Indecent Assault (No. 2388, victim Ann); Corruption of Minor (No. 0212, victim—Sally Oldman); Rape (No. 0128, victim—Sally Oldman); and Indecent Assault (No. 0124, victim—Sally).

On April 24, 1991, Winner filed a Motion for a New Trial and/or Arrest of Judgment (attached hereto as Exhibit "C"). On December 5, 1991, Winner filed a Supplemental Reasons in Support of Motion for New Trial and/or in Arrest of Judgment (attached hereto as Exhibit "D"). On June 16, 1992, Judge Herian denied post verdict motions and imposed sentence:

C.P. 89-10-0121—(Corruption of Minor—Oldman)—not less than one (1) not more than five (5) years imprisonment;

C.P. 89-10-0128—(Rape — Oldman) — not less than six (6) nor more than twenty (20) years imprisonment consecutive to #0121;

C.P. 89-12-2391—(Rape—Ann)—not less than six (6) nor more than twenty (20) years imprisonment, consecutive to #0121 and 0128;   C.P. 89-10-0121—(Corruption of Minor—Oldman)—not less than one (1) not more than five (5) years imprisonment;

C.P. 89-10-0128—(Rape—Oldman)—not less than six (6) nor more than twenty (20) years imprisonment consecutive to #0121;

C.P. 89-12-2391–(Rape—Ann)—not less than six (6) nor more than twenty (20) years imprisonment, consecutive to #0121 and 0128;

C.P. 89-12-2383—(Involuntary Deviate Sexual Intercourse—Ann)—not less than six (6) nor more than twenty (20) years imprisonment, concurrent with #2391;

C.P. 89-12-2382—(Corruption of Minor—Ann)—not less than

173

one (1) nor more than five (5) years imprisonment, consecutive to all others sentences;

C.P. 89-12-2387—(Criminal Conspiracy—Ann)—not less than two (2) nor more than ten (10) years imprisonment, consecutive to other sentences.

Thus, the total sentence imposed was not less than sixteen (16) years nor more than sixty (60) years.

Winner was represented by Gerald Humble, Esquire (hereinafter "trial counsel") at all of the above proceedings. On June 18, 1992, Winner filed Notice of Appeal in the Superior Court. On August 3, 1992, Judge Herian filed his Opinion (attached hereto as Exhibit "B"). On May 25, 1993, the Superior Court affirmed Judgement of Sentence. (The Judgment and Memorandum Opinion of the Superior Court is attached hereto as Exhibit "A").

Factual History

On August 29, 1989, Winner and Sabrina were residing in the home of Woody and Flamingo Batiler (Sabrina's sister) (hereinafter "Woody") together with Ann and their four (4) year old son Tony. Ann's friend Oldman was watching a movie on the VCR with Ann, a naked Tony, and Sabrina. Tony tried unsuccessfully to kiss Oldman. Shortly thereafter, Winner entered the basement and engaged in sexual intercourse with Sabrina. Thereafter, Winner then forcibly engaged in various acts of sexual and involuntary deviate sexual intercourse with Ann (who also testified that this had been occurring for years). Finally, Winner then forced her to engage in sexual intercourse with Oldman by threatening to strike her with a black belt. Sabrina allegedly photographed these acts involving Winner and Ann and Oldman.

Oldman said nothing for several days, but eventually related these events to her mother a bit at a time, although the story changed from day-to-day. However, Oldman's mother called Winner and Sabrina, and the Winners moved from Woody's after a confrontation with the Oldman's. Oldman's mother called the police, who interviewed Oldman, whose versions of the events in question changed each time she talked to her mother and again for the police.

Subsequently, Ann was interviewed by many prosecution aides, including social worker Wendy Pathnek (hereinafter called "'Pathnek''), Philadelphia Police Officer Michael Little (hereinafter "Little") and others. Initially, with their grandparents, she said nothing happened. Then Pathnek, had Ann placed in a foster home.

Then Ann spoke with Pathnek, but did not complain. Subsequently, Ann spoke to Gloria Mudski (hereinafter "Mudski"), a "sexual abuse expert," and began to tell of certain events. Even after, Little spoke with Ann and called her a liar. Finally, Ann told the prosecutor that Winner and Sabrina did nothing, and the prosecutor got mad at her too. Ultimately this little girl—who admitted that she was greatly influenced by others' opinion—implicated her parents.

The police searched the basement where the events were said to have occurred. They found a camera—which was never proven to be operable—but no film, no photographs, and no black belt. No other evidence was seized from the basement. Moreover, no corroboration was offered except, as discussed below, from Dr. Art Mojong (hereinafter "Mojong"), Chief of Pediatrics Medicine at Washington University Hospital.

Winner was arrested on September 9, 1989. He denied sexually assaulting either Ann or Oldman. He also presented character witnesses.

REASONS FOR ALLOWANCE OF APPEAL

This Honorable Court should grant review in this case because it presents the Court with the opportunity to decided important and heretofore unresolved questions of the law regarding (a) issues of competence for child witnesses, and (b) the admissibility of expert testimony when the expert, who has not examined the female child witnesses, relates his opinion that the medical history version of the events was consistent (that is, truthful) with his general expertise and the medical records he examined, thereby establishing nothing probative except that the female child witnesses were telling the truth.

A. THE TRIAL COURT ABUSED ITS DISCRETION IN RULING THAT CHILD WITNESSES ANN AND OLDMAN WERE COMPETENT TO TESTIFY.

——The competency of a witness is a matter for the trial court to determine, and the court's determination will not be overturned absent a abuse of discretion, *Commonwealth v. Gaerttner,* 484 A.2d 92, 98 (Pa. Super. 1984); *Commonwealth v. Knapp,* 542 A.2d 546, 551 (Pa. Super. 1988). A witness is presumed competent to testify unless proven otherwise, *Commonwealth v. Riley,* 326 A.2d 384 (1974). however, when a proposed witness is under fourteen (14) years of age, there must be a searching judicial inquiry regarding mental capacity, *Commonwealth v. Short,* 420 A.2d 694 (Pa. Super. 1980); *Commonwealth v. Stohr,* 522 A.2d 589, 591 (Pa. Super. 1987).

Years ago, this Honorable Court established a test for determining the testimonial competency of an infant witness:

> " . . . *the issue is not to be determined merely because of the capacity of the witness at the time he is called to communicate his thoughts in terms of language.* There must be (1) such capacity to communicate, including as it does both an ability to understand questions and to frame and express intelligent answer, (2) mental capacity to observe the occurrence itself and *the capacity of remembering what it is that she is called to testify about* and (3) a consciousness of the duty to speak the truth. . . ." *Rosche v. McCoy,* 397 Pa. 615, 620–21 (1959). (Emphasis added).

Moreover, it is a abuse of discretion to find a witness competent where the witness' testimony is fraught with inconsistencies and contradictions, filled with yes or no answers to leading questions, contains answers that could be only manipulated by the questions, *Commonwealth v. Mazzoccoli,* 380 A.2d 786 (Pa.1977), or is the product of undue influence by some family member or witness aide present in the courtroom, *Commonwealth v. Pankraz,* 554 A.2d 974 (Pa. Super. 1989). Finally, to determine a witness' competence, and the proper exercise of the trial court's discretion, a witness' trial testimony must be examined, *Commonwealth v. Trimble,* 615 A.2d 48 Pa. Super. 1992).

Instantly, the trial judge held a competency hearing to determine if Oldman was competent to testify. Throughout the inquiry, Oldman continually shrugged her shoulders, failed to answer many questions, failed to respond coherently to many other questions, and even failed to recall her discussion with the prosecutor about this case just days before the trial began (and the subject matter of trial was events of more than a year and a half (1–½) earlier.

Additionally, Oldman's definition of truth showed she was incompetent to testify:

BY THE COMMONWEALTH:

Q. In your own words, what is the difference between telling the truth and a lie?

A. The truth is when you say something that happens that

176

really happened and a lie is when you say that something really didn't happen.

This was insufficient to show that Oldman knew the difference between truth and lie, and Oldman's subsequent answers regarding the weather that day did not alter her incompetence. Despite these clear signs of incompetence, the trial court rules Oldman competent to testify, finding that her hesitancy in answering was grounded in her inability to recall rather than her ability to differentiate between a lie and a truth. Of course, since inability to recall is part of the definition of incompetence, the trial court essentially rules that demonstration of incompetence are a basis for a finding of competence. Obviously, such a ruling is an abuse of discretion.

After being held competent, Oldman's testimony was so halting and full of shrugs as responses that it demonstrated incompetence. Indeed, even the trial court was constrained to comment:

> THE COURT: Mr. Humble is correct in that this witness is not, on many occasions, responding to the questions. She is shrugging her shoulders and simply not responding to many questions. It is very difficult proceeding for her, obviously.

Thus, Oldman demonstrated the following pattern: she refused to answer questions; she answered by shrugging; she could not remember recent events; she constantly requested recesses; she did not remember the names of her family members; she did not remember what she told the police or her mother; she did not know what Winner allegedly had done to Ann; she did not remember testifying at the preliminary hearing (or what she said there). This pattern demonstrates a very questionable ability to perceive, an inability to remember observed events, weakness in communicating intelligent answers, and a consistent lack of consciousness of a duty to speak the truth. In other words, Oldman was incompetent and it was an abuse of discretion to rule otherwise.

Ann demonstrated a similar lack of competence. Ann was first interviewed by Little on September 9, 1989, and indicated that there was nothing wrong. Pathnek had Ann and her sibling removed from the home in September 1989. However, Ann did not complain about abuse by her parents even then. In an attempt t get Ann to repeat Oldman's story, Pathnek told Ann of her own childhood experiences. Allegedly, Pathnek did not tell Ann what Oldman had said, but somehow, surprisingly, Ann said, "whatever Oldman told you is what happened." On September 28, 1989, Pathnek arranged for Ann to be interviewed by Mudski. Finally, Ann first told Mudski of incidents of sexual abuse. On October 7, 1989, Little confronted Ann and told her she was lying.

Ann admitted being very susceptible to the opinions of others. These prosecution oriented adults brow beat her: Little told Ann that she was a liar; Mudski told her that she could get in trouble; Ann told the prosecutor that "her parents didn't do anything," and the prosecutor got made at her. Not only did she first tell the prosecutor that nothing happened, when she went to the hospital to be examined, she told the doctor that nothing happened. She told both Little and Mudski that Oldman was lying and she told another social worker that her parents did not to anything wrong. Ann told the prosecutor the same thing the first time she spoke with her. Finally, both Ann and Oldman both admitted to lying in the past and Ann's testimony showed quite clearly that she had tried on several occasions to change her recitation and exonerate Winner and Sabrina. Finally, Ann changed her story to what was presented at trial as "the truth." After that, the adults were not angry with Ann anymore. The obvious fact here is that Ann's testimony is the result of undue influence by all of these adults. Ann was clearly incompetent to testify.

This Honorable Court should accept review in this case to establish two (2) rules regarding competency of child witnesses: (a) a child witness will be declared incompetent to testify where it becomes apparent that her version of the events is a product of her will being overborne by prosecutors and their aides and associates: (b) inability to perceive and recall, and communicate intelligently will not be overlooked because of the difficult nature of the subject matter, and it is an abuse of discretion to overlook those obvious inadequacies and declare a witness competent.

B. THE TRIAL COURT ERRED IN ALLOWING EXPERT WITNESS TO TES- TIFY WEHRE THAT TESTIMONY WAS NOTHING MORE THAN A VEILED ATTEMPT TO ESTABLISH THE CREDIBILITY OF THE COM- PLAINTS.

Expert testimony is permitted only when the subject matter is within the proffered witness' scientific training and experience *Commonwealth v. Crawford,* 361 A.2d 660 (Pa. 1976). Qualification of a witness to express an expert opinion is an issue for discretion of the trial judge and will not be reversed absent an abuse of discretion, *Commonwealth v. Manquini,* 286 A.2d 482 (Pa. 1978). Moreover, it is axiomatic that determination of a witness' credibility are exclusively within the province of the jury, *Commonwealth v. Davis,* 541 A.2d 315 (Pa. 1988). Therefore, an expert witness may not be allowed to invade the province of the jury and bolster to testify directly regarding the truthfulness of witnesses who have already testified, *Commonwealth v. Seese,* 517 A.2d 920 (Pa. 1986); *Commonwealth v. Davis, supra; Commonwealth v. Rounds,* 542 A.2d (Pa. 1988); *Commonwealth v. Ferguson,* 546 A.2d 1249 (Pa. Super. 1988); *Commonwealth v. Gallagher,* 547 A.2d 355 (Pa. 1988); *Commonwealth v. Emqe,* 553 A.2d 74 (Pa. Super. 1989); *Commonwealth v. Higby,* 559 A.2d 939 (Pa. Super. 1989); *Commonwealth v. McIlvaine,* 560 A.2d 155 (Pa. Super. 1989); *Commonwealth v. Dunkle,* 561 A.2d 5 (Pa. Super. 1989), allocatur granted 574 A.2d 67 (Pa. 1990); *Commonwealth v. Cepull,* 568 A.2d 247 (Pa. Super. 1990); *Commonwealth v. Purcell,* 589 A.2d 217 (Pa. Super. 1991); *Commonwealth v. Garcia,* 588 A.2d 951 (Pa. Super. 1991); *Commonwealth v. Sees,* 605 A.2d 307 (Pa. 1992), and allowing an expert to so testify is an abuse of discretion requiring the grant of a new trial.

Experts may offer testimony based on the reports of others, *Commonwealth v. Mitchell,* 570 A.2d 532 (Pa. Super. 1990); *Commonwealth v. Thomas,* 282 A.2d 693 (Pa. 1971). Moreover, hospital records are admissible to show the facts of hospitalization and treatment, but not the diagnosis, *Commonwealth v. Garcia,* 387 A.2d 48 (Pa. 1978); *Commonwealth v. DiGiacomo,* 345 A.2d 605 (Pa. 1975). In addition, experts may rely upon the opinion and findings of other experts in forming their own opinions, but they may not rely upon unsubstantiated medical history or other materials not reasonably relied upon by other experts, in forming that opinion, *Primavera v. Celotex Corp.* 608 A.2d 515 (Pa. Super. 1992). Thus, while a medical expert may rely upon medical records and the findings of other experts, they may not rely upon rank hearsay offered by unknown persons (who may be parents, relatives, or friends of victims). In addition, because of the unique nature of child abuse cases, expert testimony in such cases must be evaluated cautiously, *Commonwealth v. Vidmosko,* 574 A.2d 96 (Pa. Super. 1990). Finally, even assuming reliance upon proper records, the experts may not express

179

an opinion based upon those records that invades the province of the injury.

Mojong was called as a pediatrician expert in research on child abuse who regularly lectured on that subject. His testimony was based upon past research projects and interpreting of medical records. After lengthy argument, the trial court overruled Winner's objections to Mojong's proposed testimony. Mojong had not examined either Ann or Oldman. Nevertheless, he reviewed their medical records, although he did not know the physicians who examined them, or their qualifications or experience or what instruments were used or measurements made. Mojong said that both Ann and Oldman had a broken hymen which he claimed was a result of injury. However, the broken hymens were consistent with (any kind of) accident and did not necessarily indicate sexual penetration. Moreover, the injury had healed by the time of the examination. Mojong also noted that each had an enlarged introits. His opinion as to the average size of the introits was based upon statistics published in medical literature. The enlarged introits went along with penetration through the hymen. There were no abnormal physical findings in the rectal area no fresh injuries found on each girl, and no indications of anal molestations were present. Thus, the only medical findings were those related to the vaginal area and the torn hymen. Nevertheless, Mojong opined that the sexual abuse history given by someone on behalf of Oldman and Ann at their examinations was consistent with the medical findings. In other words, Mojong said the inconclusive medical findings were consistent with Ann and Oldman telling the truth! As if this was sufficiently improper under the law, the Commonwealth then increased the prejudice involved by making absolutely no attempt to show the circumstances under which these histories were supplied or even that they were actually supplied by Ann and Oldman. Thus, the histories are hearsay and cannot form the basis of Mojong's opinion, *Commonwealth v. Haber,* 505 A.2d 273 (Pa. Super. 1986).

The real question is why Mojong testified. While the legal discussion of Winner's objections to his testimony demonstrates that all parties agreed that Mojong could not testify about Oldman's and Ann's credibility, that is exactly what he did. He was introduced to the jury as an expert on child abuse and a man who spent considerable time investigating specific instances, reading the literature and lecturing about this subject. Yet, the only opinion he was asked to

180

give was whether or not the physical findings were consistent with the history which was presumably given by Oldman and Ann. In other words, he was asked if, in his expert testimony, Oldman and Ann had told the truth in September when they were examined by two (2) different physicians. The result was nothing more than a thinly disguised attempt to bolster the credibility of the victims and, as such, was inadmissible, *Commonwealth v. Higby, supra.*

The Superior Court rules that Mojong did not testify regarding Ann and Oldman's credibility, and relied upon its own decision in *Commonwealth v. Hernandez,* 615 A.2d 1338 (Pa. Super. 1992) as exclusive support for its position. The Superior Court's decision in this case (and *Hernandez*) is contradictory to this Honorable Court's decisions in *Seese* and its progeny. Moreover, the Superior Court's ruling that Mojong did not testify regarding Ann' and Oldman's credibility is simple (as previously demonstrated) wrong. Both in *Hernandez* and here, the same Mojong testified that he examined records, not the complaint(s). In both cases Mojong did not offer any other probative evidence. In both cases the prosecutor offered him as a witness specifically designated not to comment on credibility. In both cases the entire import of Mojong's testimony was that, as an expert, he concluded that the medical records he examined supported (were consistent with) the complainant's allegations. In both cases the Superior Court claims this testimony "did not bolster (the victim's) credibility." Since it was not probative of any other fact, then what was Mojong offered for it if not to bolster credibility.

Our law does not act in a vacuum, and our decisions are not to be made to avoid unpleasant result. In both *Hernandez* and the instant case, the Superior Court sought to avoid a well established line of authority to avoid the unpleasant result of granting a new trial. This Honorable Court should accept review in this case and establish the rule that where an expert is offered for no other reason than to establish that, in his/her opinion, the medical history and findings are consistent, that expert is offered for the purpose of bolstering credibility.

Respectfully submitted
Dwight Goodman.
Praise God! Now the waiting game begins.

19

Pray; Don't Think!

Sabrina was thinking faithful thoughts while she waited for a break in the case at the women's prison. "O Lord," prayed Winner. "Thy will be done. ."

Sabrina and Winner had renewed the vows they made at baptism. Both had repented of all evil and made a decision to reject the clamor of evil. This entire story is a loud and continued worldly noise that has become an uproar. Satan filled many with illusions that brought forth trials and tribulations but Our Heavenly Father turns these hardships to work for his good.

Winner encouraged Sabrina to stay focused on God and truth.

Sabrina had received her miracle. Her thoughts had been transformed. She woke up; her health was improved; her attitude positive, her love for husband and children renewed. She had become a writer in jail and loved to speak on paper. Some days twelve letters would arrive from Sabrina who was kept busy washing pots and pans at the women's prison.

Poppe and nanny would visit Winner and Sabrina once a month. Both the men's prison and the women's prison were in the same mountain region. The children also lived in the area, so they would visit Winner for a few hours, then dash ten miles to see the kids. Once the visit was over, they would drive another seventy miles, rent a motel room for the night, and visit Sabrina the next day.

The grandparents were both approaching eighty years of life. This tribulation was good for them because it kept them off the rocking chair and active in life.

In the visiting room tables were provided for families. At the table the subject would always be the children. What were they doing? What were they saying? Their progress in school was good; both were A students. Nanny would say, your daughter is still brainwashed and under the complete authority of the state. We can't say a word to her about the case. Monitors watch us at our visits.

Poppe said, "We will see the kids this afternoon. Is there anything you'd like me to tell them?"

Yes dad, you tell Ann to get to confession: She needs to be right with the church. Its still my responsibility to make sure this is done."

Nanny replied, "The state doesn't want you saying anything to your daughter. These people are not interested in the Catholic faith.

Winner said, "It doesn't matter what the state wants. When it comes to religion, it's not their business. This child is a baptized child of God and needs to go to confession. I don't care what the pagans think. Tell her, go to confession, that's the best advice I can send to her. She will be relieved from sin if she obeys. What could be better than that? Nothing!"

Poppe said, "I'll give her your message"

The visit was over. Poppe and nanny left to visit the children. Winner walked back to the change room where he had to strip. The guard said, "Open yout mouth," Winner obeyed. The guard took a look inside. "Lift up your arms," Winner obeyed! The guard checked out the naked inmate! "Lift up your privates." The guard took a fast peak into this spot looking for countraband. Drugs are smuggled into prison. "Turn around and spread those cheeks" The inspection was over, "Get dressed and go back to your block."

Poppe carried the message of repentance and confession to Ann who, immediately rejected the commandment from her grandfather. Walking away she said, "I don't have to listen to this."

Poppe said to Ann as she huffed and puffed in pride, "Ann, don't turn your back on people who love you."

Two weeks passed, A letter arrived from a court-appointed attorney. The Department of Human services had scheduled a hearing to ask the court to permanently separate the children from the family. The state wanted to render capital punishment to this family and kill it dead. In his letter the attorney informed Winner what the state wanted to do but he said nothing about fighting for the Winner family. The hearing would also render a decision regarding the visits from the grandfather. He had said something to Ann about the case and the Commonwealth wanted his visiting rights terminated.

Winner walked back to his cell wondering what to do. He had heard from nanny that Ann wanted permission from the judge to speak to her mother, so letters were written to the Judge.

Your Honor, Ann has suffered long enough. Let's get on with her recovery. I the father am doing well, Sabrina the mother is also doing well but Ann is not doing well and it's your fault. You keep her in the care of false witnesses when she could be free living in a home in Cape May a few miles from the sea.

I object! Please remember, a appeal is now before the highest court in Pennsylvania. Maybe this court will overrule the bias and prejudice that has been masked as fairness. Ann wants to speak to her mother. The commonwealth does not want this to happen, so I'm telling you so you know. I have been in touch with the Attorney General's office and asked the lady in charge to investigate the entire justice department in Philadelphia. So far she hasn't replied. None of your reply because you're scared. I don't blame you for this fear because you did great evil to a baby girl child that will soon be corrected. My love will heal Ann while the malice of the commonwealth will keep her sick. This is war, without a doubt, and the soldiers on my side are much stronger, than those in your weak house of cards. One good strong wind will blow the entire case away.

I know the commonwealth will stop at nothing to continue their lies. Prideful egotists find it difficult to say, ''I made a mistake, but Your Honor, never underestimate the power of a man who is fighting for his family. Your power means nothing when it supports evil. A new development in the case is now being presented to counsel for the defense, but I can't even tell the people who are supposed to protect my rights about this development because you are all in this together and I don't trust any of you.

My court appointed attorney tells me that a hearing has been scheduled to remove the kids for good. Well, at the hearing I would like all members of the family to be present. That's poppe, he is the head of the family, and nanny. Ann with her brother Tony, and mom and dad. This is a family matter and the entire family should be present.

Ann was moved to a group home for homeless children in Philadelphia.

Flamingo is Ann's aunt and Star is her first cousin. Winner received a letter from Aunt Flamingo, it was the first letter from Flamingo in well over a year. Sabrina and Flamingo are sisters and the fanasty was born while the family was living in the basement of her house.

The letter said, "Dear Winner, Hi, It's certainly been awhile; here's the reason I'm writing. First, I need the name of your lawyer and his telephone number. I've been visiting your daughter at a homeless shelter for children at 15th and Fairmount, in Philadelphia. Surprisingly enough, the visits haven't been supervised. They were supposed to be, but weren't.

I have a lot of information that Ann has given me permission to tell someone. She's really scared, but she has told me the truth. I need to talk to your lawyer; it's so important. Ann can't tell anyone she told me because she's afraid of what they will do!

They have her locked into the system and they're all working together to keep her there.

I have information from her and Star my daughter is a witness to what Ann said. Also, Ann is willing to tell the truth. We are afraid if they (DHS) finds out she's talking, they may scare her back to their way of thinking.

Please, have your lawyer call me. 457-6161. I have to find out what can be done about this. I'm so afraid for her, Winner, *she wants to tell how they made her say what she said.*

I told her to just tell the truth.

She said, she will.

Get in touch with me. Flamingo.

Alleluia, Ann is not brain washed. She knows the truth but is not encouraged to speak the truth, instead is frightened into doing the will of those who hold her prisoner. Forcing a child to testify against her parents against her will to get a conviction. Poor America!

Winner looked at the letter. His daughter was in trouble. Help, Lord God Jehovah. In the name of Jesus Christ, send forth thy Holy Spirit to protect this child from the malace of the devil. Jehovah please also protect Tony. Mother of God, I do not hesitate to seek thy aid, please ask thy son to protect the innocent children from the corruption that surrounds them. Amen.

After praying, his daughter and son were both safe. Connecting ideas often leads to new thoughts. These thoughts when captured on paper lead the writer and the reader down a road filled with the unknown. Faith looks at the Lord, not circumstances, while the world sees situations, not the Lord. So what's next God?

Ann wants to change her testimony once more. This child needs help, but who will the Lord send to her aid? The commonwealth wants Ann to stick to her story. Ann want to change her story but she fears the people who are in charge of her. The Defense Attorney has this information. What will he do with it? The state doesn't care to have Ann speak to her father's lawyer.

This child is subject to the will of the state. The social workers need only say that Ann needs psychotherapy and into a state mental hospital she will go, so whatever is done must be done without informing the ministers of the lie.

Lord, you have defeated all fear, the enemies are on the run. Now we wait to see evil drop out of sight and justice victorious.

Winner paused at his typewriter. He knew not which way to continue. Yet, Sabrina his wife, a major character, had a a story to relate and she wanted her adventure recorded in his book.

Ok, Sabrina, the audience is ready to read your contribution. You may begin in the next paragraph!

Hi baby, I have five letters to mail to you just to let you know I miss you very much, and miss the kiddies. They are always in my heart, and always will be. I wish I had some new clothes to wear, that's enjoyment. My locker is a mess and has to be cleaned.

Winner, you might have to do your minimum (16 years). I might have to do mine—ten years. After that, most likely I'll be put in a hospital; that's what the authorities say. I hope not.

How about O.J.'s case, isn't that something? Ya never know, Do you? Our case is little; no killings, and there is no evidence against us. I look into the mirror and I think I'm pretty, I feel really great. Are you going to send me some money? Spoil me will you so I can enjoy shopping.

Winner your letters interest me, it's a bore around here. I just had a shower, cleaned up and feel good. A T. V. preacher just said, "Make sure you talk to God every day." Isn't it strange that we must make ourself love the place we hate? This will all pass in time.

I love writing, it's really interesting. I can't believe you love me that much. Isn't that funny? But I will!

My feet are healing up; finally the blisters are gone. I can walk better today.

I hope I don't get anymore write-ups because they go towards behavior. That means it could take me up to ten years if I flunk. I have got to mean business, all the way, no joking. Wouldn't that be awful?

There's nothing new around here except people going home and a lot of lifers. A lot of people get life. I'm still trying to find things to write about. Remember, I'm no big shot.

I feel great whenever I have a pencil in my hand.

Isn't it hard to keep the kids in your mind the way you want them to be? So many strange people block them out. They have nerve. I'm not quitting cause those children are my children. If you only knew the suffering behind this! I'm lucky I'm alive.

This is a sad thing to wake up to. The Bible helps fill in empty spaces. I miss them so much I could die. It was like I was dead already. I guess things will change. Winner, people have feelings and these feelings need to be recognized somehow and I can't see you going through all of this "stuff" on your own. That's why I'm helping you get through this. Nobody can do this on their own. I can't. It's strain. It's stress.

I miss my dad. I wish he was still living. He was a good man; mom's allright. Did you call the Lord today? The scriptures in Luke say: "Ye shall be filled with the Holy Ghost." That's Jesus. He will save you, seconds after being saved, ask him one time—Lord, I come to receive the Holy Ghost. Then you'll be saved. You will be re-filled this afternoon in the name of Jesus Christ. We thank you for the rock that won't go dry. I lift my husband up Lord. Bring him to God. Is Jesus doing what he promised to do? Lord, destroy the devil. Jesus, why is this happening, I'm worried because this isn't right. My husband shouldn't be in prison.

If you prayed that prayer, rejoice! You're no longer trying to forgive. You've done it! You stepped out of darkness into light. You have tapped into the supernatural never failing power of love. Shout Alleluia and let the victories manifest.

Well Winner, what have you been up to? Typing. I love your typing, it's pretty good and I love the words you type. It's nice to feel someone loves you like you love me. That's beautiful to have all the time; that keeps me together.

I miss Tony and Ann so much. I could cry now thinking of them.

There are other things to write about instead of crying for my children. I have no answers cause I don't know what to say. The kids never should have been removed from our family. It's sad to suffer like this. Lord, get my kids back home please! What else can I say? They are gone so the remorse lives on forever.

I hope you enjoy this writing. It's going to be another long week of boredom to push through. Tony is so handsome. He looks just like his daddy and so does Ann. I know our children miss us too. Isn't it something in jail? Nobody writes to you. I remember taking Ann to her first penance class; how she hated that also, cleaning the house. The summer is here and it's hot. I'm just an ordinary girl and ugly for being in jail on these charges they pinned on me, but I just have to listen to it. There's nothing I can do.

We are having a band here on Veteran's day and I'm gonna dance all day, me and Ruth, my girlfriend. I listen to the radio a lot. I think of all the clothing I put on Ann and Tony. It's a sad thing not being able to watch them grow. The judge is not going to let Ann write to me, but I pray she does. It would be nice to send her cards and allowance money but I don't see how with these charges. But you never know. Things will get better for us. You have your typing to do so you'll enjoy that until things improve ... So back to God. Amen! Did you feel His touch today. He restores everything to help get through all this mess. It takes time. Meditate on this cause his spirit is in your mouth. Stay stuck like glue to God. I miss those rascals. Here I go again. Is this a ball game that I must play to win? Well, is it? It's a rotten game.

Winner, I hope this doesn't kill me, all this worrying. I guess it's normal cause I am their mother and you're my husband. I hope I can make it through this to a happy end. I don't see their faces; my little peanuts.

Thank you for the beautiful picture of Jesus; it was beautiful. I love the picture, it lightened my eyes up. That was so nice of you. Your story with the picture was also nice. I just finished work and received a raise to $40.00 a month. Isn't that great? I'm so happy. Well things are still the same. I mailed you more letters. My report card says all A's. I'm glad of that.

My foot still hurts. I was surprised when I opened up the mail to see the picture of Lord Jesus. I always wanted a picture like that to hang on the wall. You knew I would love that picture.

This place is dreadful. I'm always trying to find things to write. I can't find anything new but I'll try cause it's the same old thing, everyday, day in day out. Well, the sun is hot. I am drinking a cup of coffee. Hold on, I'm getting another cup. I just drank a cup of black coffee. Today is my day off from working.

I'm going to see Ruthie, my friend, at 08:30. She's nice, I like her; she's my friend, an older lady. My shoes are worn out, my sandals are a mess. I miss and love you.

Where did I get such a hardworking husband and handsome as you are Winner! I mean that. Your looks can knock somebody's socks off. Your tan is beautiful. You look great. Am I pretty to you? Tell me what you think of my looks!

Holidays are nothing without the kids. The kids always liked the fireworks. Remember how Tony and Ann loved to sit in the grass and watch people celebrate. I must pray for the children. I know you are praying hard, but pray harder. Nanny and poppe are praying for the kids.

The state is making me go to sex abuse class, AA, and GED high school class. I hate it but it's mandatory. I must go. If I don't, I'll get a write up, thats a mis-conduct report that will enter my records. They can keep me here to my maximum release day with write-ups.

Praise God! I can't wait until we go to China Town again, that will be fun. Remember all the good times? I do. I'm so happy I have twenty envelopes to send to you. I want to write words that you'll enjoy. Maybe you can take a nice shower with me when we get home. Ha Ha Ha! Powder bath, doesn't that sound great. There's no sun outside. Don't know what happened to the sun. I can't wait till winter cause it's cold.

Winner, if you don't get out of prison, my life is ruined. Then What? I can't live like that with you in prison for fifteen years. I don't know what I'll do. We have to really stay close. I want you out of jail.

You should buy a radio to occupy your time, I'm still waiting for mine. Why are you so cruel to me? Not giving me some money for myself. This is a hard thing to have to accept. If you have to serve all your time, 15 years, we will bear it together, cause, I'm staying close to you all day cause this case has me really upset.

I can't believe how big Ann and Tony have grown. They both take after you, they are dolls. You have three years in, that's great and you're good. That's good.

I'm not going to work today. I'm too over worked so I'm

staying on the unit to abide time and write. That kitchen—there's about 40 girls working and it becomes tiresome really.

The only things I hate are the counts. I have to be standing by the cell door while the guards take a count to make sure no body broke out, so if I'm all the way in bed I got to get out of it. I can't sleep during the day. One day off won't hurt me. I can deal with this boredom. I have a duty to write to you my sweetie pie; that's my respect towards you and that won't stop cause I respect you. Your face is beautiful.

I have a helper in the kitchen, so it's better. There are three of us on dishes, so I'm OK. I can't believe I sleep so good at night and then open my eyes to this mess. I gave up a lot of junk food this week, no ice cream or pototo chips; just five diet yogurts, 2 small boxes of fudge brownies, 2 large M and M's and a case of diet soda.

It's very hot out. How can you stand the heat? Especially since you are so used to air conditioning. I have on a blue top, purple pants and my sneakers. I stay in this cell and watch some TV but on Sunday there are the preachers and I love those shows. I never miss Jimmy Swaggard or Mr. Copeland.

Our outdoor yard is called from: 08:00 to 10:30, 1:30 to 3:30, 6:30 to 8:30, three times a day, that's all. I wish you could just come and go like it should be cause the card room is for playing cards and I don't play cards, so, it's stay in the cell and write. I like writing to you. You're a whole part of me, the other half. I mean that to; for you I'd do anything.

Do you have many friends? My hair is getting silver again. Nerves turned the hair a different color. Poppe and nanny will be here for a visit shortly. I miss them. I always do miss them. It's two hundred miles from their home to this jail. I love visits. How long do you spend typing each day Winner?

Have you been typing any stories lately? I miss the kids and always will miss them. What goes on in your mind? Is there anything exciting to talk about? Winner, before you know what happened you'll be out of there. Years go by quickly. Remember, one day at a time. Keep waiting for the answer to your appeal. I think you'll be out soon. You're a innocent man, so why worry? I already mailed you three letters today plus will write five more tonight. I am not kidding. I'm keeping you busy if it's the last thing I have to do.

This place is relaxing when there aren't people around me.

Don't misunderstand; it's jail and I dispise prison but I'm talking about the times like this, alone, in peacefulness. Prison is really a pit but you asked me to do the best I can. Well, that's what I'm doing.

In your letters you seemed stressed-out. Why? Can't you learn to relax? I told you that you will some day be out of there. Stress is ugly. You have everything you like so why are you worried? I work like a dog here. It sounds like something's wrong to me. You are writing a fanastic story so don't spit at yourself; that's wasteful. Are you tired? Why act stressed out? Your letters are wonderful. I can't get over how beautiful those picture are of you that you sent me. You're a doll, the same doll I always owned.

Be happy, time will show you better results. Why can't I get a nice little sum of money for my account? Do I have to beg? Come on, I write you the nicest letters I know how to write and am honest with you, but what happened? Tell me! You have me confused. Nobody is trying to use you and I'm not using anybody. I don't have any plans to give money away. It's for me. Now don't be upset. Just think of what I said. Something doesn't seem right to me for some reason. You want a nice wife then explain better.

I miss you! Kiss me um. I was out in the yard and the guards made us come in because of the rain. I'm sitting here lonely as usual. I have to get ready to go to the medication line for medication; thats mandatory. Well, I just woke up. The girls are cleaning their cells and I just changed my sheets. We have to change sheets every Wednesday.

I can write stories to keep you interested till the next letter, stories that I make up. The girls here, a lot of them, are into girl girl love. I don't get involved. I don't want nobody here. Sex doesn't bother me in here. I don't focus on sex. I'm busy and wouldn't have anybody knowing my personal business,. even though I love sex, Boy, i can't believe all the women that go to each other here. Its not for me.

The thunderstorm was horrible last night. I'm in a good mood for you. My girlfriend is letting me use her radio for the day, it costs me 5 cigarettes. So, what will make you happy? I miss you shopping with me. I have to go for a breast test this week, its called a mamogram. I stay happy as best I can because depression gets you down. You're a nice man, handsome all mine. You make my day as you can see I feel so sorry for you. I know you miss the kids. I am upset about this too!

I hope you don't leave me for anyone else. I wouldn't do that because there are vows in our marriage. We've been married eleven years going on twelve. That's in writing and documented. See, I find things to write about.

I'm interested in money because I don't have any. I received your letter asking me to be a weight lifter. Well, I have two children and that wouldn't look nice. I'm too busy working anyway. I have no free time. I hate girls that weight lift. I think it stinks.

I have to be careful here. A lot of girls snitch on you around here. They tell on each other for exchanging things, and you're not allowed to swap stuff. My uniforms are stained so when I wash them they still stay stained. I have to be careful where I place my things or they will get stolen. I hate to keep asking you but are you going to send me money? Do you like my letters? Tell me if you do!

I'll be earning $40.00 a month. My boss made me a permanent dishwasher, me and another girl. I went from $28.00 a month to $40.00. Isn't that great? That's a month. So the work's worth it! Isn't it?

Ann's a beautiful girl and Tony's a beautiful boy. Soon she'll be eighteen, in four years, Tony 12. They aren't dumb kids. I'm glad you love them and are standing by them. They are the prettiest children I've ever seen. I am looking at their pictures in the photo album. We both know our children love us. I just hope you are being good in that jail. No fooling around doing bad actions. Your tan is looking terrific.

Let me create poetry. Look, he stands, the main man, he smiles, looking wild, big, he's big, plenty to see, plenty to show; him I know, so sweet, a treat, well done meat, smoking, zizzling, burning up. Him, I love. He is great. I sing my song for him. My name is Sabrina and he's my Winner.

Me and you have to get into each other more and learn about each other more and more. We are still like newlyweds. We don't know each other well. I'm a taurus zodiac. I love the gray in your hair. Don't you get any write-ups. I think I would have a heart attack if I was wrote-up. Every day I try to make this place a part time home. People come and people go, but whatever it is, I create it in the thoughts. It's beautiful here in the mountains. People take good care of this prison. You have to make the best of this situation in order to get through life.

Do you have many friends? Any? I don't need any but have Ruth. That's all. Everywhere you look up here you see green barbed wire fences. Prison is prison. We have our mail delivered at 18:30.

The story you are writing about our case is shocking. It stays with me. It's so real the way you told the story. I wonder how poppe and nanny are doing. I'd love to see you behind that typewriter. I bet when you finish a project your tummy is tickled. You put a lot of work in the book. That's nice! No real names, that's great. Fiction is better. We don't want anybody's name in the book because that will hurt us. You have a vivid imagination.

Oh by the way, weightlifting is not for me. I could never get into that. First of all, the weights are too heavy. I like me the way I am, no ugly muscles. That would ruin my build. Since when do you think girls look good like that? I'm a mother of two children. That I don't need. I'm not lazy. It's not my style, so don't be mad. I'm sorry.

I love looking into the clothing catalogs but it costs money. During the day not much good is on TV. It's junk. I can't understand how people can play cards all day long. That would drive me nuts. We had a barbecue outside, hotdogs and soda. Boy, I miss you. I hope you are feeling well with all this heat. Winner, do you ever feel like you love yourself? I do. That gives me a positive outlook in life. If you don't love yourself nobody else can. Isn't that true?

Your body is beautiful, Winner. I can't wait until I see you again in person. I'll be happy. You don't have it any harder than me. I feel good, meaning not sick. I don't get sick anymore. I'm healed! It's hard to believe. The sickness came from losing the children. I miss them and I'm glad they are getting bigger. It's healthy living in these mountains. Our unit cottage is cozy and quiet.

What would we do without our parents? It's another long day locked up in this cell but I can and will survive. I am weary all the time. Why did this have to happen? It should never have happened. I can't stand this. You have a good attorney. Many of the girls knit. I don't want to knit.

There are two guards in this cottage. Authority's making more rules, no matches or lighters. You have to get a light from the officers cause there have been too many fires. The children are out of school for the summer. I pray that they stay drug free.

194

I had a cup of soup, shrimp plus a glass of juice. I am a clean girl, always was clean. I want to see you get out of this mess. Hold tight. I feel for you dearest soul. All these years and you're still in jail but watch God grant you his promise. Look how far we have walked together. Why can't we walk the rest of the way? I hate this place. I can't stand prison. I forget what it's like to walk on the street. Its hard on me. I just sleep here and try to get along.

We don't have cable TV, just two channels. You take it easy cause you worry too much then you worry me. And another thing, people don't have many friends in jail so don't expect many. It's good to be your own friend. That's beautiful, to be that way. I mean that. Don't be too kind cause you're number one. We love you. That's all the love you need, because selfish people will walk all over you. Don't be a glutton for punishment. You should already be aware of what I'm saying. Just look at what happened to us for being nice to strangers, and it can happen again cause your a kindhearted man, that is why I love you. You don't need to worry, I'll stick by you all the way til you're out.

You need things done, I'll be your errand girl.

I would like to have some goodies to munch on. I get sick and tired of running to the medication line.

Poppe gives the children money each time on his visits to them. Ann is old enought to be into fashion. I wish I could be home doing something that I enjoy like ceramics or riding a bike or roller skating. I am wearing my sunglasses while writing to you. Be strengthened in the one Lord, touch his spirit with a prayer. Feel good, Winner. He loves us both and we are making God happy. I'm telling you I get rushes from these letters you write. They excite me a lot. I love them so much, they send rushes through me.

Your love letters spoil me, they enlighten me. The feeling I get wants me to show you Immaculate happiness.

My new clothes arrived today. I picked them up this afternoon. I have to work on the dishwasher all day long. What a drag. Did you call God to you this morning? Did you ask him for his forgiveness for everything you do. You must do that! This cell is a pest; boredom again. It's disgusting. My days off are Monday and Tuesday. I'm tired of wearing state clothing.

My clothes were cancelled til Monday again. Well, I pick up my case of soda today, that's something to look forward to. You don't tell people why you are in jail, do you? Nobody knows my business here, nobody.

You shouldn't talk about your case. I don't and not one person knows about these charges. I keep silent for my own protection. I have to be careful and watch out. I think I really look great for all the troubles I have been through, don't you? So do you? Answer me. You never answer these questions.

I could walk around these prison grounds without worrying about getting hurt. Nobody bothers me cause I don't bother anyone. That's the way to get by each day. I put my hair up in a bun. It looks cute rolled up on the top of my head.

In our old age we need to know how to pamper each other once in a while cause growing into kindness is part of maturity. Winner, I love you. I wish I could show you on behalf of my womenhood that I care about you and I know what you are experiencing and I know how you feel. Everything is wait. I place my heart on yours as long as you do the same. That makes me feel complete. Keep my love inside your heart. I'll pray forever for your soul.

Have you talked to your lawyer at all about the case? You should you know. I hope you win, I mean that, after all the money you spent. I pray most of the time.

Do you buy any snacks? They don't sell much at the commissary, it's always the same stuff. I miss my babies. You stay strong like you do, get stronger, not wronger. Deal with it as best you can. Try to give out some grace then you'll get grace back.

I wish I typed. Oh, the pictures you sent arrived. I love the one with your back turned toward the camera. Well, keep asking God into your life. He has come into my life and made me feel great. I just woke up. Saturday is a do nothing day. God is checking the situations out. Keep the faith, relax, rest your mind. You can't worry about everything because you may win and then again you may not. So stick with your love for me. You die with me and I die with you, nobody else. Every day is going to be a worry about each other. Do you ever think of sending me a greeting card? I love cards. Ask Jesus to keep us happy together and keep him with you at all times so he never leaves you. Lord clean our hearts today. I ask this in Christ's name.

You should see the corn fields here. They are six feet tall. The cows eat the corn. I was out in the yard for a hour but back writing.

Sanity is the key. Keep busy, stay occupied, don't worry! I'm not depressed, I'm happy. Prison is horrible, the guards know every move I make. It's sickening. I have to scrub this cell. I don't want to clean but do have to get the dirt up. Everything is a worry. The dust sits there. I get hyper at times but I'm OK! Do you ever get your hair cut? Mine is a mess!

I try to be good at all times and I'm going to be good, so should you!

I just mopped up the floor so it looks better. Winner, what's the name of the book you wrote. Tell me so I know. Do you start writing as soon as you wake up in the morning? My foot is healing from those blisters. I love getting presents. I can always rest with closed eyes and lighten my eyes up with peace. Do you ever take naps during the day? I can't because I'm always cleaning dishes.

I get tired of taking care of my hair, all the time constantly brushing, and it still looks horrible. But I must treat myself better or someone else has to treat me better. I mean. I need help to change these jail house feelings.

I was looking into the Sear's Catalog for winter clothing. I want to get new shoes and a winter coat. Did you hear me husband? My bed needs to be made but I'm not in the mood to make the bed. It's sad to be sad for no reason. I could understand if we did something wrong. The state has us like we're two birds in their cage. This has ruined our lives. Look at my life! Look at your life! I'm proud because I exist. I am alive. It's still difficult to cope. It has its up and downs and puts a wear on me that led me right to peace with myself. I trust you to get us out of this hell.

Be good; don't break the rules. Serving prison time is hard but even worse when you didn't do the crime.

I don't know what it is to be really happy anymore, that's for sure. Sadness never quits, it's always present, this stomach pain won't go away for nothing. I wish it would, its unbearable. So many things are wrong with me. Do you think I'll be alright or not? Please tell me. I need some assurance here no one gives me none. I feel off balance about these changes sick and irratable.

I wonder how Ann & Tony are doing? I hope fine. I hope they are ok. Things got to get better. I miss them so much. I cry for them. I hope they are eating well. Do they play many games? Do they have many toys? Its a real shame, I feel so sorry for them. They deserve the best. They are darling children.

I feel good knowing that I'm paying what these people want even though I'm innocent. It just irks me to know they did this to me & you. Its a rotten shame, really a shame, boy its a shame.

How come nobody sympathizes for me; only them self. Thats not fair. Let me finish this letter and continue another.

love Sabrina

Several separate notes arrived in the mail during the months of August and September of 94 from: Flamingo, informing Winner of the Children's well being.

Flamingo, was a reformed brand new "Child of God" who kept before her attention the virtue of diligence in her unrelenting quest to maintain sobriety.

According to Church teaching, angels act as messengers from God to man. The lord in His never disappointing magnificence assigned this charming personality that function.

Honest people, fearlessly and persistently object to the falsification of plain unvarnished truth. Dililgent beings usually are content with a continueous mindfulness of Spiritual objectives and not distracted by distractions.

Young Ann Winner had been ordered by Family Court to dwell in a group with 12 to 18 year old foster children who for various reasons couldn't live in a family setting.

Flamingo wrote; "I do what God puts before me and run in blind faith. Ann called me on the telephone. I didn't go out looking to do anything, she asked me to come and visit her in a shelter in Philadelphia. I was shocked, I couldn't believe I was actually speaking to her on the phone."

"I went to visit her. I did not bring up the case first, Ann did. I just listened. "At the least annoyance say; thank you lord, your will be done." Louis deMontfort.

Flamingo listened to her astonishment while Ann implied that her testimony in Court during the criminal trial of Mom and Dad was false. Ann is ready, willing and wants to change her testimony.

"Yes Lord," Winner wrote, with your grace Your will be done. His thoughts like a cannon ball went straight to God. O God make speed to save me, O Lord make haste to help me.

Hear-say was reaching into cell 23 on Z block. Ann had a conversation with the Judge in her chambers and retracted her sworn perjured statements. The Judge asked Ann if perhaps she was repressing her recollections.

Minister of Justice along with Social workers in the dept., of human services had been and continued to keep Ann in isolation while feeding her one side of the story. Plus, hundreds of thousands of tax payers dollars had been spent producing psychological persuasion on a child who couldn't defend herself.

Attorney Walter Cork had been appointed by the Court to represent Winner in Family Court proceedings.

Hearings were held about seven or eight weeks apart. Winner and Sabrina, Poppe and Nanny were excluded from these so-called conferences, while out siders discussed the fate of Tony and Ann. Conversations from each hearing were recorded on transcripts.

Winner writes his attorney, Mr. Cork.

Dear Walter,

Praise God. The intention of these thoughts are to bring you into readiness for the up-coming child custody hearing.

Ann Winner is asking the State to release her to her Aunt Flamingo's custody. D.H.S. will probably deny this request since Ann must be under their watchful eyes in order for the guilty to continue their mis-behavior. The State will go to any length to keep Ann from her family. In the last five years the Court hardly noticed the Father's rights to have a voice in his children's up bringing. As my voice in the hearing, please speak these words;

> "Your Honor, members of this conference, Ann wants to live with Flamingo her Aunt. You have been torturing my daughter for five years and I demand it stop. How about offering Ann some good old fashioned mercy. Come on, stop being mean to this little kid. You keep hurting her with decisions that please you, not her nor her family. You move her around like a bouncing ball. Send her to homes where she receives no love, she is left to herself, alone with strangers, no family, no stability, no Aunts, or Uncles, or Grandparents. You are making Ann into a Orphan. You certainly are permitting evil to hurt children who can't fight back or meet you eye to eye without fearing your next move. Ann needs an Attorney to represent her & this lawyer needs to be her protection and not just as an advocate or a clone for the District Attorney. She needs to be protected by law from those therapists.
>
> I the Father of Ann, will continue to shout out loud protests from a prison cell. You and your entire system is in need

of urgent reformation. The impression that you and your laws are sacred needs to be nullified. Major reform in the Judiciary of Pennsylvania Courts should be instigated immediately.''

It's still legal to Praise God, but who knows, a Judge may rule it a crime someday. The Creation is not very friendly with the Creator. The state mocks God with sinner's wisdom creating a living hell for the citizens. You don't have the slightest concern for just decisions but pretend amongst each other that your malice is justice. Truth can not penetrate into your deep rooted fanasties. Government should help citizens, but we are getting self interest; shortly freedom will be gone. You'll need a pass to walk the street at night. Crime is controlled by love of God or force of man. Love of God is the solution, but that is not in the crime bill. Our best worldly thinkers can't tell the population to pray. So the crime bill won't do any blessed positive thing, its doomed to failure before it can get started.

Prisons will be erected one after another. Who do you think are the people who will go to Prison? You or your neighbor; then the social worker will come in with their therapy solutions that never worked.

Never the less truth will not be silent or fearful or back up one inch or be pushed out of sight, by any lackadaisical voices promoting ungodly views.

Wake-up foot ball fans. We have much to lose, while you participate in games, Our freedom is just about finished.

Ann is a prisoner, a victim, forced to grow up under the teachings of a godless State. Nobody in the State is teaching Ann the power of the Rosary — O No, the devil won't like that.

But this is America. Why do you all participate and permit the State to bring sorrow to a helpless child?

Leave her alone Mr. Hey Sister—Give her back to her family who wait with love. Not one of you ever shed one teardrop over Ann Winner. She doesn't belong to you baby stealers. I want action Walter.

News has arrived; according to hear-say, Ann had a talk with the judge and recanted her testimony. Is this true Walter? You were there, please write to me and let me know, so I can move in a right direction. Why must I ask you these questions?

I'd like permission to speak or write to Ann, Walter. Ask the Judge for me. I'm sending a letter to you to give to the Judge to give to Ann.

200

(Winner wrote the following;)

Hi Ann, Hi Tony; Sabrina is doing ok, you're both ok, everybody's ok - ok, stay ok. I love you, Sabrina loves you too.

Keep doing what you're doing. You still are alive. You still exist. We love you and do not intend for a second to let those people keep abusing you with sexual harrassment.

Kids, this is your Father and your Father is teaching you to pray in the name of Jesus to be delivered from the evil that surrounds you.

Tony, most of these words are for Ann, you watch though, because you are a important member of our family but right now, Ann needs pleantly of love, so do you, but for some reason I feel Ann needs a special extra bit from Winner, I know you do too, so guess I'll speak to both of you at the same time so theres no hurt feelings by either of you.

Ann, the entire family, the folks at prayer meeting, all know you are surrounded by captors who won't ever permit you to make a phone call. Your right to free speech has been taken from you by adults who fear what you will speak. These adults could also go to prison themselves for hurting you. For now they can do as they please since nobody is there to fight them off. I am doing all that can be done from a jail cell. This book is written so you both know me and your Mother *love you,* loved you, and will continue to love you.

Ann, Tony, listen carefully, please, your Father never ever had any bad thoughts about you; nor ever will. What happened certainly is not in anyway your fault. You are victims of a family bashing by those who continue to be dead wrong. My love will help you both to love.

In my life solutions where solutions that solved problems. The Lord Jesus is a teacher who will put before your eyes a correct course to travel where defeat and evilness are conquered by your prayers, yep, thats all, your prayers.

I ask you to both pray for the therapists; pray for those who taught you to dishonor your Mother and Father. Pray for those who made you sad. Look out for wolves in sheeps clothing. Question everything. Be at peace, I hold this not against you.

Love,

Dad

Oct. 10, 1994

Flamingo was filled with great pity upon seeing the situation and circumstances Ann was forced to undergo. She made it known to the Court that she would like to be awarded custody of this child.

Bible verses come to Winners mind

O good news come to the rescue.

Lam 1:12 . . . "All ye that pass by the way attend and see if there be any sorrow like to my sorrow." Jesus being crucified. "Restore unto me the joy of thy salvation and strengthen me with a perfect spirit." Wis 8:21 "I went to the Lord, and besought him, and said with my whole heart: God of my fathers, and Lord of mercy, who hast made all things with thy word;" then to chapter 9 vs 4 "give me wisdom."

Several days later a letter arrived from Walter; "There was talk at the hearing about your daughter Ann recanting her sworn testimony, but this discovery, if it did occur, happened alone in the Judges chambers in a private conversation."

Flamingo gathered these facts and paid a visit to defense attorney Goodman. Mr. Goodman wrote a letter to a official of the State, then followed up with a phone call.

The State Representative denied any knowledge of a recantation by the witness Ann Winner. Meanwhile, Winner asked both his attorneys to get the transcripts of that hearing in the Judges chambers since a warrior aimed at victory doesn't consult the enemy for co-operation. Transcripts shouldn't lie. If Ann recanted, the recantation would be in the Court notes.

Winner sat writing & wondering what made these folks act this way then he remembered another truth from Louis deMontfort. "We must not take revenge. Let man carry on, for the Lord has commanded him to act this way. Tongue be silent, don't speak, don't resist the love of his lash for it is a great good."

So, this entire drama is God's will, ok. I surrender to thy will and thank you for the cross Amen. Prayer with God's word is the only support able to hold up a downtrodden sinner.

D.H.S. customarily rejected any and all requests from family members. Arguments appeared against Flamingo assuming custody, because she had been out of the picture for years. Folly is quite easy to discern since the Court ruled Ann would be sent to a far away place with complete strangers who never were in the picture.

Again scriptures raced around in Winner's mind; 1

John5:19 . . . "We know that we are of God and the whole world is seated in wickedness . . ." Pro 28:26 . . . "He that trusteth in his own heart is a fool . . ." 1 Tim 5:8 . . . "If any man have not care of his own, and especially of those of his own house, he hath denied the faith, and is worst than an infidel."

Ann was led out of the July 20th hearing with tears falling from her innocent eyes speaking, but nobody was listening. "You people have been ruining my life for the last five years," said Ann.

Winner wondered if the State put handcuffs on his daughter, when they moved her against her will to another detention center in the baby prisoner system.

Winner opened up a letter from Flamingo to read; Winner,

Hi; I received your letter and want you to know I've been down to see your lawyer already. The system, lawyers; humm!!! I don't have faith in any of them. God, yes. He is running the show. I put trust in God and pray something comes out of all this.

I asked Ann to write me a letter. She said she would, but the letter has to be of her own doing. She trusts me and I don't want to do anything to break her trust. I simply told Ann to tell the truth.

She did say in the Court room that she didn't believe it happened. She's scared. I'm going to see Ann tomorrow, up near Reading Pennsylvania, hopefully she'll have the letter.

I don't know whats going to happen. I'm taking this one day at a time. We'll keep this in prayer and trust in the Lord Jesus Christ and what will be, will be.

Again winner remembered God's promises: Phil 2:4 . . . "Rejoice in the Lord always. I will say it again; Rejoice . . . ." 1 Thess 5:16-18. "In everything give thanks: for this is the will of God in Christ Jesus concerning you."

Did Ann inform the Judge that she was not sexually abused in her childhood? The Commonwealth was not interested in entertaining an answer for that question. Winner knew the person who had that answer was the Judge and truthfully a matter of such importance couldn't be left to others so to the pen again, an original and two copies, one to the Judge, one to Lawyer Goodman, and the third goes to Flamingo for safe keeping.

Your Honor:

Blessed by the will of God. I have heard, and granted, its hearsay, that Ann has spoken to you in private about her memory, not being able to recollect any such incidents of sexual abuses.

203

Is this true? If yes, your Honor, please, at once pass this new information onto my attorney Mr. Goodman.

From my perspective, the Court is involved in a conspiracy to keep this child from speaking her truth to a higher authority stating her inability to recall any sexual abuse.

My intentions as always are to be straight forward, fearing God; not man. We all know that people do attempt to protect their own interests while justice revolves around just that, self interest. As far as I know, families do have the right to be protected from goose-step democracy, oppression from government, or the law. Family bashing is not what Patrick Henry had in mind when he authored the "Bill of Rights."

Mr. Abe Lincoln in 1860 said; "Neither let us be slandered from our duty by false accusations against us, nor frightened from it by menaces of destructing to the government, nor of dungeons to ourselves. Let us have faith that right makes might, and in that faith, let us, to that end, dare to do our duty."

Best Regards, Winner

Flamingo continued; I received your letter to the Judge and don't think it's wise to let them (State) know whats going on.

I'm sure they will piece it together that I informed you. I think you should keep them in the dark about what is going on.

D.H.S., has already turned me down from getting Ann to live with us. I don't think writing to the people who captured her in the first place is the answer. Its better not to let them know what is going on at this point.

I am still having un-supervised visits with your daughter. She is opening up alot to me, and shes putting it on paper. Please, be careful not to jeopardize this.

It's important that Ann feels free to speak openly to me and to trust. I do let Ann know everything I'm doing. I love your idea to send this story to the T.V. show "Hard Copy." Woody mailed the letter you wrote to "Hard Copy" and I am enclosing their mailing address.

I taped a show of 20/20 similar to your case. The daughter finally came forward and told how the therapists planted the thoughts into her mind, anyway, I am enclosing one copy of a letter Ann wrote to me. PLEASE . . . DO NOT SEND IT TO THE JUDGE . . . I HOPE YOU SEND THE LETTER TO YOUR LAW-YER. The letter definitely says a-lot.

Ann is prepared to tell the truth to whoever gets involved with this case. I'm waiting for another letter from Ann. I'll send you a copy as soon as she writes.

The State really messed with her mind. Ann needs my support in telling the truth. I'm sure the State will stop my visits in time, but for now, I see this as a small miracle from God and I think we shouldn't let D.H.S. know anything.

Let your lawyer handle the legal work. I'm sure anything you say or write to the Judge or D.H.S., they will find a way to use it against you. Remember, I'm the only one Ann is re-telling this story to, who believes her, except my daughter Star. That's why it's important she puts it on paper.

As soon as the State realizes what is going on, they'll probably stop all communications between us, so don't let them know what's happening . . . just yet.

Flamingo

Winner looked at Ann's handwriting and cried like a baby. He stood, and started to pace the floor, back & fouth, reading & crying, seeing words from his daughter. The first sign that his daughter existed in five long years.

Tony his son & Sabrina his wife both appeared in his memory. Tony didn't know his Mother or Father. Sabrina, fighting hard for her sanity; washing pots and pans like a modern slave in a woman's prison. The future looked gloomy even with a release from prison. The best that a convicted child molester can get from Society is a notice to the neighbor that a monster has moved into the neighborhood.

Folks. Convicted doesn't mean guilty, please keep that somewhere in your memory.

The tribulation ceased while the Holy Ghost brought forward the Words of the Lord Jesus, "Let your light shine before men that they may see your good works, and glorify your Father who is in Heaven." Matthew 5:16.

The Lord says to let your light shine, but this light is His Holy Spirit.

Yes, Lord. The Holy Spirit started to shine on all the fears and worries, Glory & Honor to the blessed Virgin Mary, Mother of Confidence. Shining on every anxiety, up set, injuries, angers, resentment, slander, past or present.

205

Come on, what you receive is for all. Don't act like the defective needle on a record player, stuck in a grove, repeating habitual, negative, selfish, & fearful reflections.

Jar the needle loose, move it past the defect and the song you're hearing will be more of a benefit to the entire world. Understand, the old man's mentalilty is and always will be worthless, but in Christ, in His Word, you have absolute, can't be defeated Victory.

The world is filled with unbelievers and must serve us trials and tribulations. You only need to look at Jesus, who went to Paradise through the cross. We will receive the same treatment but, never-the-less continue to return His Word that He has revealed unto you, back to Satan, and answer those illusions sin produces, defeating them easily.

Hey Devil, heres some good news HA, HA, HA - 2 Cor 10:3-5. "For though we walk in the flesh, we don't war according to the flesh. For the weapons of our warfare are not fleshly, but mighty thought God, unto the pulling down of strongholds (fortifications) & destroying counsels (imaginations), and every high thing that exalteth itself against the knowledge of God, and bringing into capivity every understanding (thought) unto the obedience of Christ.

Ann, age twelve was being put through hell & her Father could only watch and pray which was certainly enough to keep this child protected. Winner wrote to the lawyer Mr. Goodman.

I am sending you a hand-written letter from Ann Winner, written to her aunt Flamingo.

Winner had to thank Flamingo for being the dective in this case. Walking in blind faith is nothing but drama. He had to put all this hurt and upset into the blood of Jesus and continue on with truth and honesty shaking the tree of faith. Fruit would be falling, thats certain, but its not the job of the doer to investigate the fruit, but to stay focused on God an God alone. The devil was going to do some roaring, but faith alone is all that matters.

Flamingo, the original letter from Ann needs to be put in a form called an affidavit. The affidavit then needs official approval by a Notary Public. Please, have an attorney prepare your sworn affidavit, so the Court will accept this as evidence.

I think the States next move will be to dis-credit Ann, maybe say she's crazy. Just like good old mother Russia and *Gulag Archipelago* by Solzhenitsyn. What else can they do? Ann is in the Commonwealth's dog house. So expect more dirty tricks. We're going to be playing hard ball in the big leagues & these people are professional deceivers. We will keep praying & trusting Good to win out over evil in the end.

Another scripture comes to Winner's mind as encouragement. Heb 10:35 "Do not therefore lose your confidence which has a great reward. For patience is necessary for you that doing the will of God you may receive the promise. A just man liveth by faith."

Flamingo wrote:

"It's a crying shame what the system has done to us. D.H.S., is so corrupt and you can't believe anyone. I hope your lawyer cares about justice, because no one else who is involved seems to give a dam, anyway here is another scream for help from Ann, please, don't send these letters to the Judge. Inform your lawyer of your actions at all times. Trust God & stay humble. Let God direct this play, and ask for His guidance.

Pro 3:5-6 "Trust in the Lord with all thine heart; and lean not unto your own understanding(s). In all your ways acknowledge Him, *and He shall direct your paths.*"

A few more weeks passed by. Winner waited for the signed affidavit to arrive. A hearing was set for the middle of September. Mr. Cork was sent copies of Ann's recantation. Mr. Goodman like wise was sent copies.

While all this was happening, a New York publishing House called Rivercross, was busy type-setting the first eighteen chapters of this massacre of truth.

The Supreme Court had the appeal for 16 months & it doesn't take that long to say No.

Flamingo wrote:

I just came back from visiting Ann and she asked me for your lawyers phone number. I didn't know if I should give the number to her, so Ann asked the social worker if she could have the number.

He said, "Yes" so I gave her Mr. Goodman's card. Ann said in Court that she was talking to the Judge, and the stenographer was told by the Judge not to put what she was speaking, in the record. So you see, this is why you mustn't tell them anything; don't ever let them know what you're thinking. Always ask your lawyer's advice before you do anything, ask God to guide your attorney's thoughts. Your lawyer knows how to work the system.

It's hard not to want to shout out at these people. It's in God's

Hands, I'm just an instrument. Being powerless is the best place to be; God takes over at that point.

Ann has hope today, of maybe a new trial & to tell the truth as she understands the truth.

Ann only remembers good times with her Father and she remembers loving you. The greatest part of it all right now is, Ann can talk about it openly to someone who believes her. So, as frustrating as it may be and as scary as it is, I just do God's work and remain humble and willing. If I stay patient; God will lead the way. Keep praying. I put the original letters from Ann in a safe place and I expect another letter shortly.

This is what the affidavit and cover letter look like.

September 15, 1994

I, Flamingo, in good faith, present this affidavit and these enclosures to Mr. Goodman & Mr. Cork, for Mr. Winner. And I do affirm that during the month of August, in 1994, I received (2) two letters from Miss Ann Winner.

These letters are respectfully submitted to Mr. Winner's lawyers. For easy reading of her letters, a typed copy is also submitted with a photo-copy of her letters to me, her aunt Flamingo.

Sincerely,

_____

Flamingo

cc: Mr. Goodman
     Mr. Cork
     enclosures 1. typed copy/ 2. photo-
     cpies of (hand written letter)

AFFIDAVIT

COMMONWEALTH   OF
PENNSYLVANIA   :

                        :

COUNTY
OF_____   :   _____

                        :

                        :

Before me, the undersigned personally appeared before me.

_____, who being duly sworn according to law, deposes and says that he/she is the affiant in the fore-going statement, and that the facts set forth therein are true and correct to the best of their knowledge, information, and belief.

s/_____
Affiant

Sworn and subscribed to before me
this _____ day of
_____, 19____

_____
Notary Public

Ann's two letters to Flamingo.

"Aunt Flamingo,

I can remember the day all this stuff started, I tell you exactlly how I knew it. I was going roller skating with Sally Oldman and my Dad. I don't remember going, but, I do remember Sally Oldman not being allowed to go and she threw a temper tantrum, then my Dad got home from work and ate lunch.

I KNOW HE (MY DAD) DIDN'T HAVE SEX WITH SALLY OLDMAN BECAUSE I WOULD HAVE REMEMBERED IF MY OWN FATHER HAD DONE SOMETHING LIKE THAT.

My Dad & Mom decided to go up to Sally Oldman's house and talk to her parents. We walked up to her house with my brother. Then, I remember Dad knocking on the door. Sally's Father answered. Sally was standing behind her Dad. He came out of the door, and said something; I don't remember exactly what he had said; but, the next thing I knew, her Dad hit my Dad and jumped on top of him and started to beat him up.

My Mom grabbed my brother and ran us back to aunt Flamingo's house. We got my uncle Woody, he went up there & broke up the fight.

I forgot to write about my Mom wearing her blue lace panties and sports bra, and me and Sally went downstairs. My Mom told us to go back and we did, anyway, a few days later, my Mom & Dad, had to bring my brother and I down to the Dept., of Human Services for questions. When we got there, my Mom & Dad were talking to social worker Wendy Pathnek about what happened, they

209

came out, my Mom was crying. They told Tony and I to say goodby and that we would see them (Mom & Dad) the following Friday.

Me and my brother were hysterical. We never did see our parents again.

Then I went to see Gloria Mudski (sex expert). Social worker Pathnek was in the room. Gloria asked me what my parents had done to Tony. And I remember not knowing what she was talking about.

She asked me again. I said nothing. Then, she gave me dolls to act out what they did. I can remember not knowing what to do with them, then she said, "did your Dad do this to you?" And she put the father doll's penis in the daughter doll's vagina. I said "NO" then she said, "If you are telling the truth, then you could blow out a match." She struck it and I couldn't blow it out; then she asked me again if my Dad had intercourse with me.

I REMEMBER SAYING NO SEVERAL TIMES UNTIL I FINALLY TOLD HER *WHAT SHE WANTED TO HEAR.*

I also know she said something like, "What else." I told her "NOTHING."

I can remember exactly what I said in court. I can remember also details of the day my Dad was charged with raping Sally Oldman, but I HAVE NO MEMORY AT ALL OF BEING SEXUALLY ABUSED AS A YOUNG CHILD.

I REALLY WANT TO CONTACT MY PARENTS AND LIVE WITH MY AUNT FLAMINGO.

SINCERELY,

Ann Winner.

(Letter # Two)

Wednesday
8-10-94
Aunt Flamingo,

EVERYTHING I SAID IN COURT WAS WHAT I WAS TOLD TO SAY, *NOT WHAT I REMEMBER OR REMEMBERED.*

I ALSO FORGOT WHAT D.A. (SLIM VIM) DID. SHE TOOK ME OUT AND SPENT $140.00 ON ME AND SAID IT WAS MY REWARD FOR DOING GOOD IN COURT.

SINCERELY,

Ann Winner

20

Good Memories

Emotions fought each other in a battle to see which would be the strongest. Inside Winner, in his mentality, in his thoughts, vivid recollections of the last five years brought forth his current feelings towards life; his life. Winner learned the hard way through pain and suffering that selfishness is the cause of just about all the ills in life. "Yes", he had not handled the situation very well but his pride kept looking for a victory that didn't come; he kept doing what couldn't work and kept receiving back what he didn't want.

Anger certainly manifested early. Anger at self for being un-prepared in protecting his family from sudden evil. Anger with the neighbor Oldman, the police, social workers, courts, Judges, prisons, but did this unkindly emotion produce good? "No", it did not. Anger created more anger. Clearly a new approach would be more beneficial. Winner had to drop the negative thoughts that bad memories kept producing in the present circumstances. The battle in Court continued but changes had to be made. The feelings and the emotions from this difficult situation had to be changed and they needed to be changed immediately. He couldn't continue to bring what was not into realty. There is no guilt nor is there innocence to something that never occurred. With this enlightenment Winner closed his eyes and drifted back into the happier moments that he shared with his family in the past.

"Lets leave the city and go on a holiday." Who wants to go to the seashore?", asked Winner. "I do", said Sabrina. "Me too", "I want to go to the ocean, yea yea yea", both kids were excited and ready to leave immediately.

"We'll go to Atlantic City to see your Grandmother, then we will drive to Wildwood to see the boardwalk, and go on the amusement rides. Who wants to go ride the amusements on the boardwalk," questioned Winner. "Lets Go!"

In the Holiday Market van, Tony asked, "We almost there yet Daddy?". "Yea, Tony. I Can hear the fish jumping, listen, can you hear the fish splashing in the water, they must be pretty big fish to hear them from the truck?". Tony listened and listened. Two hours later the family was in Wildwood by the sea after deciding to visit Atlantic City on the return trip.

Sabrina made sure the children had towels and she brought along sun-tan lotion. A parking spot was found far away from the beach since Winner didn't want to put his money into parking meters, he found a free space and the family walked towards the beach.

The sun was blazing in a clear, cloudless, blue, pollution free sky. White and black two colored sea birds flew towards the breaking waves of the Atlantic Ocean. Sabrina had a two piece bathing suit that caught the attention of walking sailors heading the same way. Stress from over-crowded city living disappeared.

The ramp leading to the boardwalk entered the scene. Ann saw the ocean, she took off running with Tony a few steps behind her, up the ramp, running free. Winner and Sabrina stepped up the pace.

Sabrina shouted, "Ann, Tony, don't get lost, stay close enough to us so you can know where we are at all times". The kids made a swooping circle and ran back towards Sabrina and Winner.

"Lets walk down the boardwalk and you kids tell me what you see. Did anybody bring the camera?", Winner asked. Sabrina answered, "Yes, I have the camera, let me take a picture of you and the kids with the ocean in the background!". Winner, Ann and Tony smiled for Sabrina into the camera and picture number one was on the film.

"Look, Daddy Look!", Tony pointed towards a fishing boat three hunded yards in the sea.

Ann countered, "Daddy, the amusement rides, lets go to the amusement rides". "The first thing that we will do", said Winner, "is take a ride on the hobby-horse, you wait here and I'll buy the tickets!".

Moments later, "I have the tickets, come on, listen kids, as we ride the hobby-horse, we will pass a spot that has a machine that will be holding a ring. If you reach out when we pass this spot and grab the ring, then, you will get a prize, follow me!''.

Tony and Ann were placed on the toy horses. Sabrina and Winner stood close by so the children wouldn't fall. The hobby-horse started to spin, around and around it went, the horses went up and went down, music was playing, Ann reached for the ring but missed. Tony reached for the ring and missed. Sabrina snapped a picture. Winner grabbed a ring. The ride ended.

"Lets go pick up our prize", said Ann. "We have a ring, Sir", said Winner to the operator of the hobby-horse.

The operator looked at the children, smiled a great big smile, and said, "Today is bonus day, you get two prizes, what will it be?" He held up a Teddy Bear that said, "I Love my daddy". Ann said, Daddy, that one, Daddy, the teddy bear". Then the operator held up a hockey stick. Tony requested the hockey stick.

"Give me the camera Sabrina", said Winner. He took a picture of the man giving Tony his hockey stick, then off the family walked up the boardwalk.

"Whats that?", asked Ann as she watched a group of people go past in a specially made boardwalk car that traveled up then down the boardwalk so people who are tired of walking or elderly people can ride instead of walk. Winner answered, "It's called a jitney, Ann". "Watch the car please, watch the car", said the driver as the vehicle passed. Ann said, "Daddy take a picture of the jitney!", "Okay Ann, here you take the picture". Winner handed the camera to Ann who aimed then snapped the photo. The family continued their journey into a perfect holiday.

Eyes were filled up with different objects of attention. The ocean to the right, boardwalk stores to the left, thousands of people walking without a destination. There were: Ice cream stores, gift stores, stores that sold tee shirts with your own printing on the front, fudge shops, peanuts stores, salt water taffies, beach balls, sand shovels with buckets, postcards, fortune tellers, artists drawing portraits, a movie theater, the house of mirrors, the fun house, a tunnel of love and the Roller Coaster.

"Who wants to ride Thunderbolt, the ride that travels seventy miles per hour, out over the ocean, up and down steep hills, twisting around, turning up side down?" Weeedo, Weeedo''. Tickets were purchased, the roller coaster man released the brake, "Take a picture

Sabrina'', said Winner. Up the coaster creeped. Tony held his Father's arm saying, ''I'm scared Daddy''. ''Tony, a lot of people are scared, thats why people ride the roller coaster,''. Up over the houses, over the trees, over the telephone poles, sixty feet, eighty feet, the ocean was in full view, then over the top of the hill then down, swoop, people screamed, down the coaster twisted, zoom, screams from excited customers produced excitment in the air. Thunderbolt turned sharply headed out towards the ocean, sharp turn, down, up another hill, twist, down. then it was over, everyone was glad to be safe and secure back on the ground.

Tony said, ''I no like that thunderbolt. I no ride that no more''. Winner said, ''Lets all surprise Poppe and Nanny in Cape May''. The children were tired of walking; they loved their house in Cape May. Each child had their own bedroom that was three blocks away from the bay.

Sabrina said, ''Winner I want to take the children to the beach before we leave''.

''Sure, lets go''. The family walked down to the sea. ''I have a idea family, I'm gonna buy a house on wheels, one of those big expensive RV's that you turn the key and move your house any place you like. Living in a crowded city is not the way I like to live. On the way home, I'm gonna stop in a dealer and put a down payment on a fancy first class motor home'', said Winner. Sabrina was cautious, the kids said yes. ''Take the last picture Tony of Ann looking out into the ocean then we are going to a place where yesterday meets tomorrow''

''Ann will you say grace please?'', inquired Winner

Ann made the sign of the cross and said, ''In the name of the Father and the Son and the Holy Spirit, Thank You O Lord for these thy gifts that we are about to receive from thy bounty, through Christ Our Lord. amen.

Poppe sat at the head of the table, Tony next to him, he made sure his grandson was well served at table. Winner was next with Ann to his right, then Sabrina. Nanny started to bring the food from the kitchen and place it on the round dinning room table. Today was special, Tony was celebrating his birthday with a dinner birthday party.

Sabrina with Nanny had spent most of the day in the kitchen preparing the twenty pound turkey with all the trimmings.

Winner had been going to a recovery group called Overeater's

Anonymous where he was told that compulsive over eating was a disease and that this disease could be checked if certain steps were initiated to combat the compulsions to over eat.

Sabrina also was watching her weight by attending Weight Watchers. Both Parents were losing weight and this meal was a challenge to their recovery. In OA, a member agrees to plan each meal, write a food plan, no in-between meal snacks, foods are to be measured and weighed. It is a scientific approach that teaches discipline; that works.

Poppe and Nanny both wore birthday hats. The dining room was decorated with streamers of different colors taped to the ceiling and wall: red, green, blue and pink air filled balloons put a extra touch to the interior of the celebration room.

Nanny served the meal, Sabrina excused herself from table to assist her mother-in-law bringing in the dinner.

Nanny carried in the Roasted Turkey. Sabrina followed with seasoned bread dressing and peas. Both were placed in the center of the table, then they returned to the kitchen. Nanny re-appeared carring wipped potatoes; behind her Sabrina with cranberry sauce.

Poppe said, "That looks real good".

Ann said, "My Mommy and Daddy are on a diet".

Nanny said, "They can break their diets today"

Winner pulled out his food plan, looked it over, it said: today I will eat for dinner a quarter pound of turkey, no potatoes or gravy, one cup of peas, yes, all I need to do is follow this plan". He had on his lap his scale for weighing food and his measuring cup. He could lose weight and fast.

Sabrina entered with steaming hot dinner rolls and butter. Nanny said, "for desert we will have Old fashioned pumpkin pie with whipped topping and ice cream!".

Ann said, "Lets all sing Happy Birthday to Tony!". Winner nodded and said "Good idea" He started to sing, the family joined in, Happy birthday to you, happy birthday dear Tony, Happy birthday to you. The family applauded Tony who smiled with a face, lighted up with happiness.

"Lets break the fast", said Poppe, "start passing the food around the table".

Winner put Ann's turkey on her plate while Poppe helped Tony. Winner said, "I guess since you went to all this trouble I will start back on the diet after this meal, you went to alot of effort fixing this banquet"

The conversation around the table usually touched on the news of the day, the state of the nation, religion and who was doing what in the neighborhood. Poppe and Nanny would share their wisdom offering advice or guidance to Winner who was learning how to be the leader in the home.

Tony was a quiet lad who looked at Winner when he held out his hands about a foot apart and said, "Tony, I don't love you this much", then, Winner held his arms out spread about three feet saying, "I don't love you this much, then, he opened his arms as far as possible and shouted, "I Love you this much". Tony beamed in the innocence of a child, his face a picture of peaceful serenity with no trace of care.

Thirty minuets later the meal over consumed. Poppe said, "Lets wait for desert". Everybody agreed, the people stood up, left the table. Sabrina begins to clear the table, Poppe starts to rock on his rocking chair in front of the TV set.

Ann asked, "Daddy, can we go to Kiddy City? "Not now Ann, wait, I'm tired after that meal". Tony jumped in, "Daddy, take us to Kiddy City to play with the toys" "OK, we'll go, put your jackets on, lets get moving, were gonna have some fun looking at the toys", said Winner, both kids jumped around with excitement yelling, "yea yea, were going to kiddy city".

Kiddy City was a mile drive away. Ann and Tony argued with each other over who was going to sit next to their Father. "Kids", said Winner, "please, Ann you sit next to me on the way to Kiddy City and Tony, on the way home, you can sit next to me, Tony you ride shotgun, look out the windows, help me drive, your job is to make sure that your daddy stops at red lights and stop signs, you make sure no cars hit us, will you do that for me, I need your help?", asked Winner. Ann said, "Can I help you look to Daddy?" "You sure can, I need all the help you can give me, Ann, you look for little kids who might be running in the street, we don't want to have a accident".

The van pulled into Kiddy Cities parking lot. The children were trying to get out the door before the truck came to a stop. "Stop, wait til we stop the van before you get out", said Winner. "I would like both of you to walk with me. Hold my hand until we are in the store. Do you understand?"

216

Ann an Tony were moving towards the door. Ann had her hand on the handle, Tony was trying to put his hand on the door handle. The van stopped. Winner put the gear shift in park, turned off the motor, opened his door, jumped out of the truck while saying, "Don't move til I open the door". He double-timed to the children's side to open the door. Both tried to exit at the same time, each wanted to be first.

"Knock it off will you", Winner said, impatiently

After a brief pushing and shoving match, the three entered the doors of this children's paradise. Upon entering this store customers had to walk past a electronic eye device that beamed a light that couldn't be seen. Once this light was interfered with by a passing object, the doors automatically opened. Ann and Tony thought this was a toy and they ran around in circles, breaking the beam and opening the door. "Come on kids, you can't play with this door because its not a toy, the toys are inside, lets go".

Inside the toy store, racks and racks of items of interest to children came to view. There were baby strollers, car seats for kids, cribs, fire truck beds, footballs, dolls, bikes. Tony noticed a tricycle. Adults were being walked by children throughout the store. Ann took off to the doll section; Tony enjoyed riding a bike, he peddled down lane three. God help anybody who was in his way. "Daddy. look at me ride my bike will you buy it for me?" Ann came a running asking, "Daddy when are you going to look at all the pretty dolls with me?" Both children wanted Winner to be with them at the same time which is impossible! One hour past, it was time to go home.

"Kids" you both get three presents each. Ann, since you are a lady, you get to go before Gentlemen, What do you want?". asked Winner Ann responded, "Daddy, I want a Barbie Doll, a coloring book and a box of crayons". "Good Ann, you go get them sweetheart and meet me and Tony at the bike department", answered a weary tired Daddy who was ready to get started on the road to home. "Tony, what presents do you want?". Tony said, "I like to have that bike daddy". "Go get the bike, its yours". Tony went after his new red bike. Winner pulled out his billfold, counted $100.00 dollars, yes, he had enough to cover the cost.

Tony rode his bike to the check out counter, Winner stood in line that was seven deep. The wait would be another twenty minuets. "Daddy, can I have this game?" "No Ann you reached your limit".

Tony asked, "Can I buy a gun?". "Yes Tony, but don't you go shooting anybody in this store. You could go to jail or some cop might shoot you for pointing that toy at him, you have one more present Tony". The line moved ever so slowly ahead. Both kids disappeared while Winner wondered what they were up to, they explored the scene, finally, at the cash register. Tony asked. "Can I have a taffy?". "Yes you can." Winner paid the bill then struggled with a bike under his arms and both kids holding his hands, staggered towards the van watchful for speeding cars that might run them down in the parking lot.

Two hours of fun wore Winner out. He was beat. The children too sat passive in silence all the way home but Tony ran into Poppe's house excited, "Poppe come see the new bike my daddy buy me" Poppe asked, "Did you get a new bike?" "Yes daddy bring it in right now, look, here it comes". Winner placed the bike on the living room floor. Tony immediately mounted and started to ride. Nanny asked, "Are you ready for pumpkin Pie?".

Winner walked over to Sabrina, spoke into her ear, "I am going to a AA meeting, you have to watch the kids until I return. I'm beat and need a break". Sabrina happily said, "Go ahead Winner, Ann has a coloing book, me and Ann will color". Poppe asked, "Tony, do you want to go to the park to ride your bike?" "Yea Poppe! Winner walked out the door, saying, "See you kids later, I'm going to AA". God grant me the serenity to accept the things I cannot change; courage to change the things that I can and the wisdom to know the difference.

Winner and Ann walked out the door heading for Ann's new experience with the first grade. She had spent one semester in kindergarten. Winner walked Ann to the flower shop, purchased a bunch of assorted flowers that cost three dollars, handed them to Ann so she could give them to her teacher, then off they went to travel two blocks to grade school.

"Ann, don't worry, I will take you to school and pick you up after school. keep thinking positive, Honey!".

Father and daughter walked into the school yard. "Come on Ann, this is exciting, I want to show you your new playground".

"Daddy, I like the playground. Can we go play?"

"Yes Ann, we can play for ten minutes, then we have to come back and you need to get ready for your first grade class."

After playing on the swings, it was time to get into position with Ann at least close to the school building.

Other Mothers and a few Fathers also spent the last minutes convincing their young ones that school was good, when the door to the school building opened. Ann watched.

A few teachers walked out the door and into the school yard. They began to mingle with the children. "OK, all you adults, its time to say good by to your children, we'll take good care of them" The clock struck 08:30 then the school bell sounded.

A teacher announced: "I'd like all the first graders to line up in front of me". "Ann, that is your teacher", said Winner. "Go give her the flowers". Ann obeyed, she handed the teacher the flowers and the teacher was pleased, she made a fuss over the flowers then said a few words to Ann who walked over to Winner who said, "OK honey, this is it, you're ready to go. I want you to be brave and walk over to that line and stand behind the person in front of you, you can do it Sweetheart!".

Ann left, walked over, and did as she was told. She stood there, looking at the back of the head of the girl in front of her who moved to her left, Ann moved to her left, then she moved to the right, Ann moved to the right. The boys were harder to discipline. The teacher showed impatience and raised her voice, Ann bolted out of line, crying, she grabbed Winner and said, "I don't want to go to school Daddy". Winner said, "Ann, the teacher did yell but you little girl, will learn that what people say is what you need to hear; not how they speak, some people get excited quickly. You listen to what is said and don't pay attention to how it is said; that is why you are going to school, to learn how people are different. I don't know why she yelled at the boys but she will not hurt you. I promise, go ahead back get in line, all by yourself.

Ann did, she went back in line, the line started moving into the school with Ann glancing at Winner. She walked out of sight into the building for her first day in school.

Ann at the age of six had her own computer. A friend of the family was her instructor who would play computer games with the child two nights per week inside his basement that he also used as a office. Winner would drive over to pick Ann up after the two hour lesson but before he knocked on the door, he'd peek in the window to see his daughter having a ball, learning how to concentrate, then he knocked on the door. Ann looked up to see her Father's face then said, "Go home Daddy, this is fun".

In the living room was a toy box just plum filled up with dolls. One evening when Ann was three, Winner emptied the contents of the box on the living room floor. He and Ann sat down to play dolls. In this game the toys come to life and speak to Ann while they are in her father's hand. Ann looked at Barbie doll, then heard her say, "Hi Honey, my name is Barbie, will you listen to what I say?" Ann sat spellbound, laughing, talking back to her doll. "He He He, me listen Barbie". Barbie started to move around in Winner's hands, Barbie too acted in a excited manner and said, "Ann, you are a beautiful baby, I love you, me and all your doll babies want you to say no to drugs". Ann said, "Me say no Barbie", and Ann started cracking-up!

"Bye Ann, I'll see you later. I am going back into the toy box, Mr. Potato Head wants to sing you a song".

"Good Morning Ann, I'm Mr. Potato Head, do you like me?" "Yes, me like you", Ha Ha Ha". "I feel good today, everythings OK, do you want to play?". "Yes, me do", Okay Ann, little sweetheart, "Don't take drugs to feel good".

The toys in the box acted as teachers since education, that is, the ability to think for yourself, begins as soon as you can think for yourself; why not from the beginning, at least that was Winner's intention, to teach this child to meditate and make considerations for herself at the earliest possible moments of her life.

Ann was pushed around the neighborhood in a English Tram, a baby coach with large wheels in the rear and in the front smaller wheels. She'd ride like a queen in her chariot being pushed by a slave down and through the shaded path of the park, looking at dogs and squirrels. We usually made a stop at the playground where Ann would make her first encounters with other children on the see-saw, or the sliding board. For some reason, many of the parents would suspect that their child would meet harm as they stood 15 feet below watching their children mustering the courage to slide down the steel sliding board. Winner kept his mouth shut but prepared to catch Ann if she fell off the slide. Sabrina was different, she'd say, "Winner, that is a little three year old girl you have 15 feet in the air and she is going to get hurt". "Come on Sabrina, Ann is not going to get hurt, Come on Honey, show your Mother how you can come down the sliding board by yourself!''. Well, she did and the lesson was learned.

Usually when the family was traveling about, Winner encouraged his family to be on the lookout for a good picture. This family had a camera close by when outdoors. Sabrina, Ann and later Tony did just that which made the experience more interesting since it gave everybody a reason to pay attention to what was going on around them.

Ann had expensive taste when it came to dressing up. We were walking in a shopping center looking into store windows when Ann noticed a dress she liked on a store manikin. This dress was for a teenager, nevertheless, Father and daughter walked into the shop. Ann tried on the dress that cost sixty bucks, then, we walked out of the store with the oversized garment. The idea was to take Ann and have a tailor custom fit her with her first dress but there was too many alterations for the tailor to make, so, we ended up returning the item, but you see, it was the experience that counted; not the dress. If the idea would have worked. everyone would have been happy.

This family did most of the things the average family would probably do but there were exceptions. Remember, Winner had no experience whatsoever at being a Father, so it was trial and error, especially when it came to outside activity. For instance, some parents teach their children to come in the house when it starts to rain; not so with Winner's family, when the rain started to fall, this was a sign to put Ann in her yellow rain gear then head out doors with umbrellas opened. No, Winner did not think and never did think for a second that weather was responsible for sickness, no matter what the opnion of others was, Winner spent most of his life outdoors and snow, rain, cold or wind never caused illness.

Teaching the children to earn a living was initiated at a early age. The idea to teach Ann to sell developed and what better way to teach then to demonstrate by example. We needed a product. All Saint's Day was a few day away. That's Halloween. Well Nanny spent the better part of a week hand making Ann's custom-made costume. Ann was going to go out trick-or-treating as a good witch but during the day, he and Ann went to a wholesale store and purchased thirty pictures of pumpkins that neighbors could hang on their windows to generate some excitment for the kids.

The idea was to have Ann go door to door with one of her

friends selling pumpkins for a quarter each. One kid would start on one side of the block, the other kid would start across the street and they would have a race to see who could sell more pumpkins in the shortest period of time. The business was successful, each girl sold out, most homes were decorated with a pumpkin in the window, sold to them by a salesgirl who was thrilled by her successful achievement.

Most mornings, the day began with the children hearing a tape by a Gospel singer belting out a inspirational tune like, "Rise and shine, give God the Glory, Glory, rise and shine. The kids would sing and dance along with the song.

As the day progressed, during the school year, Winner walked Ann to school, picked her up, cooked lunch for her and took her back to school. After school it was a fast trip to Chuckie Cheese Pizza time theater, or a ride on a bike that was converted to carry a small child, meaning, a seat was installed on the bar directly in front of the driver so the child could go along for new adventures.

Ann's first report card showed her need for a tutor. She failed three subjects out of five, but Winner with positive thoughts as a guide saw the good since he let his daughter learn by her own initative initally but the F's showed a need for action. Winner looked at the F's, then remembered how hard it is for a child to go to school by herself, put together with strangers, frightened by yourself, insecure, learning how to get along. He said, "Ann lets celebrate your F's, you earned them they are yours, lets go to Chuckie Cheese's to celebrate your first report card. Ann, you know what you need to do to make improvements and I know what needs to be done, you need to learn to concentrate, listen, and pay attention. Would you like one of my friends to teach you the computer? Ann was agreeable so a tutor was hired. In Ann's next report card, she went from three F's to the top 10 percent in the state of Pennsylvania because to her, she was doing this on her own which was what Winner wanted her to believe.

During these development years, Winner insisted on employment that enabled him to bring his children with him to work. The kids helped their father deliver groceries, often, he'd drive his delivery van to the neighborhood swimming pool were Sabrina and Flamingo watched the children play in the water, then one or the other would come along to deliver groceries. One customer handed Ann a two dollar tip. Outside the house Winner said, "Give me the money Ann". Ann replied, "Daddy that's my tip. That lady gave me the money".

Often Ann invited her young friends to the house to play. One friend stayed overnight on weekends for four straight months. Winner wondered if she was ever going to stay home on the weekend.

There were hours of family fellowship, drawing, coloring, teaching, talking into a tape recorder since this taught the children not to fear their own voice and it also taught communication skills. Ann went to church, attended prayer meetings with Nanny, and at times would go along to the restaurent for a after the prayer meeting snack. She enjoyed video movies, making her own decisions, and at night Winner taught her the fundamental principles of meditation. The family would say their prayers together and soon thereafter the kids would fall to sleep.

Old head, left his memory, returned to focus on reality. A prison guard was standing at his cell door with an envelope in hand saying, "You have a letter from the Supreme Court!".

Winner made up his mind, from this second forward, he would **STOP THINKING OF EVIL BY THINKING OF GOOD!**

THE END